T0273833

# ROUTLEDGE LIBRARY EDITIONS: ARTIFICIAL INTELLIGENCE

Volume 3

# ARTIFICIAL INTELLIGENCE

# ARTIFICIAL INTELLIGENCE
## The Case Against

Edited by
### RAINER BORN

Routledge
Taylor & Francis Group

LONDON AND NEW YORK

First published in 1987 by Croom Helm
New in paperback 1988
Reprinted 1989 by Routledge

This edition first published in 2018
by Routledge
2 Park Square, Milton Park, Abingdon, Oxon OX14 4RN

and by Routledge
711 Third Avenue, New York, NY 10017

*Routledge is an imprint of the Taylor & Francis Group, an informa business*

*British Library Cataloguing in Publication Data*
A catalogue record for this book is available from the British Library

ISBN: 978-0-8153-8566-0 (Set)
ISBN: 978-0-429-49236-5 (Set) (ebk)
ISBN: 978-0-8153-5118-4 (Volume 3) (hbk)
ISBN: 978-1-351-14152-9 (Volume 3) (ebk)

**Publisher's Note**
The publisher has gone to great lengths to ensure the quality of this reprint but points out that some imperfections in the original copies may be apparent.

**Disclaimer**
The publisher has made every effort to trace copyright holders and would welcome correspondence from those they have been unable to trace.

# ARTIFICIAL INTELLIGENCE
## THE CASE AGAINST

Edited by
Rainer Born

ROUTLEDGE
London and New York

© Rainer Born 1987
Croom Helm Ltd
New in paperback 1988

Reprinted 1989
by Routledge
11 New Fetter Lane, London EC4P 4EE
29 West 35th Street, New York NY 10001

Printed and bound in Great Britain by
Biddles Ltd, Guildford and King's Lynn

British Library Cataloguing in Publication Data

Artificial intelligence: the case against.
  1. Artificial intelligence
  I. Born, Rainer
  00.63      Q335
  ISBN 0-415-00289-3

# CONTENTS

# ACKNOWLEDGEMENTS

I wish to express my sincere gratitude to all those who helped me in preparing this collection, who offered comments and criticism and helped me to formulate my ideas; especially to Ilse Born-Lechleitner, Alfred Kobsa, Hans Mittendorfer, Otto Neumaier and Stuart Shanker. For permission to reprint articles I am indebted to H. Putnam and J. Searle. I am also heavily indebted to the patience of the editors of Croom Helm. Special thanks go to Hertha and Herwig Lechleitner.

# INTRODUCTION

## Rainer P. Born and Ilse Born-Lechleitner

Initially, Artificial Intelligence (hereafter, AI) was a sub-section of the computer sciences — and it is not even a very young science, for all its recent popularity. Already in 1956, at the Dartmouth Conference in Hanover, New Hampshire, John McCarthy and Marvin Minsky introduced the name 'Artificial Intelligence' for this particular branch of the computer sciences (Charniak and McDermott, 1985, 9). Simply by its provocative name (often regarded as a *contradictio in adjecto*), a series of discussions were triggered off which today increasingly attract even commercial interests through the development of so-called expert-systems (whose success is claimed to be due to developments in AI). AI also zoomed into the limelight of public interest through the use of computer-based early warning systems and anti-missile (missile-defence) systems, resulting in a series of false alarms that were disquieting enough at least to make the public aware of these problems (cf. Parnas, 1986, 49–69).

A meaningful discussion of the justification of this choice of words for characterizing a new field of science cannot be conducted from an external point of view; we have to take internal concerns of this science into account. Even more important in this context is the *tension* between everyday considerations (i.e. external considerations) and the insights of the computer sciences. If we pay no attention to this, the mere name 'AI' evokes impressions and causes misunderstandings both of which present the subject in a false light.[1]

We could, of course, give an (approximate) definition of AI (and we shall do so a little later, though with certain precautions/qualifications), yet it would soon become evident that the misunderstandings caused by associations evoked by the name 'AI' cannot be clarified by giving a *definition* of AI. The discussion created by these misunderstandings is in many cases based on completely different presuppositions which cannot be grasped by or formulated in a comprehensive and neutral account of the nature of AI. Yet though we have to be aware of its limitations, such a definition does fulfil an important function. It is surprising that AI is able to influence today's world to such an extraordinary extent. One possible explanation for this is an (of course not openly conceded) projection of the conception of human intelligence into machines which could be prevented by a generally accepted, neutral definition. We might wonder why human intelligence is so quickly assigned to computers. The role of AI in our life depends on our expectations in regard to the performance of these machines, and our expectations are predominantly based on our misguided conceptions of the potentiality of the machine and not on its technical performance.

As a possible solution I therefore wish to present, as a definition of AI, a slightly modified form of Feigenbaum's definition (cf. Feigenbaum, 1981, 3), namely that 'AI is that part of computer science concerned with designing intelligent computer systems, i.e. systems that exhibit the characteristics which *we* associate with *intelligence* in human behaviour — e.g. understanding language, learning, reasoning, solving problems etc.'

Earlier than Feigenbaum, Marvin Minsky maintained that a machine is intelligent 'if the task it is carrying out would require intelligence if performed by humans'. Again, this does not allow the reverse inference that the machine actually *manifests* intelligence; it might use other, purely technical, means to arrive at the same result. Yet Minsky does not define intelligence: he presupposes a common-sense understanding of the term, according to the motto 'I cannot define it but I know it when I see it', and leaves a scientific definition to psychologists or cognitive scientists. His definition, therefore, not only eliminates a projection of the concept of human intelligence onto computers but was actually devised with just this purpose in mind.[2]

A change in the conception of the nature of AI (which, however, still does not prevent the above-mentioned projection), is reflected in the more recent formulation of AI by Eugene Charniak and Drew McDermott (1985, 6): 'Artificial intelligence is the study of mental faculties through the use of computational models.' The discussion ensuing from this, already hinted at by Patrick Winston (1984, 1: 'AI is the study of ideas that "enable" computers to be intelligent') resulted from the fact that one wishes to understand the *principles* which allow for the *possibility* of intelligence (a seemingly Kantian turn). I shall return to this theme below.

As an attempt to sum up the various definitions of AI, I would like to categorize sophisticated programming techniques (the so-called 'smart programs') as syntactical approaches, and the search for 'principles of intelligence' as a semantical approach.[3] A further development would then be a pragmatical approach which I would like to consider as a new paradigm (or working philosophy). The central idea of this approach is that AI programs should be sophisticated (or smart) programs which allow for (or even themselves take care of) an *intelligent* use, application or interpretation of computational models (i.e. results), insofar as they are open to revision in accord with new information or insights by the (end-) user. We have to create computer programs, the results of which can be evaluated against our experiences (background knowledge) in order to fit into our ways of attuning to the world. They should also allow for a possible change of our views of the world. They should fit in between *processor intensive* and *memory intensive* programs,[4] and allow for a controllability via our human intellectual abilities. This is especially important if we use object-oriented programming languages which allow for an immediate evaluation of the results and which — in using e.g. icons and menus — place the emphasis on the 'human user' and not on the machine.

This means that the *intelligent use* of computers in artificial information processing contains a strong ethical component which includes a scientist's responsibility for the influence of her/his results upon the development of mankind.[5]

Actually, I see little sense in a battle with definitions as they sometimes have the same effect as 'cleaning up an empty room'. The conclusions derived from definitions are, above all, derived from the picture evoked by the words used in them,[6] and therefore from what has been *said* and only in a minority of cases from what one *sees* respectively from what *shows* itself in reality. I shall therefore try to build up an understanding of the nature of AI on the following pages by using the tension between the common-sensical world-view and the scientific world-view as a frame of reference for the discussion, and I shall try to acquire an understanding of AI by identifying its place within this frame.

My approach already presupposes a certain understanding of the role of philosophy in the area of tension between common-sense knowledge versus scientific theory. An explanation of this role would, however, lead us too far away from the main topic, necessitating a long philosophical deviation. It therefore seems to be more reasonable to test this implicitly presupposed understanding of philosophy in its practical application and to measure the significance of this approach against its *success*. The success should not simply consist of a better understanding of the nature of AI — i.e. of having gained a *knowledge by content* (or participative knowledge) — or an informal (in contrast to formal) understanding of the 'significance' of the matter. It should also consist in one's ability to handle AI in a more creative way and to offer not only negative philosophical criticism to the computer scientist but also *constructive* support (at least in a conceptual form). I want to put this constructive (but by no means patronizing conception of the role/importance of the philosophy of science for the daily routine of the working scientist) at the centre of my considerations. With this approach, we could solve especially those questions which worry any scientist because they recur in the course of his work and to which he cannot find satisfactory answers.[7]

I shall introduce, therefore, in order to substantiate these somewhat ambitious claims, a *general scheme* LIR into which the problems of the inter-relation between everyday knowledge and the insights of any specific scientific discipline can be placed, and which therefore facilitates a discussion and proper understanding of them. This scheme will explicitly deal with the relation between language, information and reality. I shall not substantiate this scheme but hope that its meaning becomes clear through its use, and that a successful application is sufficient explanation of its use.

After this, I shall briefly hint at the fact that it is possible (and is already done in a more or less unconscious way) to gain a new working philosophy (or paradigm) for the general pursuit of science through dealing with the information sciences and AI in particular.[8] Such a working philosophy might lead to a particular view of the world which could influence philosophical discussions in various areas (such as mental models, the mind–body problem and questions of human rights). More specifically, I am interested in the way in which the working philosophy of AI could reflect back on our everyday philosophy and influence the acceptance of certain suggestions for the solution of philosophical problems in respect of basic attitudes towards this world.

Furthermore, I shall concern myself briefly with the opportunities and dangers posed by the development of the computer sciences, and I am going to comment on the possibilities offered by expert-systems. These systems, handled with appropriate discretion, would enable us to create a so-called 'human window' (cf. Michie, 1985, 56ff, 214) which could lead to better means of controlling the autonomous dynamics of technical developments.

I shall then discuss the problem of a 'realistic' *working philosophy* for the understanding and handling of technical developments in a way which results from my previous considerations.

One final preliminary remark: The following considerations are not intended as an introduction to the technical aspects of AI, but rather as a personal introduction to the problems and debates triggered off by AI. This does not mean, however, that no technical considerations will be provided. Technical considerations should always be employed if one talks of, for example, the fact that a certain working philosophy of AI is not in accordance with what is *said* about AI; i.e. it may be completely different from one's *practice,* i.e. from what one *does* in AI.

I am now going to develop, in an intuitive way, the interpretative scheme or lattice LIR (Language–Information–Reality).[9] I shall proceed in two steps: I shall first present, in several stages, a general idea of the relation between science and common sense (*T* and *V* in Figure 1). I shall then try to make this idea more precise by illustrating it with examples from AI.

At the same time, the scheme LIR is also intended as a *theoretical frame or abstract model* (with a lot of practical consequences) of the more general *relation* between language, information and reality. The scheme should analyse our ways of investigation. Since the scheme is intended to reflect the relation between philosophy and information respectively computer sciences, I prefer to call it a meta-philosophical approach.[10]

The basic idea I am going to use is, roughly speaking, a 'contrast'[11] between reality **W** and some representational system **R** as well as one between two views of the world, namely one using scientific, theoretical and/or technical concepts (*T*) and one using vernacular and/or folk-theoretical concepts (*V*). *T* and *V* mediate between **W** and **R**.[12]

Figure 1

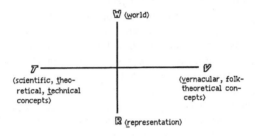

The choice of this system of co-ordinates can be taken as a quasi-empirical hypothesis.[13] **W**, **R**, *T* and *V* therefore serve as undefined basic terms, their exact meaning is defined implicitly, i.e. by the relation of the terms to each other. To begin with, we use the respective everyday concepts for **W**, **R**, *T* and *V* which only afterwards become more precise and exact (analysis of revelation and standardization). For further discussions we restrict ourselves to a section (part) **B** of **W** (see Figure 2) which can be *related* (resp. referred to) with a concrete depiction **D** as part of **R**. We can take a linguistic description of **B** as a special case of an arbitrary depiction **D** of **B**. In our case, we instantiate **D** by means of the natural language *L*.

We assume that fixing of reference of some **D** (=*L*, a depiction of some part of **B** of **W**) can be established and conveyed in at least two different ways. One procedure uses a theoretical background knowledge **A**[14] as an instantiation of *T* (see Figure 2); the other way of fixing this reference uses a common-sensical everyday knowledge **C**, an instantiation of *V*.

Figure 2

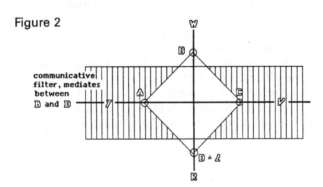

We could also imagine the role which *T* and *V* play in fixing the reference of **D** in **B** as 'rival language games' *à la* Wittgenstein. The tension between *T* and *V* seems to be decisive for the way in which the relation of **D** to **B** is established. It is pointless to consider a dominance of one of the two language games over the other and make the dominant one the supreme judge with respect to understanding the meaning of linguistic expressions (cf. *L*). It is much more important to pay attention to the contribution of the respective language games to fixing the reference of **D** in **B** and to identify those misunderstandings which result from an unconscious shift into a different language game.[15] Yet these so-called mistakes can also have positive, creative consequences, since they often open up new aspects of analysis or new possibilities of classification which have to be understood and taken into account.

These theoretical considerations demonstrate the (trivial) fact that certain linguistic expressions, which are here understood as elements of **D**, can, according to the *background-knowledge* (context of communication) in use, refer in completely different ways to **B** as part of **W**. An example for this would be a term such as 'intelligence', which has different meanings in the context of everyday life and in cognitive science.

There are some philosophers who, possibly influenced by a misconceived empiricism, think that these differences of meaning could nevertheless be completely translated into ordinary language, e.g. by using indexicals. More precisely, we would no longer talk about 'intelligence' but about 'intelligence$_n$' in the sense of, for example, a psychologist. If this translation by indexicals were possible, any difference in the use of the information about the world encoded in the respective indexed terms would have to disappear. The primacy of ordinary language and its world-view presupposes that, after a successful translation, the reaction of a cognitive scientist (A-background knowledge) and a layman (C-background knowledge) to the term 'intelligence' is indistinguishable in any situation if this situation is specified in terms of a natural language.

The claim of the primacy of ordinary language also presupposes that *any insight* can be translated into ordinary language and therefore be reduced to the concepts available within ordinary language. The meaning of those concepts and therefore of any possible insight can be given any time within *L* (i.e. via the background knowledge **C**). This attributes a universal status to *L*. A possible objection against this claim would be to maintain that there could be (scientifically) *meaningful* statements which cannot be gained by an appropriate deduction[16] from expressions of ordinary language (which encode the background knowledge of ordinary language). The standard immunization against this objection is to test the translation procedure in situations which from the beginning do not allow for different reactions according to A- or C-background knowledge; that is in trivial everyday situations.

If a depiction could be given in such a way that A could be *reduced* completely to C — A could be translated completely into C in such a way that it would make no difference whether one referred (in a truth-functional way) to B via C or via A — then there would be no difference in the use of the encoded information. The C-meaning of a sign (information carrier) for D would be identical with the A-meaning of this sign.[17] As a consequence of this presupposition, science as routine could be *pursued* with a C-view of the world, but I doubt whether serious new scientific insights can be gained in this way.

Some might think that this state of affairs would be ideal. Science could be pursued as a mere system of rules, and a deeper or hidden meaning of scientific results other than that directly and realistically accessible via a C-interpretation (meaning) of those signs need not exist. Only what could be expressed adequately in *L* (ordinary language) would make sense.

As responsible philosophers, however, we should leave room in our analyses for the possibility that not everything can in any case be translated into *L*; i.e. can be reduced to an understanding via a common sensical background knowledge C. In retrospect, we can often give the corresponding translations from the scientific to the vernacular understanding; we can, within our given (vernacular) background knowledge, make clear (in a rudimentary way) what the scientific insights we have gained are about. Yet the question remains whether we could ever have reached these insights with a vernacular background-knowledge only: i.e. whether we would, from the very beginning, have been able to *recognize* the significance of these insights without a scientific background-knowledge. The *process* of gaining knowledge cannot be translated; at least not without enriching some ordinary language with scientific terms or without keeping the scientific connotation of a vernacular term in mind.

'Processing' scientific results with the help of a vernacular background-knowledge only means that one does not learn anything new, does not gain any additional knowledge. At best, one has made an insight conscious by exhausting the deductive possibilities of the given vernacular background-knowledge **C**. The fact that, theoretically speaking, the validity (technical meaning) of scientific results can be checked in a vernacular context does not allow for the assumption that scientific insights can be gained with ordinary language and everyday background-knowledge only.[18]

I therefore propose that for a *reconstruction* of the manner in which we study the relation of **D** to **B** a split into at least two components is necessary: namely **A** and **C**. Their combination should contribute to the understanding of the effective relation of **D** to **B**. In addition to this, I propose that **A** and **C** have to be split up even further, namely into the components *knowledge by rules* and *view of the world* (or knowledge basis) (see Figure 3a). Knowledge by rules can either be of a *theoretical* nature (expressed in mathematical calculi) or be of a more practical nature: the sort of experience which appears in heuristics or in rules of thumb and in this way guides the actions of experts. The component 'view-of-the-world' (knowledge basis, knowledge representation), can be dominated more scientifically (**A**) or in a primarily vernacular way (**C**). For reasons which will be explained later I introduce the signs **L**, **F** for knowledge by rules and **M**, **E** for knowledge basis, according to the emphasis on **A** or **C** respectively.

Figure 3a[19]

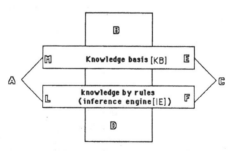

We can imagine **L** and **F** as a theoretical and practical information processing (inference-engine) of a natural language *L*, and **M** and **E** as theoretical and practical *assessment* (or judgement/representation) of the results (knowledge gained) reached by **L** and **F** within Figure 3b, respectively by a given view of the world. The assessments lead to a concrete building up of a *relational* and *operational* knowledge basis, which can either be of a theoretico-explanatory nature or of a predominantly descriptive nature, i.e. related to actions. A is then split up into a theoretical knowledge of calculi **L** and an explanatory structural knowledge **M**; C is split up into a practical knowledge of rules **E** (in which e.g. the knowledge of experts is expressed) and an ordinary or everyday view of the world **F**.

Figure 3b

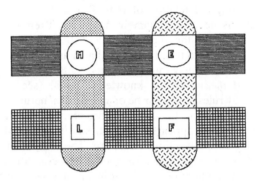

A first summing up of these explications is the scheme PLIR (Figure 4), a preliminary version of the final scheme LIR which can be understood, in a technical way, as *structural analysis* of the *relation* between language (means of depiction), information (knowledge and meaning) and reality. It can help to find rules for acting, for the transformation, the building up and above all the *use* of knowledge about our world.

Figure 4: (PLIR)

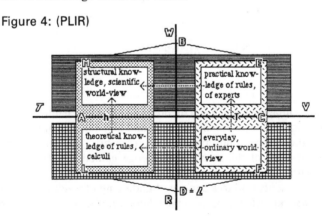

Occasionally the individual parts of the scheme merge into one another. The emphasis of the concept's structural knowledge and calculus knowledge lies on the *explanatory* aspect, while the right side of the scheme is supposed to express the *directly descriptive* aspect which is orientated towards action. The scheme is intended to prevent one of the crucial misunderstandings about the nature of theoretical and explanatory knowledge, namely to (mis-) understand it as directly (literally) descriptive and therefore as immediate instructions for acting (i.e. applying scientific results to reality).[20]

As a last step towards LIR, I would like to enrich PLIR (Figure 4) with a *technical distinction* which originates in an analysis of the way in which scientific results are achieved.[21] It is concerned with an inherently *theoretico-explanatory* and therefore NOT a *directly descriptive* component of scientific results in general, which has to be distinguished from the concrete models contained in the practical rules of experts.

No direct correspondence for this technical distinction can be found in the everyday world.[22] This is because, in general, in an everyday context and therefore also in the *prose*[23] a scientist uses to talk or think about his subject (in a meta-language) or which he uses to communicate the significance of his results, the *abstract dimension* of the significance (or meaning) of these results is suppressed. One pretends that, just as in everyday thinking, scientific results describe certain (causal) connections of events and that one can, step by step (in a literally descriptive way), trace the consequences of an insight which is supposed to lead to the solution of a problem, just as one can visibly trace the running of a computer program. The ambivalence of scientific results with respect to their abstract or effective significance is generally neglected. In applying the results, in evaluating them and in looking at their consequences we tend to use our everyday conceptions and ideas about these results only. We tend to disregard the fact that scientific results are also abstract, theoretico-explanatory 'structure'-models with a primarily systematic character. They are intended to make possible a deeper understanding of causal connections even if these from time to time run contrary to our *prima facie* impressions.[24] Yet I want to emphasize that all this does not by any means plead for a dominance of the scientific world-view over common-sense. I consider them as the different but supplementary sides of the coin. I am therefore primarily concerned with mediating between them, so

**Figure 5**

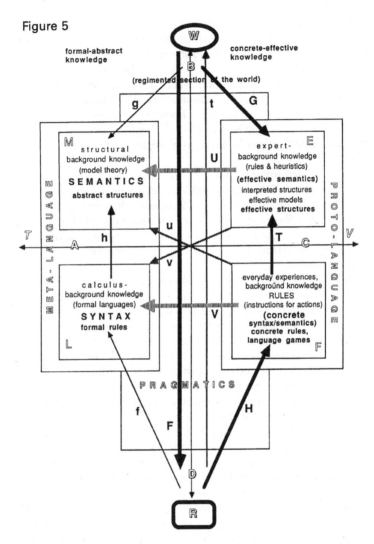

that positive aspects of both approaches can be developed in a *constructive* way.

I therefore propose to split up the content **M** of the scientific world-view ***T*** into an *abstract* and an *effective* part. This means that the scheme PLIR experiences a certain transformation of meaning: the *world of experts* **E** becomes a mixture of scientific abstract and practical knowledge (i.e. knowledge concerned with effective or interpreted structures). The *effective* part of **M** is identified as part of **E** and externally merges with it. **A** = {**L**, **M**} is considered as an instantiation of the scientific world-view (e.g. a concrete theory). The *effective part* of **M**, now identified as an essential part of **E**, contains those statements and results, i.e. *effective models* which we normally regard as positive in scientific progress, that is e.g. the knowledge of a doctor, a geologist, a computer scientist and other specialists or so-called experts. It is, so to speak, the practical, interpreted and applied part of a scientific discipline and represents an intersection (overlap) between the abstract, theoretico-explanatory models in **M** and the concrete, literally (intuitively) descriptive rules and realistic instructions characterizing our ways of interacting with the everyday world. Therefore, **M**, in contrast to **E**, is given the status of an *abstract explanation*, which primarily explains the success of the models used with the help of **E** and, in doing so, **M** uses structures which are NOT *literal descriptions* of reality.

My claim is that the AI computer programs have just that status of abstract explanation. The structure models they use have to my mind a primarily analytic purpose. The scheme LIR, now that it is fully developed, enables us to distinguish[25] between AI programs and 'normal' computer programs. AI programs often contain, especially if they are intended as 'expert systems', the distinction between a representation of knowledge (knowledge basis) and an inference-engine for the processing of knowledge, i.e. for drawing conclusions from some given knowledge which can be made sense of against the background of some knowledge basis. These programs can therefore be understood in the following way: they reach a certain flexibility if the algorithms they use (are able to) function in such a way that they can evaluate computed results against the background of either a certain global knowledge or (interpreted) empirical data.

If an expert reads a general introduction into his special field, he reads the words and specific expressions used in it with his experiences and specific knowledge at the back of his mind. This also influences his reactions and the application of the information.[26] A student, however, who uses this general introduction to study the subject does not have the expert's special knowledge. The conceptions he forms about the world presented in the book are based on the elements of his experiences. The result is that identical situations and identical prose can lead to different reactions in the expert and the student. An expert could then say that the student has not grasped the core of the subject.

I suppose that it is not possible to represent this (expert) *knowledge*, which is only apparent in real situations and actions, in a computer in such a way that the use of (computed) results by a layman does not differ from that of an expert. Participative knowledge cannot be reduced completely to instructions for the handling of real situations and actions.

'Clever' users of the programs will (after some mistakes and negative experiences[27]), learn to take the results the programs generate with a grain of salt. They learn to relate the results to reality with the help of their newly developed 'participative knowledge' which is needed for an adequate application of the programs. In this way, new user-'experts' crop up who develop concepts about that part of reality they refer to. They re-invent the wheel, so to speak, and are then guided by this wheel in their practice.

At first sight, this is not really worrying, just clumsy. Yet most sciences which today use computer programs, such as, for example, economics, are interactive disciplines, they influence politics and society in general. In many cases we do not realize that misconceived conceptions such as out-dated ideas about economic growth, built into the computer programs via the theories underlying them, also seep into our world through these channels.

It is therefore essential to find out those basic assumptions or 'identities' that are the guiding concepts for AI-specialists when they create programs such as, for example, expert systems like MYCIN.[28] *In concreto*, expert systems work with the idea that the human way of information processing uses certain *rules* to draw conclusions from certain facts.[29] Yet the syntactical rules of computing do not exhaust every aspect of the human way of information processing.

Just as with logic in philosophy of science, pure syntax, an inference-engine only, is not sufficient. What we need here is a kind of semantics, i.e. a way of representing knowledge[30] to which computed results can be referred; a representation of knowledge that gives *meaning* to computed results, so to speak. After this, we discover that mere data-banks are not sufficient either, they should be replaced by a kind of *dynamic* representation of knowledge. We realize that we need programs which allow for conclusions[31] which obtain their meaning from a participative knowledge.

The necessity of knowledge representation is at first (similar to model theory) a technical necessity, since we want to construct computer programs with an input/output behavior similar to the way in which experts process information.[32] This technical necessity[33] quickly becomes an assumption about how information processing works with human beings. This is a projection of explanatory structures onto human beings, i.e. a literal operationalization of these structures. The identification of explanatory and descriptive structures guides the scientist in the search for technical realizations of his ideas. Therefore, the guiding principles of AI-experts are reflected in their programs, in which certain technical details are regarded *as representation of knowledge.*[34]

We can now use the expressive power or cognitive resolution level of the scheme LIR to clarify some further points important for the debate about the significance of AI. Let us at first identify some of the essential aspects of the computer sciences with the respective parts of the scheme: Computer programs are written in formal languages and therefore take place in **L**. **F** contains the everyday concepts corresponding to **L**, and **E** contains the (effective) semantics for **L** as far as concrete (effective) concepts of scientific disciplines about the meaning of the algorithms operating in the programs are concerned. **M** contains the abstract semantics of the programs (in **L**).

A concrete application of a computer program would, for example, be the situation of a doctor who is confronted with a sick patient for whom he has to prescribe some medicine. We can understand his situation as β in **B** as part of **W**. The way in which a doctor finds the answer to his problem is simulated by a communication with the computer. This means that we have to describe the situation β as precisely as possible in **D** or rather *L* (F(β)=Φ) and enter it into the computer via **L** (f(Φ)=φ ). We understand the confirmation of our input, given in the form φ, as Φ from *L*, which to us makes sense in **B**, i.e. we attribute a meaning to it, a situation or problem β in **B**. We achieve this by either using our background knowledge (built on rules and therefore of an inferential nature) or our special experiences, our own experts' background knowledge **E** (built on contextual, participative knowledge). For us, Φ therefore refers to something which is the case in **B**.

As a result of our input we expect an expression ψ screen which we can understand as the concrete statement Ψ[35] in the natural language *L* (respectively in the description **D**) used by us and which at the same time represents the solution of the problem posed as β in **B**. Precisely spoken, Ψ is a linguistic expression from *L* (or **D**) which contains the solution of the problem posed in β, i.e. instructions for acting, and which is referred by us via **F** (and sometimes via **E**) onto **B**. It would therefore also be possible that the expression Ψ contains a solution which is, in the long run, meaningful but which is not understood (at the moment), i.e. which cannot be understood in the normal linguistic context.[36] It is decisive for our understanding of the communication with the computer (Man–Machine interface) to keep in mind that internally (inside the computer), a machine *computes* the symbol ψ from the symbol φ with the help of some well-specified algorithms.

We can understand the elements φ, ψ in **L** as parameter 'values' for the concrete linguistic descriptions Φ and Ψ in *L* which are used to calculate ψ (as value of Ψ) and which yield a corresponding meaning if interpreted by the user of the natural language *L* and given a meaning in **B**. It is important to once again stress the fact that the algorithms instantiated by the machine in order to compute ψ from φ describe neither the structure of the brain processes of a human being nor the structure of inferring Ψ from Φ. On the level of the machine, calculating ψ from φ has nothing in common with an effective algorithm for solving problems based on the background knowledge **E** which we, as human beings, would use to produce Ψ as a solution for Φ.[37] On a scientific level, such a human system of rules in which every single step is literally descriptive and can be understood as a causal connection between events would consist in a doctor's exact classification of his patient in regard to his symptoms and in his reaching his diagnosis via a process of case-differentiation and -elimination. The methods of calculation used by the machine (and by us, via **F**) have as much (or as little) in common with these descriptive rules for the generation of instructions as the blackened silver atoms on a photo with the depicted objects.

If one has constructed *one* (universal) machine, however, then it is possible to build a suitable, formally adequate machine which uses, for directing the calculation of ψ from φ, a computer language which is so far removed from the original machine language and so close to the natural rules of inferring that one then has the *impression* that the calculation of ψ from φ corresponds to human processes of inferring (information processing). This is what happened with the computer language LISP, which has developed accordingly through several stages or with the programming language smalltalk, which has a high level of expressiveness but is very slow.

A computer can on the one hand be employed to *simulate* and on the other hand to *instantiate* intelligent problem solutions. The way in which this is done corresponds neither to the everyday understanding of the applications of scientific achievements to real life problems nor to the usual 'working philosophy' of a computer scientist, i.e. the unreflected concepts which direct or guide his work. These concepts must not be confused with those concepts which explain and/or predict the success of his programs.[38]

This is particularly important because the different interpretations of these two concepts become apparent in the *use* of the computer programs. In an everyday context we classify computer programs according to their applicability to real life problems. This depends on the background knowledge of our *Lebenswelt*, which is responsible for an understanding of Φ, i.e. it depends on an everyday (or rule-) semantics (F in the scheme LIR) which is also responsible for the evaluation of the computed solution Ψ (produced by the program).

Everyday semantics is also responsible for the *prose* of the scientist, i.e. for a computer expert's understanding or acceptance of a program P in L[39] as a solution for the problem Φ. This F-semantics is, however, primarily a semantics of rules or one based on processes, i.e. the meaning of the signs in L is given by rules for their use (in their relation to B).[40]

The unconscious use of a scientist's everyday background-knowledge which is mapped (cf. T in LIR) into his E-background knowledge, which reflects his everyday expectations or understanding in a transformative way is decisive in regard to an internal clarification of the meaning (in the sense of an adjustment to their scientific world-view) of scientific achievements. The arguments via F, with which the consequences of everyday meanings are tested, also play an important role.

The result of these considerations is that philosophy is assigned a special importance. It should on the one hand attempt to make clear how certain results of, say, the computer sciences are to be understood at all with the help of arguments (respectively argumentations) working with an F-semantics (making an F-sense of certain results). On the other hand, it should also try to discover the extent of the influence of everyday concepts on the work of scientists — yet some philosophical approaches neglect this concern of philosophy.[41] Other philosophical approaches attempt to find such F-argumentations (i.e. considerations based on an F-semantics) as are either supposed to show that **E** can, in principle, be completely reduced to **F**.[42]

In any case, philosophical considerations can be beneficial to the scientist if they help him to consider the consequences of the *labels* he uses for his activities, e.g. 'artificial intelligence'. Yet philosophers are often far too little concerned with what scientists could have meant precisely and under what conditions a scientist arrives at an *interpretation* (or understanding) of his results (which might be entirely justified from his point of view). Philosophers tend to concentrate on the scientists' prose, using their own F-semantics and their own (philosophical) E-semantics without taking the scientists' E-semantics[43] into account. In scientific research, however, the E-semantics of a scientifically meaningful expression[44] can lead to a prose which is completely clear to a scientist but causes considerable confusion in the context of an F-semantics.

Yet it is often a mixture of E- and F-understanding which influences a scientist (via his prose) in the choice of the direction in which he searches for a solution of his specific problems. In the case of AI programs, the mixture concerns, e.g., the concepts[45] about the '. . . intuitions of people who normally do the tasks that the program is doing' (Schank, 1979, 218).

Thus, the direction of AI-research can also be understood in the following way: First of all, scientists developed programs that could solve problems for which a human being would, in an everyday context, normally use intelligence. Then, they interpreted these programs as 'instantiations of artificial intelligence', and hoped to find abstract *principles of intelligence* which are, in the 'machine code' of the human brain,[46] simply realized differently. Yet they were confronted with greater difficulties than anticipated. Guided by the everyday understanding of the term 'intelligence', they concluded that they had, on the one hand, to represent meaningful background-knowledge (knowledge basis) and, on the other hand, to separate it from the rules for information processing (cf. inference-engine).[47]

Refined common sense had its consequences, and we are now faced with the question of how the interaction between A- and C-background knowledge can be controlled in a meaningful way.[48] In any case, I think there is a point in considerations about the way in which we grasp and solve problems in regard to their content with automatic, formal systems (Haugeland, 1985, 47–86). There is also a point in a certain correction of the self-conception of scientists as well as of philosophers. There is no danger of receiving obtrusive concepts (cf. McCarthy, 1979, 161–195).

I would now like to analyse how it is possible that a computer can simulate human information-processing. Let us assume that in $L$ we have a numerical representation of some facts about $B$. We now want to calculate new data with these numbers which we can use in a meaningful way. We would like to know, for example, how many boards of wood we need to cover some floor. The arithmetical rules we need for this task belong to the type 'human information-processing' and are located in $F$. If we use a computer, the result of the application of these arithmetical rules has to be reproduced by an 'interpreted, automatic and formal system' (Haugland, 1984, 48) implemented in the computer.

Basically, this is made possible by the discovery (by Leibniz) of an *abstract principle* which makes explicit, in a modern language, the algebraic structure of calculating with numbers. This algebraic structure can be regarded as an abstract structure model (expressed in $M$); i.e. as the abstract, mathematical meaning of what talking about *adding* numbers amounts to and what computation by a computer and computation by a human being[49] have in common.[50]

Furthermore, this algebraic structure (usually a Boolean algebra) can be considered as an abstract (mathematical) explanation of how it is possible that a binary system of numbers can be used to compute. The Boolean algebra which underlies both the computations of people in the decimal system and the dual system of the machine, can be placed into $M$. It was decisive for the development of modern computers that the abstract model (or principle) could on the one hand be used to select a formal (dual) system equivalent to the formal (decimal) system underlying our natural ways of calculation; and on the other hand could be realized in an electronic machine (based on physical principles).

Similarly, one tries to find a formal system for human information-processing which is to be instantiated in a computer. One of the conditions for this is that human information-processing actually *is* an automatic formal system,[51] and that the results of human information processing can be reproduced by some formal system.[52]

Just as in the case of computation, in the case of (formal) intelligence[53] we would first need abstract principles (in $M$) that can be assigned a formal system (in **L**) as instantiation of those principles. This system (in **L**) needs to be formally equivalent to our natural intelligent information processing (in **F**). Furthermore, we would need a proof that there exists an interpreter for this instantiation, i.e. a computer program which translates the formal system into the machine code of the computer. The interpreter allows the computer to imitate the input/output behavior of the formal system (in **L**), which is considered as virtual machine.[54] The input/output behavior of the formal system is actually imitated by simulating the manipulation of strings of signs in a higher programming language.[55] This is the way in which the input/output behavior of human (intelligent) information-processing can be imitated. But we still do not know whether our interpreted formal system (the computer) is an instantiation of a structure model (or an abstract principle in **M**) *common* to **L** and **F**.[56]

One thinks that, just as in the case of calculation/computation one need not be aware of the principles that explain why it is possible to use machine-code and how to turn the latter into the commands for a real machine, one need not be aware of the unifying principles between **F** (intelligent, human information processing) and **L** (formal intelligence). One more or less tacitly presupposes the existence of that structure in **M**. While in calculation/ computation one knows the structure, in AI one does not. One simply assumes the formal system in **L** to be complete with respect to **F**, and then adjusts reality to it.[57]

I think that what least influences the construction of AI programs are concepts about what intelligence *is*. Instead of this, what is built into the programs are (participative) concepts about *how* people solve problems.

One possible explanation for the fact that Newton's physical concepts, for example, were able to achieve general acceptance is that his abstract, theoretical concepts (such as position and momentum and, above all, force) permit literally descriptive (common-sensical) interpretations which even today govern the application of theoretical insights of physics within an everyday realm of experience — a human window into the world. This is also true for some central concepts of AI such as knowledge, inference, or such metaphors as 'something is hardwired into our brains'.

To identify these concepts, one could try to *analyse* the way in which existing programs such as Winograd's Block's World or natural language parsing programs work. One should, however, consider the requirements these concepts should meet before starting an analysis. One (central) requirement could be that the concepts lie within the narrow band in which the abstract and the concrete meet, i.e. one should try to identify those explanatory concepts which can be used in an immediately descriptive way.

In the computer sciences, this happens when processor- and memory-intensitivity[58] of programs are close and therefore allow for a better human understanding (at least at the surface) of the way they work.[59] These programs are to some extent closer to human thinking and can therefore much easier be controlled and applied.

This fact leads to the following theoretical considerations:[60] a formal system, which is at the basis of a given computer program in a higher programming language can be imitated by a universal Turing machine in regard to its computational input/output behavior. It is just a conjecture (Turing thesis), however, that there exists a Turing machine for any of these formal systems (in L with regard to F). It is therefore not unlikely that formal systems exist which would be suitable for grasping important aspects of human information-processing but for which no Turing machine (computer instantiation) exists. This possibility is ignored in AI. Only those formal systems are accepted which allow for a realization in a computer, i.e. have an interpreter or assembler for the given higher programming language that contains the formal systems. For some it is insignificant whether the formal system, which is reduced to computability by the machine, is in most cases incomplete. One dangerous consequence of this[61] is that human thinking might lose its flexibility and creativity, since human thinking might mimic the computer. Another consequence is that, in a restricted area of observation, reality is changed in such a way that it contains only facts which confirm the theory that, finally, 'thinking and computing' are made 'radically the same' (Haugland, 1985, 2).

Unfortunately, it is unrealistic to expect that functioning (yet incomplete) programs are put aside in search of principles that allow the selection of suitable formal systems which cannot be simulated by a computer. Instead of this, the formal systems underlying such computer programs are used as approximations of the formal systems at which we aim.

The only way out of this situation is to be aware of the use of incomplete (formal) systems and to permit a correction of their results which can then be fitted into and evaluated in our world. This is easier with processor-intensive programs than with memory-intensive programs, which work with very abstract concepts. The creation of a human window should include a narrowing of the gap between processor- and memory-intensive programs.

Yet this solution also has its dangers. The transparency of these programs and the application of their results is based on a certain background knowledge (**E** and/or **F**). Yet **E** background-knowledge plays an important part in the construction of programs. I suspect that neither the **M**-representation nor the **E**-expression of knowledge are completely grasped by computer programs. A sensible application of the programs (interpretation in **B**) demands an **E** background knowledge which is able to eliminate those results which do not make sense in **B** (via **E**). But the main problem is the use of the programs via **F**. Now, one would have to presuppose that **E** knowledge can be reduced completely to an **F** knowledge, i.e. all **E** meaningful arguments could be justified by **F** arguments. To my mind, this is possible neither in principle nor is it practicable. Any solution of this problem depends on our epistemological and philosophical assumptions. It can be neglected, however, if we concentrate on creating programs which do not lead to serious mistakes if applied with an **F**-background knowledge only. What we need is a compromise between **E** and **F** for the evaluation of computational results. Since in general **E** at least locally uses a higher resolution level as **F** and therefore has more expressive power, **F** is incomplete in regard to **E**. Again we have to build possibilities of evaluation and correction into the programs that prevent mistakes of application. Basically, this can only be solved in a pragmatical way (cf. p. v above).

So far, we have not dealt with the question of a concrete working philosophy for the AI scientists. In this context, I would like to consider four aspects:

(1)  The philosophical pillow: Some scientists do the opposite of what they claim to do. Certain physicists, e.g., argue that their theoretical insights are derived from their experiments only, while others (like the later Einstein) admit that physical theories are free conceptual creations. In the case of AI, there are some who want to sell their subject by claiming that with the help of AI 'principles of intelligence' can be investigated. Actually, they can only specify what is necessary for constructing programs that can feign intelligence in a regimented area of application.

(2)   The use of the computer by the programmer: In this case it can happen that for constructing a good program the programmer falls back onto everyday concepts, for example, he assumes that the computer has *intentions* that are, however, by no means necessary for writing good programs and for working with the finished programs. These guiding concepts stemming from the context of discovery are easily stylized as realistic assumptions about the computer.

(3)   Idealizations: There are some idealistic concepts which can guide our programming activities but do not interfere directly. These are certain F-concepts about intelligence, such as that intelligence has to do with, e.g., learning and flexibility in applying certain solutions to different situations. These concepts become the guiding principles for evaluating AI programs since the latter have to embody those F-characteristics of intelligence. Sometimes even F-concepts about human approaches to problem-solving are used, but this is rather a simulation of formal characteristics of intelligence (as understood via F). The F-concepts concern the acceptance of a program as an AI-Program. They do not influence the practice of computer scientists directly. Yet calling the programs 'intelligent' prepares for the assumption that the principles successfully influencing the construction of AI programs are also realized in human thinking.

(4)   Effective knowledge (by programmers and experts): In a program like MYCIN, the knowledge (expertise) of doctors is directly implemented into the computer in an attempt to reproduce participative problem solving. The problem of what intelligence is and how intelligence can be implemented in the computer is then a minor one.

In this context, the task of philosophy should be to expound the concrete concepts influencing the construction of the programs, and to pave the way for an intelligent use of the programs (in the sense of the pragmatic approach, cf. p.v above).

I presume that only (3) and (4) lead to a fruitful working philosophy for the programmer as well as the user of a computer. The central assumption of the information processing sciences is to equalize knowledge, information and meaning and to analyse the world under this aspect. The relation of these concepts is explicated in the scheme LIR, which supports the positions (3) and (4) and could prevent the negative consequences of the attitudes underlying (1) and (2).

On the one hand, the scheme does not interfere with a normal working practice, it helps the scientist to see his problems in the right perspective. On the other hand, the scheme helps to identify possible problems if they are caused by misconceived and wrongly implemented expertise. An example for such a misconception, for example, is to employ memory-intensive programs to control nuclear power stations (cf. Michie, 1984, 56–60). In such a case, the complexity of the information, given as a normal set of data, can be decisive for losing control over the system. The lesson is clear: 'Unless a technical system is designed in every detail so as to be comprehensible to the humans operating it, unless the way information is presented fits in with the way human eyes and minds work rather than the way the machinery works, then once the system starts to malfunction it will tend to become unmanageable' (Michie, 1984, 58).

Another very important example concerning the philosophy for pursuing AI is Winograd's Block's World. With the help of LIR, we can analyse the structure of the program and can understand its conceptual environment (relying on the expressive power of LISP). It also becomes clear how the positive results of the program are to be understood, e.g. not as descriptions of how humans have to act or react in a Block's World.

If we now look at the contributions to this volume, we can identify their respective topics in the scheme LIR. Chapter 1 belongs to the interrelation between **M**, **E** and **F**; Chapters 2 and 3 are concerned with **E** and **F**. A specifically psychological approach is presented in Chapter 4, which deals with the relation between **E** and **M**. Chapter 5 is again concerned with the relations between **M**, **E** and **F**, and Chapter 6 takes up the interaction of **M** and **F**. Chapter 7, however, deals with the interests of the specialist in AI and is primarily — but not solely — concerned with the relation between **E** and **L**. Chapter 8 tries to deal with **L**, **M** and **F**.

**Legend of symbols used in Introduction**

**B** regimented part of the world
**E** semi-formal expert-knowledge
**F** folk-knowledge
**F** concrete mapping (representational aspect), linguistic classification
**f** abstract mapping (truth-functional evaluation), logical classification (analysis)
**G** concrete evaluation (in **E**)
**g** abstract mapping, measurement function
**H** concrete interpretation (via expert background-knowledge)
**h** abstract interpretation (via structural models of the world)
**L** logical language
*L* natural language
**M** structural models of the world
**R** representational system
**T** concrete mapping, translation of expert background-knowledge into folk-knowledge
**t** identification, referring linguistic expressions onto **B**
**U** concrete-formal transformation
**u** abstract-semi-formal
**V** concrete-abstract conveyance
**v** abstract formal-conveyance
**W** reality or world

**Notes**

1. Ultimately, even insiders might think that they are dealing with 'intelligence' in an everyday sense of the word and not merely with a powerful computer program. This aspect of the topic of 'AI' and the general interest in it might be due to an, at least seemingly possible, revival of mankind's old dream of creating a 'Golem'. Yet a detailed analysis of this side of the problem would lead us too far from the *content* of our topic and would not cede those insights into the functioning of AI in regard to its consequences (in everyday life and in science) which we would expect to gain or perhaps wish to convey to the reader.

2. This can have a dangerous influence on the application of the results of AI to reality and its problems.

3. Since the structure of successful programs should yield general insights into what the meaning of intelligence amounts to.

4. Cf. the concept of a 'human window' (Michie, 1985, 69ff.).

5. Cf. Parnas (1986, 49–69). If someone produces an AI program that decides complex economic situations with certain data, wrong conclusions have to be disentangled from correct ones with the help of a sound intuitive knowledge about the

situation, a knowledge that rests upon participation or factual content. But if someone without this background knowledge bases his decisions on such programs, he relies on the theory at the bottom of the program. The theories, however, are more or less unknown to a blind user of the programs and are therefore immune to revision. They may be built upon a completely mistaken representation of the world, even if the programs themselves produce good results at the beginning. The results may even be similar to an evaluation of the situation by experts and the programs therefore meet the expectations of the experts. But experts know how to eliminate nonsensical results as soon as they crop up and they do so with their background knowledge and their experiences. Yet people who use the programs without this possibility of correction are liable to consider all results as correct and meaningful. It is therefore irresponsible to continue to produce such AI programs, even if they sell well (cf. Schank, 1984, 146ff.).

6. And this at a time when we know little or nothing about the subject.

7. The traditional philosophical response to these questions is to dismiss them as insignificant or unimportant, although for ethical considerations constructive support would be a far better attitude.

8. By the term 'working philosophy' I understand those concepts which guide a scientist in his enterprises.

9. This scheme should by no means be understood as an (axiomatic) foundation.

10. Cf. also Wang, 1986, 191ff.

11. I use quotation marks in order to draw additional attention to the special meaning of the term in question.

12. In object orientated LISP programming, for example, the communication (in a technical sense) between $W$ and $R$ establishes the relation between sign and object (message) in those programs.

13. A successful solution of the problems we are here concerned with will justify its application.

14. Some of the signs I use are not directly derived from the terms they stand for. In the case of $A$, I have taken over a convention of mathematical model-theory.

15. According to a paradigm given by Haugland (1985, 230), 'intelligence is essentially symbol manipulation'. A common-sensical understanding of the term 'intelligence' might emphasize, for example, flexibility in solving complex problems in new situations.

16. A deduction makes something conscious which is already known. Therefore, no new insights can be gained by this process (creative semantics).

17. Be $\theta\varepsilon$ $D$; A-meaning: = (defined as) that $\beta$ $\varepsilon$ $B$ for which it is valid that (g $(\beta)$, h f $(\theta)$) $\varepsilon$ $A$. An analogous procedure is valid for $C$. This means that $A$ and $C$ select that same object of reference in $B$. This is to be reached by differentiation (indexicalization) in $L$ (via $C$).

18. A child can make complicated manoeuvres with a desk calculator once he or she has been told to press the right buttons — he or she need not understand anything about mathematics.

19. $E := KB \cap C; F := IE \cap C; L := IE \cap A; M := KB \cap A$.

20. Of course it is easier to look for such theories as do not have to be transformed by a lengthy process. This means, however, an irresponsible restriction of the available solution space via $T$ which carries severe scientific consequences. It would only be justified if one could be sure that $T$ can be 'reduced' completely to $V$. It is, in this context, of little use to talk about the supposed freedom of applying all possible means of gaining knowledge in the realm $T$ if only what is immediately accessible via $V$ is taken up for further discussion.

21. This differentiation between theoretico-explanatory (abstract) and operational insights or contents is to my mind especially important because the application of the results depends in a central way on this understanding of results. What does

it actually mean, for example, if we say that the summing up of integers is a mapping of the Cartesian product of the set of integers onto itself — a binary mathematical (number) operation — which attributes an integer to a pair of integers? This operation has to realize certain formal characteristics, e.g. the commutativity (3+4=4+3; the attribution of a number onto a pair of integers does not depend on the sequence of numbers in the pair). The knowledge about these abstract characteristics is essential for a generalization and for the construction of new models (which are realizations of these abstract structures). The formal aspects of given real systems (e.g. our personal, concrete experience in calculating) can then be transferred to other fields in a semantically meaningful way. If we ignore this differentiation, we arrive at a grave misunderstanding of the results of scientific endeavours, especially those of AI. To my mind, this has happened in occidental thinking. Explanatory concepts were misunderstood as immediate instructions for actions, as immediately applicable. Now that we have realized that 'something' went wrong, that our operationalizations are unfit for this world, all we do is to search for new paradigms, new approximations which are, however, still based on this essential misunderstanding.

22. The question remains whether we could not identify something within everyday experiences that corresponds to this distinction. I think that this is possible, but only after we have successfully introduced and used this distinction in a scientific or technical context. The theory of relativity could not have been developed with an everyday background knowledge only. Yet after it had been developed, it was possible to enrich everyday language at certain points with carefully selected and defined terms of the scientific background and to talk about the theory of relativity in an everyday context without too many serious misunderstandings. Yet for solving technical problems in e.g. the computer sciences, the everyday world-view and everyday language are not sufficient. We cannot, therefore, use the *everyday world-view* and its *concepts* for talking about the distinctions I am going to introduce. We would not be able to realize their significance if we made these distinctions within an everyday world-view only. We are also not able to justify these distinctions with the help of vernacular concepts. *Conveying* scientific results is not identical with *justifying* them.

23. Wittgenstein discusses the influence of a scientist's prose on this subject (cf. *Remarks on the Foundations of Mathematics*; *Lectures on the Philosophy of Mathematics*).

24. Such as the fact that the earth is an irregular rotational ellipsoid which circles the sun on an elliptic path.

25. Cf. Schank, 1979, 218ff.

26. Of linguistic expressions in everyday language, yet in his special field.

27. At present, mistakes are still possible. The danger is, however, that formal systems are stylized as reality, and whatever does not fit in is simply left out — cf. Charlie Chaplin, who cuts away everything that does not fit into his suitcase in 'Goldfever'.

28. This is actually also an approach to find out aspects of mapping reality onto a theory; and therefore also the categories of classification (or characteristics) and simplifications of any scientific discipline.

29. At the bottom of this we find the concept that in logic we are also confronted with rules for the production of inferences. Actually, these rules are algorithms to justify the validity of intuitive inferences, and we have to find the concrete rules which operationalize those algorithms.

30. Knowledge has to be represented as a structure model, respectively a structure model is at the basis of any knowledge-representation.

31. Such inferences are not accepted as valid within ordinary logic.

32. Once we accept a connection between statements by relating them to knowledge (structure model), we can in retrospect give a new algorithm, a rule for

proceeding from one meaningful statement to a new meaningful statement.

33. Which, from a different point of view, is a sufficient condition for a reconstruction.

34. It is often said that the context of a situation has to be taken into account, yet if we look at the actual programs, we find finite decision trees based on syntactical rules.

35. A statement that describes a procedure to produce a solution!

36. A real-life example for this would be to give technical instructions (printed in Chinese) for the construction of a gun to an eskimo who is attacked by a hungry polar bear.

37. I believe that we resort to such algorithms to a greater extent than we are aware of even in so-called everyday situations. In the scheme, human algorithms would be found in F (everyday semantics of rules), while those used by the machine are located in L.

38. It is not possible to gain directly applicable instructions for solving real-life problems out of our attempts to understand how the construction of solutions with automatic, formal systems (i.e. computer programs) is possible. An (intelligent) solution is supposed to tell us what should be done in a concrete situation.

39. P applied to $\psi$ yields $\psi$ ($\psi$ is understood as $\Psi$).

40. Some philosophers might have their doubts about the existence of anything other than an F-semantics. They might be satisfied with interpreting the E- and M-semantics as different language games. We then once again face the problem of a possible translation of M-meanings into F-meanings.

41. E.g. theoretical analyses about whether all those *E-concepts* which function as explanatory hypotheses for the difference in a behavior of users — all E-concepts giving an E-meaning in B to the results $\Psi$ which lead to a use in B which is different from a use of $\Psi$ via the F-meaning only — can be mapped onto or, as some would say, reduced completely to F-concepts.

42. Many philosophers are, I think, simply not aware of the fact that in general they do *not* use, for their philosophical considerations, a language with a different resolution level as the language they use to convey their results. This leads to the mistaken impression that the means for gaining an insight are the same as those used for its conveyance. I have here deliberately replaced the 'context of justification' by 'context of conveyance'.

43. Which accounts for the technical meaning of the terms.

44. Depending on a specific aspect of representation.

45. They are also the intuitions and/or folk-psychological ideas which a computer scientist implements in the computer.

46. 'Neuronese', Flanagan (1984, 227); 'mentalese', Putnam, this volume, and Pylyshin (1984).

47. Cf. Schank, 1979, 220.

48. The reciprocal influence such as that of scientific results onto internal philosophical considerations and of these considerations onto the prose of the scientist has to be analysed very carefully.

49. Who applies the rules of calculation internalized in F during his school days.

50. This idea of 'something in common' haunted Wittgenstein all his life. In the *Tractatus* he assumed that it was *the* logical structure which the world and language have in common which was considered to be responsible for the application of, say, inferences drawn in language to the world. Due to the fact that both rested on or were instantiations of the same abstract structure, those inferences had to apply to reality.

51. This prerequisite for Turing's thesis that for any deterministic automatic formal system whatever, there exists a formally equivalent Turing machine, is often neglected; cf. Haugeland, 1985, 133–40.

52. Yet logically speaking this does not imply that human thinking is nothing but a formal, automatic system of symbol manipulations. It is only analysed in this way.
53. Just as we could talk of formal computation as artificial computation, we could talk of formal intelligence as artificial intelligence.
54. Defined as computer-plus-interpreter, cf. Churchland, 1984, 103ff.
55. That is, one considers the instantiated formal system as a computer, cf virtual machine.
56. There is no proof that for an arbitrary 'deterministic automatic formal system' there exists a formally equivalent Turing machine since Turing's thesis is not proven. But if there is an appropriately specified formal system which is realized as a Turing machine then there exists a universal Turing machine which can mimic the first one move by move.
57. Cf. n. 27, above.
58. Cf. Michie, 1985, 56–75.
59. These programs can, so to speak, be used in certain areas with an F-understanding only.
60. And has long-term practical and ethical consequences.
61. Which can be seen in the wrong application of the program MYCIN.

# References

Barr, A., and Feigenbaum, E.A. (1981) *The Handbook of Artificial Intelligence*, Vol. 1, Stanford.
—— (1982) *The Handbook of Artificial Intelligence*, Vol. 2, Stanford.
Charniak, E., and McDermott, D.V. (1985) *Introduction to Artificial Intelligence*, Reading MA.
Churchland, P.M. (1984) *Matter and Consciousness: A Contemporary Introduction to the Philosophy of Mind*, Cambridge MA.
Cohen, P.R. and Feigenbaum, E. A. (1982) *The Handbook of Artificial Intelligence*, Vol. 3, Stanford.
Flanagan, O. J. Jr. (1984) *The Science of the Mind*, Cambridge MA.
Haugeland, J. (1985) *Artificial Intelligence: The Very Idea*, Cambridge MA.
Michie, D., and Johnston, R. (1985) *The Creative Computer: Machine Intelligence and Human Knowledge*, Harmondsworth.
Parnas, D.L. (1986) 'Software Wars, Ein offener Brief', in *Kursbuch 83, Krieg und Frieden — Streit um SDI*, Berlin, 49–69.
Pylyshyn, Z. (1984) *Computation and Cognition*, Cambridge MA.
Ringle, M. (1979) *Philosophical Perspectives in Artificial Intelligence*, Brighton.
Schank, R. (1979) 'Natural Language, Philosophy and Artificial Intelligence', in M. Ringle (ed.), *Philosophical Perspectives in Artificial Intelligence*, Brighton.
—— (1984) 'Intelligent Advisory Systems', in P.H. Winston and K.A. Prendergast (eds.), *The AI Business*, Cambridge MA.
Turing, A. (1950) 'Computing Machinery and Intelligence', *Mind*, 59, 434–60.
Wang, H. (1986) *Beyond Analytic Philosophy: Doing Justice to What We Know*, Cambridge MA.
Winograd, T. (1972) *Understanding Natural Language*, Edinburgh.
Winston, P.H. (1984) *Artificial Intelligence*, 2nd ed, Reading MA.
—— and Pendergast, K.A. (eds.) (1984) *The AI Business*, Cambridge MA.
Wittgenstein, L. (1976) *Wittgenstein's Lectures on the Foundations of Mathematics*, ed. C. Diamond, Brighton.
—— (1978) *Remarks on the Foundations of Mathematics*, eds. G.H. von Wright, R. Rhees and G.E.M. Anscombe, Oxford.

# 1 COMPUTATIONAL PSYCHOLOGY AND INTERPRETATION THEORY

Hilary Putnam

I once got into an argument after dinner with my friend Zenon Pylyshyn. The argument concerned the following assertion which Pylyshyn made: 'cognitive psychology is impossible if there is not a well-defined notion of *sameness of content* for mental representations'. It occurred to me later that the reasons I have for rejecting this assertion tie in closely with Donald Davidson's well-known interests in both meaning theory and the philosophy of mind. Accordingly, with Zenon's permission and (I hope) forgiveness, I have decided to make my arguments against his assertion the subject of this paper.

## Mental Representation

Let us consider what goes on in the mind when we think 'there is a tree over there', or any other common thought about ordinary physical things. On one model, the computer model of the mind, the mind has a 'program', or set of rules, analogous to the rules governing a computing machine, and thought involves the manipulation of words and other signs (not all of this manipulation 'conscious', in the sense of being able to be verbalized by the computer). This model, however, is almost vacuous as it stands (in spite of the heat it generates among those who do not like to think that a mere device, such as a computing machine, could possibly serve as a model for something as special as the human mind). It is vacuous because the program, or system of rules for mental functioning, has not been specified; and it is this program that constitutes the psychological theory. Merely saying that the correct psychological theory, whatever it may be, can be represented as a program (or something analogous to a program) for a computer (or something analogous to a computer) is almost empty; for virtually any system that can be described by a set of *laws* can at least be *simulated* by a computer. Anything from Freudian depth psychology to Skinnerian behaviorism can be represented as a kind of computer program.

Today, however, computer scientists working in 'artificial intelligence', and cognitive psychologists thinking about reference, semantic representation, language use, and so on, have a little more specific hypothesis in mind than the almost empty hypothesis that the mind can be modelled by a digital computer. (Even that hypothesis is not wholly empty because it does imply *something*: the causal structure of mental processes; it implies that they take place according to deterministic or probabilistic rules of sequencing according to a finite progam.) The further hypothesis to which workers on computing machines and cognitive psychologists have been converging is this: that the mind thinks with the aid of *representations*. There seem to be two different ideas, actually, which are both involved in talk of 'representations' today.

The first idea, based on experience with trying to program computers to simulate intelligent behaviour is that thinking involves not just the manipulation of arbitrary objects or symbols, but requires the manipulation of symbols that have a very specific structure, the structure of a *formalized language*. The experience of computer people was that the most interesting and successful programs in 'artificial intelligence' *typically* turned out to involve giving the computing machine something like a formalized language and a set of rules for manipulating that formalized language ('reasoning' in the language, so to speak).

The second idea associated with the term 'representation' is that the human mind thinks (in part) by constructing some kind of a 'model' of its environment: a 'model of the world'. This 'model' need not, of course, literally *resemble* the world. It is enough that there should be some kind of *systematic relation* between items in the representational system and items 'out there', so that what is going on 'out there' can be read off from its representational system by the mind.

Once a reference definition has been given for a formalized language, a set of sentences in that language can serve as a 'representational system' or 'model of the world'.

Suppose, for example, we wish to represent the fact that the city of Paris is bigger than the city of Vienna. If we have a predicate, say $F$, which represents the relation *bigger than* (i.e. if the open sentence which we write in the formal notation as '$Fxy$' is correlated to the relation which holds between any two things if and only if they are both cities and the first is larger — in, say, population — than the second), and if we have 'individual constants' or proper names, say, *a* and *b*, which represent the cities of Paris and Vienna (i.e. '*a*' is correlated to Paris and '*b*' is correlated to Vienna by the reference definition for the language), then we can represent the fact that Paris is a bigger city than Vienna by just including in our list of accepted sentences (our 'theory of the world') the sentence '*Fab*'. In a similar way, any state of affairs, however complex, that can be expressed using the predicates, proper names, and logical devices of the formal language can be asserted to obtain by including in the 'theory of the world' the formula that represents that state of affairs.

When our 'representational system' is itself a *theory*, and when our method of employing our representational system involves *making formal deductions*, we see that *one and the same object* — the formalized language, including the rules for deduction — can be the formalized language that computer scientists have been led to postulate as the brain or mind's (the difference does not appear particularly significant, from this perspective) medium of computation, and, simultaneously, the medium of representation. *The mind uses a formalized language* (or something significantly like a formalized language) *both as medium of computation and medium of representation.* This may be called the working hypothesis of cognitive psychology today.

Part of this working hypothesis seems to me certainly correct. I believe that we cannot account at all for the functioning of thought and language without regarding at least some mental items as representations. When I think (correctly) 'there is a tree in front of me', the occurrence of the word 'tree' in the sentence I speak in my mind is a *meaningful* occurrence and one of the items in the *extension* of that occurrence of the word 'tree' is the very tree in front of me. Moreover, the open sentence '*x* is in front of me' is correlated (in the correct semantics for my language) with the relational property of being in front of me, and the entire sentence 'there is a tree in front of me' is, by virtue of these and similar facts, one which is *true* if and only if there is a tree in front of me.

Where there is room for psychologists to differ is over *how many* mental items are representations, how useful it is to postulate a large and complex *unconscious* system of representations in order to explain conscious thought and intelligent action, etc.

### The Verificationist Semantics of 'Mentalese'

So far what I have said is in line with the thinking of Pylyshyn and other 'propositionalist' cognitive psychologists. For the sake of the argument, we shall assume all this is right. Of course, the actual story may be much more complicated. The mind may employ more than *one* formalized language (or, rather, formalized-language-analog). Different parts of the brain may compute in different 'media'. And both sentence-analogs and image-analogs may be used in the actual computational procedures, along with things that are neither. But let us assume the best case for Pylyshyn's view: a mind which does *all* its computing in *one* formalized language.

In what does the mind's *understanding* of its *own* medium of computation consist? It will do no good to say, as Fodor (1975) has, that we should not apply the word 'understand' to 'mentalese' itself. ('Mentalese' is a name for the hypothetical formalized-language-analog in the brain.) For 'mentalese' and 'formalized-language-in-the-brain' are *metaphors*. They may be scientifically useful and rich metaphors; but *as* metaphors they are inseparable from the notion of *understanding*. Something cannot literally be a language unless it can be *understood*; and something cannot be a language-*analog* unless there is a suitable *understanding-analog*. If some representations in the brain are sentence-analogs and predicate-analogs, then what is the corresponding *understanding-analog*?

The answer, I suggest, is this: the brain's 'understanding' of its own 'medium of computation and representation' consists in its possession of a *verificationist semantics* for the medium, i.e. of a computable predicate[1] which can represent acceptability, or warranted assertibility, or credibility. Idealizing, we treat the language as interpreted (in part) *via* a set of rules which assign *degrees of confirmation* (i.e. subjective probabilities) to the sentence-analogs relative to experiential inputs and relative also to other sentence-analogs. Such rules must be computable; and their 'possession' by the mind/brain/machine consists in its being 'wired' to follow them, or having come to follow them as a result of learning. (I do *not* assume that mentalese must be *innate*, or that it must be disjoint from the natural language the speaker has acquired.)

But why a verificationist semantics? Why not a meaning theory in Davidson's sense?

Obviously, if we interpret mentalese as a 'system of representation' we do ascribe extensions to predicate-analogs and truth conditions to sentence-analogs. But the 'meaning theory' which represents a particular interpretation of mentalese is not *psychology*. In fact, if we formulate it as Davidson might, its only primitive notion is 'true', and 'true' is not psychological notion. To spell this out: the meaning theory yields such theorems ('T-sentences') as (pretend that mentalese is English): ' "Snow is white" is true in mentalese if and only if snow is white'. This contains no psychological vocabulary at all.

We might try to say 'well, the understanding consists in the brain's *knowing* the T-sentences of the meaning theory'. But the notion of *knowing* cannot be a *primitive* notion in sub-personal cognitive psychology.[2]

Suppose we try to say: the mind understands *without using representations* what it is for snow to be white, and it knows the representation 'snow is white' is true if and only if that state of affairs holds. Not only does this treat the mind as something that 'knows' things, instead of *analyzing knowing into more elementary and less intentional processes*, but it violates the fundamental assumption of cognitive psychology, that understanding what states of affairs are, thinking about them, etc., *cannot be done without representations*. At bottom, we would be stuck with the myth of comparing representations directly with unconceptualized reality.

On the other hand, if we say, 'the brain's/mind's *use* of the sentence "Snow is white" (or the corresponding sentence-analog) is such as to warrant the interpretation that "Snow is white" is true in mentalese if and only if snow is white, *and this is what it means to say that the brain (implicitly) "knows" the T-sentence*', then we do not give any theory of what that 'use' consists in. This is what a *verificationist* semantics gives (and, as far as I can see, what *only* a verificationist semantics gives). I suggest, then, that verificationist semantics is the natural semantics for functionalist (or 'cognitive') psychology. Such a semantics has a notion of 'belief' (or 'degree of belief') which is what makes it *cognitive*; at the same time it is a *computable* semantics, which is what makes it functionalist.

Of course, we want the semantics to connect with *action*, and this means that the model must incorporate a *utility function* as well as a degree of confirmation function. This function, too, must be computable (or, strictly speaking, semi-computable). This idealization is, of course, severe: we are assuming that the belief-analog (represented by the degree-of-confirmation function) and the preference-analog (represented by the utility function) are both *fully consistent*. The actual (neurologically realized) analogs of both belief *and* preference (or belief-representations and preference-representations) may well be *inconsistent*, as long as there are procedures for resolving the inconsistencies when practical decisions have to be made. In a terminology used by Reichenbach in another context, consistency may be '*de faciendo* and not *de facto*'. What significance this has for philosophy of mind, I shall discuss briefly at the end of this paper.

For now, the problem is this: if the *brain's* semantics for its medium of representation is verificationist and not truth-conditional, then what happens to the notion of the 'content' of a mental representation?

**Two Ruritanian Children**

Imagine that there is a country somewhere on earth called Ruritania. In this country let us imagine that there are small differences between the dialects which are spoken in the north and in the south. One of these differences is that the word 'grug' means silver in the northern dialect and aluminium in the southern dialect. Imagine two children, Oscar and Elmer, who grow up in Ruritania. They are as alike in genetic constitution and environment as you please, except that Oscar grows up in the south of Ruritania and Elmer grows up in the north of Ruritania. Imagine that in the north of Ruritania, for some reason, pots and pans are normally made of silver, whereas in the south of Ruritania pots and pans are normally made of aluminium. So northern children grow up knowing that pots and pans are normally made of 'grug', and southern children grow up knowing that pots and pans are normally made of 'grug'.

We may suppose that Oscar and Elmer have the same 'mental representation' of 'grug', that they have the same *beliefs* in connection with grug, etc. Of course some of these beliefs will differ in meaning even if they are identical in verbal and mental representation. For example, when Oscar believes 'my mother has grug pots and pans' and when Elmer believes 'my mother has grug pots and pans' the indexical word 'my' refers to different persons, and hence the term 'my mother' refers to different mothers. But unless such small differences in collateral information are already enough to constitute a difference in the *content* of the mental representation (in which case it would seem that the ordinary distinction between the meaning of a sign and collateral information that we have in connection with the sign has been wholly abandoned),[3] then it would seem that we should say that the content of the mental representation of 'grug' is exactly the same for Oscar and for Elmer at this stage in their lives.

I do not mean to suggest that the *word* 'grug' has the same meaning in Oscar's idiolect as it does in Elmer's idiolect at this stage; I've argued elsewhere (Putnam, 1975a) that the difference in reference in the two communities should be regarded as infecting the speech of the individual speakers. To spell this out: when Oscar tries to determine what *is* grug he will ultimately have to rely on 'experts'. These experts need not necessarily be scientists, he may simply ask his parents (who may in turn consult store owners or even scientists). But the point is that since the extension of 'grug' is in fact different in the two communities, and since, on the theory of meaning that I have defended in other places, difference in extension constitutes difference of meaning, and since extension is fixed collectively and not individually, it ends up that the *meaning* of the word 'grug' in the idiolects of Oscar and Elmer is not the same even though there is nothing 'psychological', nothing 'in their heads', which constitutes the difference in meaning. *Meanings aren't in the head*. There is a difference in the meaning of the word 'grug' in this case; but it is in the *reference* of the word, as objectively fixed by the practices of the community, and not in the conceptions of grug entertained by Oscar and Elmer.

But the concept of content that Pylyshyn is interested in and that Chomsky[4] has expressed an interest in is one that would factor out such objective differences in extension. What Pylyshyn is looking for is a notion of the content of a mental representation in which 'water' on earth and 'water' on Twin Earth would be said to have the same content for speakers who had identical conceptions of 'water' even though it might be the case that 'water' on earth referred to $H_2O$ and 'water' on Twin Earth referred to XYZ. And what I have said so far is that on *any such notion of content it would seem that 'grug' in Oscar's mind would have the same content as 'grug' in Elmer's mind*.

Not only would the words have the same content; any mental

signs or predicate-analogs that the brain might use in its computations and that corresponded to the verbal item 'grug' would have the same content at this stage. But if the word 'grug', and the mental representations that stand behind the word 'grug' on a theory of the kind Pylyshyn advocates, have the same content at this stage, then *when do they come to differ in content?* By the time Oscar and Elmer have become adults, have learned foreign languages, and so on, they certainly will not have the same conception of grug. Oscar will know that 'grug' is the metal called 'aluminium' in English (I assume that everybody in Ruritania learns English as a second language in High School), and Elmer will know that the metal called 'grug' in his part of Ruritania is the metal called 'silver' in English. Each of them will know many facts which serve to distinguish silver from aluminium, and 'grug' in the south Ruritanian sense from 'grug' in the north Ruritanian sense.

However, on a verificationist model of the kind described in the first section of this paper there is no stage at which the word 'grug' or the corresponding mental representation in the mind of Oscar (or in the mind of Elmer) is ever treated as changing its reference. *Internally* to treat a sign as changing its reference is to treat it as, in effect, a different sign. This never happens; in the internal point of view all that happens is that Oscar acquires more information about grug. At one time he knew only that pots and pans are made of grug; that grug is a metal; and that grug has a certain color. Later he learned additional facts about grug (e.g. what it is called in English). When the use of a word is modified by the continual acquisition of collateral information, without it being supposed that at any stage the word is being committed to a new extension, all that happens (in the verificationist model) is that the degree of confirmation of various sentences containing the word changes. Moreover, this change in the degree of confirmation of various sentences containing the word is a *continuous* change; it is continuous because it is brought about merely by the conditionaliza-tion of prior probabilities to added information. What this simple example shows is that there is nothing in a functionalist model of the use of a language (or even of a system of internal represen-tations) which automatically gives us a decision as to when we should say that a representation has changed its 'content'. We can have a complete description of the use of mental signs without thereby having a criterion which distinguishes changes in the con-tent of mental signs from changes in collateral information. So we have a problem with synonomy *for mental signs.*

## Possible Solutions

In 'The meaning of "meaning" ' I proposed to decide whether or not words of a certain kind (natural kind words) are synonymous by looking at two things: the extension and the correlated *stereotype.* By the stereotype I meant a certain set of beliefs, or idealized beliefs, which all speakers are expected to have in connection with the word. For example, if all speakers are expected to believe that a tiger is striped (or that idealized tigers are striped) then stripes are part of the 'stereotype' of a tiger. Can the idea of a stereotype be extended to mental representations, and can *sameness of stereotype* provide us with a criterion for the synonymy of mental representations? To explore this, let me again imagine an Oscar, only this time let me imagine that Oscar lives in an experimental research station very near the North Pole. Perhaps this is a community of scientists and engineers experimenting with finding oil in extreme arctic conditions. I shall imagine that in this community, for some reason, there are no green plants, but that there are artificial plants and even artificial grass which people have introduced in order to make the place look more hospitable.

Now consider the word 'grass' in the idiolect of Oscar and in the idiolect of an ordinary American child, whom we shall call Elmer. If we take the stereotype of grass to be simply the perceptual prototype, then the stereotype of grass may be exactly the same in Oscar's mind as in Elmer's mind; but Oscar does not know that grass is in any sense a living or growing thing. I think we would regard it as wrong in such a case to suppose that the mental representation, or *the word* 'grass', had the same content in Oscar's mind as in Elmer's mind.

Perhaps we should require that in addition to having the same perceptual prototype for 'grass', Oscar and Elmer should have the same 'markers': for example, they should both believe that 'grass is a plant'. But this simply raises what I shall call the *infection problem.* If they do believe that grass is a plant, how similar do their notions of a *plant* have to be in order for their belief that *grass is a plant* to be relevantly the same belief? I think that in actual *interpretation* our policy is not to let infection go very far; i.e., for the purposes of deciding that an Oscar and an Elmer have the same notion of grass we may require that they both believe that grass is a plant *without* requiring that their notion of a plant be exactly the same. But this is already to accept the stance that interpretation is an essentially informal and interest-relative matter.

If we try for a notion of *exact sameness of content of mental representations*, which is what Pylyshyn is arguing for, then the infection problem becomes an infinite regress problem. Suppose, for example, that Oscar and Elmer are two children who both live in the United States and who both know that grass is a plant; but that Elmer knows that plants can be microscopic, whereas Oscar's notion of a plant involves being of visible size, being green, etc. Then the problem of distinguishing what is a difference in the content of the representations and what is a difference in collateral information re-arises again at the level of the marker 'plant'.

The point is that while discovering whether or not stereotypes are the same is good methodology for translation, it is nothing like an *algorithm*. Stereotypes themselves are beliefs expressed in *words*. Once we have accepted translations, however tentative, for some words or representations, then stereotype theory may give us a handle on how to translate other words or representations; but it cannot serve to *define* a notion of sameness of content for words or mental representations.

Nor can *sameness of perceptual prototype*, another notion that we have mentioned. We have seen that even if two words are associated with the same perceptual prototypes they may differ in meaning; for the meaning of the word is not just a function of associated perceptual prototypes, but also of various more or less abstract beliefs that one has in connection with the word ('grass is a plant'). Not only would it be wrong to say that two words (or two mental representations) have the same content when they are associated with the same perceptual prototypes; it would be wrong to take sameness of perceptual prototype as even a *necessary* condition for sameness of content of mental representations. For two speakers may have exactly the same meaning for the word 'bachelor', i.e. male adult human of marriageable age who has never been married, and have quite different perceptual prototypes associated with the word. On any intuitive notion of semantic content, to count every difference in perceptual prototype as a difference in semantic content would be just as unnatural as to count every difference in collateral information as a difference in semantic content.

Chomsky's response to my 'The meaning of "meaning" ' was to suggest that one might be able to save the Fregean notion of an 'intension' by giving up the principle that 'intension determines extension'. On Chomsky's proposal, as applied to my Twin Earth example, we should say that the word 'water' has the same *intension* on earth and on Twin Earth even though it has a different *extension* on earth than on Twin Earth. In terms of what has just been said, however, it would seem that this is the wrong way to go. For if we go the way I went in 'The meaning of "meaning" ', and take the extension of a term as one of the components of its 'meaning vector', then we have a clear reason for saying that 'grug' has a different meaning in north Ruritanian and in south Ruritanian. Since the word 'grug' clearly has a different reference in the two dialects of Ruritania, it also has a different meaning. Once we decide to put the reference (or rather the difference in reference) aside, and to ask whether 'grug' has the same 'content' in the minds of Oscar and Elmer, we have embarked upon an impossible task. Far from making it easier for ourselves to decide whether the representations are synonymous, we have made it impossible. In fact, the first approximation we have to a principle for deciding whether words have the same meaning or not in actual translation practice is to look at the extensions. 'Factoring out' differences in extension will only make a principled decision on when there has been a change in meaning totally impossible.

On the other hand, if we do decide to take extension as a factor in determining synonymy, either of words or of mental representations, then we still will not arrive at anything like an algorithm. For, just as determining the stereotype involves determining the meanings of other words, so determining the extension of a term always involves determining the extension of other terms. That words should not be regarded as the same in content if they have different extensions is a useful principle in translation after we already have the enterprise of interpretation underway. But until we have started interpreting a language we don't have any idea what the extension of a term is.

How then do we ever get started in interpretation? The answer that I would defend is one which has been vigorously urged by Donald Davidson and by Quine. (David Wiggins has pointed out that the germ of this view can already be found in Vico.) This is the view that *interpretation is essentially a holistic enterprise.* To interpret a language (and it makes no difference whether the language be a public language or 'mentalese', assuming the existence of 'mentalese') involves finding a translation scheme, an 'analytical hypothesis', which is capable of being learned, capable of yielding ready equivalents in our home language to the expressions being translated, and, most important, which is such that when we interpret the speakers of the alien language as meaning what the translation scheme says they mean we are able to 'understand' their purposes, beliefs, and behaviour. As Vico put it, in interpretation we seek to maximize the *humanity* of the beings being translated. If this is right then the only criteria that we actually have for the 'content' of any signs, or sign-analogs, are our intuitive criteria of successful interpretation; and to *formalize* these would involve formalizing our entire conception of what it is to be human, of what it is to be intelligible in human terms (see Putnam, 1976).

The discussion is not meant to suggest that interpretation theory is something incapable of study. Interpretation is something that can be studied in many ways and from many perspectives. But it is meant to suggest that, contrary to Pylyshyn's suggestion, the theory of interpretation and cognitive psychology deal with quite different projects and that to a large extent success in one of these projects is independent of success in the other. What the example I have developed shows is that it may be possible to give a complete functionalist psychology, including a complete verificationist semantics for mentalese, without in any way solving the problem of interpretation, or even the problem of reference-preserving translation (assignment of extensions). To have a description of how a system of representations works in functionalist terms is one thing; to have an *interpretation* of that system of representation is quite another thing.

The difference between functionalist psychology and interpretation theory is in part due to this: functionalist psychology treats the human mind as a computer. It seeks to state the rules of computation. The rules of computation have the property that although their interactions may be complicated and global, their action at any particular time is local. The machine, as it might be, moves a digit from one address to another address in obedience to a particular instruction, or to finitely many instructions, and on the basis of a finite amount of data. Interpretation is never local in this sense. A translation scheme, however well it works on a finite amount of corpus, may always have to be modified on the basis of additional text.

Let me illustrate this point by means of what may seem to be a digression. Some years ago Hartry Field (1972) advocated the view that *reference* is a physicalistic relation between sign-uses and things (including properties). When he commented on my paper 'Language and reality' (Putnam, 1975b) at Chapel Hill some years ago, Field spelled this out a little further with some examples. Considering the case of a Newtonian scientist who used the term 'gravitation', Field suggested that the decision we should make as to which objects or properties this term refers to should be based on finding which objects the scientist had better be referring to as a matter of objective fact, if his theory as a whole is to be a rationally acceptable approximation to the truth. The reason I mention this is that, although the notion of interpretation involved here is as different from Pylyshyn's notion of finding 'content' as could possibly be imagined, the same considerations turn up. It turns out that the 'physicalistic relation' that Field is looking for is one whose very definition will involve *interpreting the language as a whole*, and not just individual signs (since what constitutes an interpretation of a theory that makes the theory rationally acceptable depends on looking at the *whole* theory), and is a relation whose very definition involves an analysis of rationality in its normative sense. Whether any relation whose definition involves these elements is properly called 'physicalistic' I shall not inquire: but the point is that *every* project for analyzing the notion of *interpretation* sooner or later involves recognizing that the analysis of the notion of interpretation is inseparable from the analysis of either the normative notion of rationality, or from some such notion as Vico's 'humanity'.

To expect anything like complete success at stating in a completely rigorous and formal way what the correct procedures are in interpretation would obviously be utopian. This may not, in itself, seem like a terribly important point. After all, complete success at stating the laws of physics may well be a utopian project; certainly complete success at describing the functional organization of a human brain is a utopian project. But physics is possible, even though complete success eludes us, because the laws of physics can be successively approximated; and functional psychology is possible because (we hope) the functional organization of the human brain can be partly described and approximated. Similarly, one might hope that one could obtain partial success in describing the practices and procedures of interpretation.

I have no doubt that this is true; indeed I have no doubt that each of these subjects can be studied at more than one level (physics, after all, is not just elementary particle theory; it is also magneto-hydrodynamics, solid state physics, and many things besides) and in connection with many different projects requiring many different notions of precision and many different vocabularies. The important point is that the kind of partial success that is realistically foreseeable in cognitive psychology and the kind of partial successes that is realistically foreseeable in interpretation theory are quite different.

In one sense, I hope the present paper is a contribution to interpretation theory. The interesting successes that we are likely to have in interpretation theory are more likely to be philosophical discussions than technical 'results'. But even if we confine attention to the sorts of contributions to interpretation theory that are likely to come from computer science and related areas, then, as Marvin Minsky (1975) has pointed out, these successes are likely to be by their very nature partial. When we mechanize interpretation, Minsky points out, what we typically do is *restrict* it to a definite set of texts which are on a specific subject matter and which share a common vocabulary, a common set of projects, and a common set of empirical or other assumptions. The reason that partial successes in interpretation theory are always so limited is that any global success, any program for interpretation of sentences in a variable language, a variable theory, on variable topics and with variable presuppositions, would involve an analysis of the notion of humanity, or of the notion (which in my view is closely related) of rationality. The function of limiting interpretation to a specific frame is to avoid having to tackle the totally utopian project of algorithmic analysis of these notions.

The kind of partial success we are likely to have in cognitive psychology, however, is quite different. Here what we might hope for are the identification of the kinds of physical states that realize various functional roles. If the hypothesis that the brain computes in something analogous to a formalized language is correct then we might hope to identify such things as predicate-analogs and sentence-analogs in the brain, or to say something about the computation rules for manipulating these. I think that anyone who has a clear idea of what these two kinds of partial success amount to, and who does not allow himself to be carried away by utterly utopian dreams of a complete mathematical analysis of what it is to be human (or what it is to be rational), will see at once that they are independent projects and neither really presupposes the other at all.

Nelson Goodman (1978) has advocated 'pluralism' as opposed to 'monism'. In this terminology, the view that we should aim for a single science of cognitive psychology which solves the problems of syntax and semantics together and at one stroke (and which solves the problems of semantics both in the sense of verificationist semantics and in the sense of interpretation) is a species of monism. In opposition to it I suggest that we should let a hundred flowers blossom, that we should let them blossom in their separate ways, in their separate seasons, and even in their separate gardens.

### Relevance to Davidson's Philosophy of Mind

I think that the points that I have made have a certain 'Davidsonian' quality. It may be appropriate in this place to bring out more explicitly how this is so. In 'Mental events', Davidson (1970) put forward the thesis of 'anomalous monism'. This is the thesis that there are token—token identities between physical events and mental events (i.e., events described in the vocabulary of belief and desire), but no type—type identities. The argument that he gives for the non-existence of type—type identities has been widely misunderstood. To many it has seemed like a 'howler'; Davidson has been charged with arguing for the non-existence of type—type identities from the mere fact that mental concepts and physical concepts owe allegiance to different criteria. (Such an argument would be fallacious since it would block all type—type identities, even the identity 'water is $H_2O$', or 'light is electromagnetic radiation'. For certainly, before the reduction, 'water' and '$H_2O$' owed allegiance to different criteria, as did 'light' and 'electromagnetic radiation'.) This is simply a misreading, however; Davidson does have an argument, and it is both a subtle and an interesting one.

Davidson is very familiar with the work of Amos Tversky (see Tversky and Kahneman, 1975, 1982). Thus he is extremely aware that *preferences* cannot be read off from even *sincere verbal reports*. As Tversky's very careful empirical research shows, people's sincere verbal reports of their own preferences are totally incoherent. If we acted on the maxim of ascribing to people all of the preferences they say (sincerely) they have then we would be unable to interpret their behaviour at all, for *expressed* preferences are totally contradictory (e.g. they violate the logical property of the transitivity of preference very badly). Now, and perhaps this is the step that Davidson should have spelled out a little more explicitly, there is no reason to think that the availability of a 'cerebroscope' which enabled us to directly read off the subject's 'mentalese' could make things any better. Sincere verbal reports presumably correspond to mental representations that are present in the subject's brain. There is no reason to believe that the patient's 'mentalese' representations are any more consistent than his sincere verbal reports. If we could *read* the 'mentalese' we would undoubtedly find coded in the brain itself such reports as 'I prefer A to B', 'I prefer B to C', 'I prefer C to A', on certain occasions. What we do when we discover such reports in a discourse is look at the subject's total behavior and try to decide on the basis of his total behavior, and also on the basis of further linguistic material, further 'corpus', what is the most reasonable *reconstruction* of the patient's behavior and talk. A reasonable reconstruction accounts for the subject's behavior, or for most of his behavior, in terms of preferences which may be a subset of those he avows or which may even be slightly different from any that he avows, and accounts for those expressed preferences which we decide the patient does not really have as being confusions of various kinds. We may decide that some of the patient's expressed preferences were the product of suggestion in the particular context, for example.

Of course, someone may say that at a deeper level than even the patient's mentalese there must be a level of what we might call Platonic mentalese which records in the form of neurologically salient representations in a hidden code what the subject's *true* preferences are. But there is absolutely no reason to believe this. People may just be computers which are wired so that most of the time what they end up doing admits of some rational explanation or other; it need not be the case that the rational explanation which is the best *rational reconstruction* of the behavior is itself actually physically coded in their brains somewhere.

In short, Davidson's point is that what is true of public language is almost certainly going to be true of any 'mental representations' or salient neurological states which stand causally *behind* public language. Just as we have to say that a person's true preferences are not exactly the same as the preferences he *avows*, so we will have to say that a person's 'true preferences' (i.e. the ones it would be best to ascribe to him in rationally reconstructing his behaviour) are not the same as the one's coded in his brain representations. Belief–desire explanation belongs to the level of what I've been calling *interpretation theory*. It is as holistic and interest relative as all interpretation. Psychologists often speak as though there were *concepts* in the *brain*. The point of my argument (and, I think, of Davidson's) is that there may be *sentence-analogs* and *predicate-analogs* in the brain, but not concepts. 'Mental representations' require interpretation just as much as any other signs do.

## Notes

1. Strictly speaking a *semi-computable* (*partial* recursive) predicate; in *psychology*, as opposed to idealized inductive logic, we cannot require that degrees of belief be always *defined*. Let me emphasize also that in a psychological model not all learning is a matter of *induction* even in the wide sense in which inductive logicians use that term. We learn many things just by being *told* them or *shown* them: believing things that other people tell us or show us (to some extent) must be incorporated into the 'degree of confirmation' function whether or not one thinks this is good 'inductive logic'.

2. The reason is that, as both Fodor and Dennett have emphasized, cognitive psychology is *computational* psychology. It is alright to have 'homunculi' who make inferences, etc., as part of one's explanations provided the homunculi are eventually 'discharged' (as Dennett puts it), i.e. explained away as computer algorithms. But this means 'knowing' must eventually be 'discharged'.

3. The reason that we cannot count every difference in the collateral information we have as difference in the meaning of a *word*, is that to do so abandons the distinction between our 'concepts' and what beliefs we have that contain those concepts, and just this distinction is the *basis* of the intuitive notions of meaning, synonymy, analyticity, etc. To give up the meaning/belief distinction amounts to agreeing with Quine that we may as well give up the notion of *meaning* altogether. The same goes for the distinction between the 'content' of our mental representations and our beliefs involving them; this is nothing but a *picture*, a picture of 'words in the head'. Pictures are not always a *mistake*; they can be useful models. But if the picture of 'mental representations' and their 'content' is to have any use, then 'content' must remain stable under *some* changes of *belief*.

4. Chomsky wrote me a long letter after the appearance of 'The meaning of "meaning" ' defending this way out. Fodor (1979) defends the same program.

*Note*: A Bibliography is included in Further Reading.

# 2 MINDS, BRAINS AND PROGRAMS

John R. Searle

Abstract: *I distinguish between strong and weak Artificial Intelligence (AI). According to strong AI, appropriately programmed computers literally have cognitive states, and therefore the programs are psychological theories. I argue that strong AI must be false, since a human agent could instantiate the program and still not have the appropriate mental states. I examine some arguments against this claim, and I explore some consequences of the fact that human and animal brains are the causal bases of existing mental phenomena.*

What psychological and philosophical significance should we attach to recent efforts at computer simulations of human cognitive capacities? In answering this question I find it useful to distinguish what I will call 'strong' AI from 'weak' or 'cautious' AI. According to weak AI, the principal value of the computer in the study of the mind is that it gives us a very powerful tool. For example, it enables us to formulate and test hypotheses in a more rigorous and precise fashion than before. But according to strong AI the computer is not merely a tool in the study of the mind; rather the appropriately programmed computer really is a mind in the sense that computers given the right programs can be literally said to *understand* and have other cognitive states. And, according to strong AI, because the programmed computer has cognitive states, the programs are not mere tools that enable us to test psychological explanations; rather, the programs are themselves the explanations. I have no objection to the claims to weak AI, at least as far as this article is concerned. My discussion here will be directed to the claims I have defined as strong AI, specifically the claim that the appropriately programmed computer literally has cognitive states and that the programs thereby explain human cognition. When I refer to AI, it is the strong version as expressed by these two claims which I have in mind.

I will consider the work of Roger Schank and his colleagues at Yale (cf. Schank and Abelson, 1977), because I am more familiar with it than I am with any similar claims, and because it provides a clear example of the sort of work I wish to examine. But nothing that follows depends upon the details of Schank's programs. The same arguments would apply to Winograd's (1972) SHRDLU, Weizenbaum's (1965) ELIZA, and, indeed, any Turing machine simulation of human mental phenomena.

Briefly and leaving out the various details, one can describe Schank's program as follows: the aim of the program is to simulate the human ability to understand stories. It is characteristic of the abilities of human beings to understand stories that they can answer questions about the story even though the information they give was not explicitly stated in the story. Thus, for example, suppose you are given the following story: 'A man went into a restaurant and ordered a hamburger. When the hamburger arrived, it was burned to a crisp, and the man stormed out of the restaurant angrily, without paying for the hamburger or leaving a tip.' Now, if you are given the question 'Did the man eat the hamburger?', you will presumably answer, 'No, he did not.' Similarly, if you are given the following story: 'A man went into a restaurant, and ordered a hamburger; when the hamburger came, he was very pleased with it; and as he left the restaurant he gave the waitress a large tip before paying his bill,' and you are asked the question 'Did the man eat the hamburger?', you will presumably answer, 'Yes, he ate the hamburger.' Now Schank's machines can similarly answer questions about restaurants in this fashion. In order to do so, they have a 'representation' of the sort of information that human beings have about restaurants which enables them to answer such questions as those above, given these sorts of stories. When the machine is given the story and then asked the question, the machine will print out answers of the sort that we would expect human beings to give if told similar stories. Partisans of strong AI claim that in this question-and-answer sequence, not only is the machine simulating a human ability but also:

(a) the machine can literally be said to *understand* the story and provide answers to questions; and
(b) what the machine and its program do *explains* the human ability to understand the story and answer questions about it.

Claims (a) and (b) seem to me totally unsupported by Schank's work, as I will attempt to show in what follows.[1]

A way to test any theory of the mind is to ask oneself what it would be like if one's own mind actually worked on the principles that the theory says all minds work on. Let us apply this test to the Schank program with the following *Gedankenexperiment*. Suppose that I'm locked in a room and suppose that I'm given a large batch of Chinese writing. Suppose furthermore, as is indeed the case, that I know no Chinese either written or spoken, and that I'm not even confident that I could recognize Chinese writing as Chinese writing distinct from, say, Japanese writing or meaningless squiggles. Now suppose further that after this first batch of Chinese writing, I am given a second batch of Chinese script together with a set of rules for correlating the second batch with the first batch. The rules are in English and I understand these rules as well as any other native speaker of English. They enable me to correlate one set of formal symbols with another set of formal symbols, and all that 'formal' means here is that I can identify the symbols entirely by their shapes. Now suppose also that I am given a third batch of Chinese symbols together with some instructions, again in English, that enable me to correlate elements of this third batch with the first two batches, and these rules instruct me how I am to give back certain Chinese symbols with certain sorts of shapes in response to certain sorts of shapes given me in the third batch. Unknown to me, the people who are giving me all of these symbols call the first batch 'a script,' they call the second batch a 'story,' and they call the third batch 'questions.' Furthermore, they call the symbols I give them back in response to the third batch 'answers to the questions,' and the set of rules in English that they gave me they call 'the program.' To complicate the story a little bit, imagine that these people also give me stories in English which I understand, and they then ask me questions in English about these stories, and I give them back answers in English. Suppose also that after a while I get so good at following the instructions for manipulating the Chinese symbols and the programmers get so good at writing the programs that from the external point of view — that is, from the point of view of somebody outside the room in which I am locked — my answers to the questions are indistinguishable from those of native Chinese speakers. Nobody looking at my answers can tell that I don't speak a word of Chinese. Let us also suppose that my answers to the English questions are, as they no doubt would be, indistinguishable from those of other native English speakers, for the simple reason that I am a native speaker of English. From the external point of view, from the point of view of someone reading my 'answers,' the answers to the Chinese questions and the English questions are equally good. But in the Chinese case, unlike the English case, I produce the answers by manipulating uninterpreted formal symbols. As far as the Chinese is concerned, I simply behave like a computer; I perform computational operations on formally specified elements. For the purposes of the Chinese, I am simply an instantiation of the computer program.

Now the claims made by strong AI are that the programmed computer understands the stories and that the program in some sense explains human understanding. But we are now in a position to examine these claims in light of our thought experiment.

(a) As regards the first claim it seems to me obvious in the example that I do not understand a word of the Chinese stories. I have inputs and outputs that are indistinguishable from those of the native Chinese speaker, and I can have any formal program you like, but I still understand nothing. Schank's computer for the same reasons understands nothing of any stories whether in Chinese, English, or whatever, since in the Chinese case the computer is me; and in cases where the computer is not me, the computer has nothing more than I have in the case where I understand nothing.

(b) As regards the second claim — that the program explains human understanding — we can see that the computer and its program do not provide sufficient conditions of understanding, since the computer and the program are functioning and there is no understanding. But does it even provide a necessary condition or a significant contribution to understanding? One of the claims made by the supporters of strong AI is this: when I understand a story in English, what I am doing is exactly the same — or perhaps more of the same — as what I was doing in the case of manipulating the Chinese symbols. It is simply more formal symbol manipulation which distinguishes the case in English, where I do understand, from the case in Chinese, where I don't. I have not demonstrated that this claim is false, but it would certainly appear an incredible claim in the example. Such plausibility as the claim has derives from the supposition that we can construct a program that will have the same inputs and outputs as native speakers, and in addition we assume that speakers have some level of description where they are also instantiations of a program. On the basis of these two assumptions, we assume that even if Schank's program isn't the whole story about understanding, maybe it is part of the story. That is, I suppose, an empirical possibility, but not the slightest reason has so far been given to suppose it is true, since what is suggested — though certainly not demonstrated — by the example is that the computer program is irrelevant to my understanding of the story. In the Chinese case I have everything that artificial intelligence can put into me by way of a program, and I understand nothing; in the English case I understand everything, and there is so far no reason at all to suppose that my understanding has anything to do with computer programs — i.e. with computational operations on purely formally specified elements. As long as the program is defined in terms of computational operations on purely formally defined elements, what the example suggests is that these by themselves have no interesting connection with understanding. They are certainly not sufficient conditions, and not the slightest reason has been given to suppose that they are necessary conditions or even that they make a significant contribution to understanding. Notice that the force of the argument is not simply that different machines can have the same input and output while operating on different formal principles — that is not the point at all — but rather that whatever purely formal principles you put into the computer will not be sufficient for understanding, since a human will be able to follow the formal principles without understanding anything, and no reason has been offered to suppose they are necessary or even contributory, since no reason has been given to suppose that when I understand English, I am operating with any formal program at all.

What is it, then, that I have in the case of the English sentences which I do not have in the case of the Chinese sentences? The obvious answer is that I know what the former mean but haven't the faintest idea what the latter mean. In what does this consist, and why couldn't we give it to a machine, whatever it is? Why couldn't the machine be given whatever it is about me that makes it the case that I know what English sentences mean? I will return to these questions after developing my example a little more.

I have had occasions to present this example to several workers in artificial intelligence and, interestingly, they do not seem to agree on what the proper reply to it is. I get a surprising variety of replies, and in what follows I will consider the most common of these (specified along with their geographical origins). First, I want to block out some common misunderstandings about 'understanding'. In many of these discussions one finds fancy footwork about the word 'understanding'. My critics point out that there are different degrees of understanding, that 'understanding' is not a simple two-place predicate, that there are even different kinds and levels of understanding, and often the law of the excluded middle doesn't even apply in a straightforward way to statements of the form 'x understands y,' that in many cases it is a matter for decision and not a simple matter of fact whether x understands y. And so on. To all these points I want to say of course, of course; but they have nothing to do with the points at issue. There are clear cases where 'understanding' applies and clear cases where it does not apply; and such cases are all I need for this argument.[2] I understand stories in English; to a lesser degree I can understand stories in French; to a still lesser degree, stories in German; and in Chinese, not at all. My car and my adding machine, on the other hand, understand nothing; they are not in that line of business. We often attribute 'understanding' and other cognitive predicates by metaphor and analogy to cars, adding machines, and other artifacts, but nothing is proved by such attributions. We say, 'The door *knows* when to open because of its photoelectric cell,' 'the adding machine *knows how* (*understands how*, is *able*) to do addition and subtraction but not division,' and 'the thermostat *perceives* changes in the temperature'. The reason we make these attributions is interesting and has to do with the fact that in artifacts we extend our own intentionality;[3] our tools are extensions of our purposes, and so we find it natural to make metaphorical attributions of intentionality to them; but I take it no philosophical ice is cut by such examples. The sense in which an automatic door 'understands instructions' from its photoelectric cell is not at all the sense in which I understand English. If the sense in which Schank's programmed computers understand stories is supposed to be the metaphorical sense in which the door understands, and not the sense in which I understand English, the issue would not be worth discussing. Newell and Simon write that the sense of 'understanding' they claim for computers is exactly the same as for human beings. I like the straightforwardness of this claim, and it is the sort of claim I will be considering. I will argue that in the literal sense the programmed computer understands what the car and the adding machine understand, viz. exactly nothing. The computer understanding is not just (like my understanding of German) partial or incomplete; it is zero.

Now to the replies:

I. *The Systems Reply* (Berkeley): 'While it is true that the individual person who is locked in the room does not understand the story, the fact is that he is merely part of a whole system and the system does understand the story. The person has a large ledger in front of him in which are written the rules, he has a lot of scratch paper and pencils for doing calculations, he has "data banks" of sets of Chinese symbols. Now, understanding is not being ascribed to the mere individual, rather it is being ascribed to this whole system of which he is a part.'

My response to the systems theory is simple: Let the individual internalize all of these elements of the system. He memorizes the rules in the ledger and the data banks of Chinese symbols, and he does all the calculations in his head. The individual then incorporates the entire system. There isn't anything at all to the system which he does not encompass. We can even get rid of the room and suppose he works outdoors. All the same, he understands nothing of the Chinese, and *a fortiori* neither does the system, because there isn't anything in the system which isn't in him. If he doesn't understand, then there is no way the system could understand because the system is just a part of him.

Actually, I feel somewhat embarrassed even to give this answer to the systems theory because the theory seems to me so implausible to start with. The idea is that while a person doesn't understand Chinese, somehow the *conjunction* of that person and bits of paper might understand Chinese. It is not easy for me to imagine how someone who was not in the grip of an ideology would find the idea at all plausible. Still, I think many people who are committed to the ideology of strong AI will in the end be inclined to say something very much like this; so let us pursue it a bit further. According to one version of this view, while the man in the internalized systems example doesn't understand Chinese in the sense that a native Chinese speaker does (because, for example, he doesn't know that the story refers to restaurants and hamburgers, etc.), still 'the man as formal symbol manipulation system' *really does understand Chinese*. The subsystem of the man which is the formal symbol manipulation system for Chinese should not be confused with the subsystem for English.

So there are really two subsystems in the man; one understands

English, the other Chinese, and 'it's just that the two systems have little to do with each other.' But, I want to reply, not only do they have little to do with each other, they are not even remotely alike. The subsystem that understands English (assuming we allow ourselves to talk in this jargon of 'subsystems' for a moment) knows that the stories are about restaurants and eating hamburgers, etc.; he knows that he is being asked questions about restaurants and that he is answering questions as best as he can by making various inferences from the content of the story, and so on. But the Chinese system knows none of this; whereas the English subsystem knows that 'hamburgers' refers to hamburgers, the Chinese subsystem knows only that 'squiggle-squiggle' is followed by 'squoggle-squoggle'. All he knows is that various formal symbols are being introduced at one end and are manipulated according to rules written in English, and that other symbols are going out at the other end. The whole point of the original example was to argue that such symbol manipulation by itself couldn't be sufficient for understanding Chinese in any literal sense because the man could write 'squoggle-squoggle' after 'squiggle-squiggle' without understanding anything in Chinese. And it doesn't meet that argument to postulate subsystems within the man, because the subsystems are no better off than the man was in the first place; they still don't have anything even remotely like what the English-speaking man (or subsystem) has. Indeed, in the case as described, the Chinese subsystem is simply a part of the English subsystem, a part that engages in meaningless symbol manipulation according to rules in English.

Let us ask ourselves what is supposed to motivate the systems reply in the first place — that is, what *independent* grounds are there supposed to be for saying that the agent must have a sub-system within him which literally understands stories in Chinese? As far as I can tell, the only grounds are that in the example I have the same input and output as native Chinese speakers, and a program that goes from one to the other. But the point of the example has been to show that that couldn't be sufficient for understanding, in the sense in which I understand stories in English, because a person, hence the set of systems that go to make up a person, could have the right combination of input, output, and program and still not understand anything in the relevant literal sense in which I understand English. The only motivation for saying there *must* be a subsystem in me which understands Chinese is that I have a program and I can pass the Turing test; I can fool native Chinese speakers (cf. Turing, 1950). But precisely one of the points at issue is the adequacy of the Turing test. The example shows that there could be two 'systems' both of which pass the Turing test but only one of which understands; and it is no argument against this point to say that since they both pass the Turing test, they must both understand, since this claim fails to meet the argument that the system in me which understands English has a great deal more than the system which merely processes Chinese. In short, the systems reply simply begs the question by insisting without argument that the system must understand Chinese.

Furthermore, the systems reply would appear to lead to consequences that are independently absurd. If we are to conclude that there must be cognition in me on the grounds that I have a certain sort of input and output and a program in between, then it looks as though all sorts of noncognitive subsystems are going to turn out to be cognitive. For example, my stomach has a level of description where it does information processing, and it instantiates any number of computer programs, but I take it we do not want to say that it has any understanding. Yet if we accept the systems reply, it is hard to see how we avoid saying that stomach, heart, liver, etc. are all understanding subsystems, since there is no principled way to distinguish the motivation for saying the Chinese subsystem understands from saying that the stomach understands. (It is, by the way, not an answer to this point to say that the Chinese system has information as input and output and the stomach has food and food products as input and output, since from the point of view of the agent, from my point of view, there is no information in either the food or the Chinese; the Chinese is just so many meaningless squiggles. The information in the Chinese case is solely in the eyes of the programmers and the interpreters, and there is nothing to prevent them from treating the input and output of my digestive organs as information if they so desire.)

This last point bears on some independent problems in strong AI, and it is worth digressing for a moment to explain it. If strong AI is to be a branch of psychology, it must be able to distinguish systems which are genuinely mental from those which are not. It must be able to distinguish the principles on which the mind works from those on which nonmental systems work; otherwise it will offer us no explanations of what is specifically mental about the mental. And the mental—nonmental distinction cannot be just in the eye of the beholder — it must be intrinsic to the systems, for otherwise it would be up to any beholder to treat people as nonmental and, e.g. hurricanes as mental, if he likes. But quite often in the AI literature the distinction is blurred in ways which would in the long run prove disastrous to the claim that AI is a cognitive inquiry. McCarthy, for example, writes: 'Machines as simple as thermostats can be said to have beliefs, and having beliefs seems to be a characteristic of most machines capable of problem solving performances' (McCarthy, 1979). Anyone who thinks strong AI has a chance as a theory of the mind ought to ponder the implications of that remark. We are asked to accept it as a discovery of strong AI that the hunk of metal on the wall which we use to regulate the temperature has beliefs in exactly the same sense that we, our spouses, and our children have beliefs, and furthermore that 'most' of the other machines in the room — telephone, tape recorder, adding machine, electric light switch, etc. — also have beliefs in this literal sense. It is not the aim of this article to argue against McCarthy's point, so I will simply assert the following without argument. The study of the mind starts with such facts as that humans have beliefs and thermostats, telephones, and adding machines don't. If you get a theory that denies this point, you have produced a counter-example to the theory, and the theory is false. One gets the impression that people in AI who write this sort of thing think they can get away with it because they don't really take it seriously and they don't think anyone else will either. I propose, for a moment at least, to take it seriously. Think hard for one minute about what would be necessary to establish that that hunk of metal on the wall over there has real beliefs, beliefs with direction of fit, propositional content, and conditions of satisfaction; beliefs that have the possibility of being strong beliefs or weak beliefs; nervous, anxious or secure beliefs; dogmatic, rational, or superstitious beliefs; blind faiths or hesitant cogitations; any kind of beliefs. The thermostat is not a candidate. Neither are stomach, liver, adding machine or telephone. However, since we are taking the idea seriously, notice that its truth would be fatal to the claim of strong AI to be a science of the mind, for now the mind is everywhere. What we wanted to know is what distinguishes the mind from thermostats, livers, etc. And if McCarthy were right, strong AI hasn't a hope of telling us that.

II. *The Robot Reply* (Yale): 'Suppose we wrote a different kind of program from Schank's program. Suppose we put a computer inside a robot, and this computer would not just take in formal symbols as input and give out formal symbols as output, but rather it would actually operate the robot in such a way that the robot does something very much like perceiving, walking, moving about, hammering nails, eating, drinking — anything you like. The robot would, for example, have a television camera attached to it that enabled it to see, it would have arms and legs that enabled it to act, and all of this would be controlled by its computer brain. Such a robot would, unlike Schank's computer, have genuine understanding and other mental states.'

The first thing to notice about the robot reply is that it tacitly concedes that cognition is not solely a matter of formal symbol manipulation, since this reply adds a set of causal relations with the outside world. But the answer to the robot reply is that the addition of such 'perceptual' and 'motor' capacities adds nothing by way of understanding, in particular, or intentionality, in general, to Schank's original program; and to see this, notice that the same thought experiment applies to the robot case. Suppose that instead of the computer inside the robot, you put me inside the room and you give me again, as in the original Chinese case, more Chinese symbols with more instructions in English for matching Chinese symbols to Chinese symbols and feeding back Chinese symbols to the outside. Suppose unknown to me, some of the Chinese symbols that come to me come from a television camera attached to the robot, and other Chinese symbols that I am giving out serve to make the motors inside the robot move the robot's legs or arms. It is important to emphasize that all I am doing is manipulating formal symbols: I know none of these other facts. I am receiving 'information' from the robot's 'perceptual' apparatus, and I am giving out 'instructions' to its motor apparatus without knowing either of these facts. I am the robot's homunculus, but unlike the traditional homunculus, I don't know what's going on. I don't understand anything except the rules for symbol manipulation. Now in this case I want to say that the robot has no intentional states at all; it is simply moving about as a result of its electrical wiring and its program. And furthermore, by instantiating the program, I have no intentional states of the relevant type. All I do is follow formal instructions about manipulating formal symbols.

III. *The Brain Simulator Reply* (Berkeley and MIT): 'Suppose we design a program that doesn't represent information that we have about the world, such as the information in Schank's scripts, but simulates the actual sequence of neuron firings at the synapses of the brain of a native Chinese speaker when he understands stories in Chinese and gives answers to them. The machine takes in Chinese stories and questions about them as input, it simulates the formal structure of actual Chinese brains in processing these stories, and it gives out Chinese answers as outputs. We can even imagine that the machine operates not with a single serial program but with a whole set of programs operating in parallel, in the manner that actual human brains presumably operate when they process natural language. Now surely in such a case we would have to say that the machine understands the stories; and if we refuse to say that, wouldn't we also have to deny that native Chinese speakers understood the stories? At the level of the synapses what would or could be different about the program of the computer and the program of the Chinese brain?'

Before addressing this reply, I want to digress to note that it is an odd reply for any partisan of artificial intelligence (functionalism, etc.) to make. I thought the whole idea of strong artificial intelligence is that we don't need to know how the brain works to know how the mind works. The basic hypothesis, or so I had supposed, was that there is a level of mental operations that consists in computational processes over formal elements which constitute the essence of the mental and can be realized in all sorts of different brain processes in the same way that any computer program can be realized in different computer hardwares: on the assumptions of strong AI, the mind is to the brain as the program is to the hardware, and thus we can understand the mind without doing neurophysiology. If we had to know how the brain worked in order to do AI, we wouldn't bother with AI. However, even getting this close to the operation of the brain is still not sufficient to produce understanding. To see that this is so, imagine that instead of a monolingual man in a room shuffling symbols we have the man operate an elaborate set of water pipes with valves connecting them. When the man receives the Chinese symbols he looks up in the program, written in English, which valves he has to turn on and off. Each water connection corresponds to a synapse in the

Chinese brain, and the whole system is rigged up so that after doing all the right firings — that is, after turning on all the right faucets — the Chinese answers pop out at the output end of the series of pipes.

Now where is the understanding in this system? It takes Chinese as input, it simulates the formal structure of the synapses of the Chinese brain, and it gives Chinese as output. But the man certainly doesn't understand Chinese, and neither do the water pipes, and if we are tempted to adopt what I think is the absurd view that somehow the *conjunction* of man *and* water pipes understands, remember that in principle the man can internalize the formal structure of the water pipes and do all the 'neuron firings' in his imagination. The problem with the brain simulator is that it is simulating the wrong things about the brain. As long as it simulates only the formal structure of the sequence of neuron firings at the synapses, it won't have simulated what matters about the brain, namely its causal properties, its ability to produce intentional states. And that the formal properties are not sufficient for the causal properties is shown by the water pipe example: we can have all the formal properties carved off from the relevant neurobiological causal properties.

IV. *The Combination Reply* (Berkeley and Stanford): 'While each of the previous three replies might not be completely convincing by itself as a refutation of the Chinese room counter-example, if you take all three together they are collectively much more convincing and even decisive. Imagine a robot with a brain-shaped computer lodged in its cranial cavity; imagine the computer programmed with all the synapses of a human brain; imagine that the whole behavior of the robot is indistinguishable from human behavior; and now think of the whole thing as a unified system and not just as a computer with inputs and outputs. Surely in such a case we would have to ascribe intentionality to the system.'

I entirely agree that in such a case we would find it rational and indeed irresistible to accept the hypothesis that the robot had intentionality, as long as we knew nothing more about it. Indeed, besides appearance and behavior the other elements of the combination are really irrelevant. If we could build a robot whose behavior was indistinguishable over a large range from human behavior, we would attribute intentionality to it, pending some reason not to. We wouldn't need to know in advance that its computer brain was a formal analogue of the human brain.

But I really don't see that this is any help to the claims of strong AI, and here is why: according to strong AI, instantiating a formal program with the right input and output is a sufficient condition of, indeed is constitutive of, intentionality. As Newell (1980) puts it, the essence of the mental is the operation of a physical symbol system. But the attributions of intentionality that we make to the robot in this example have nothing to do with formal programs. They are simply based on the assumption that if the robot looks and behaves sufficiently like us, we would suppose until proven otherwise that it must have mental states like ours which cause and are expressed by its behavior, and it must have an inner mechanism capable of producing such mental states. If we knew independently how to account for its behavior without such assumptions, we would not attribute intentionality to it, especially if we knew it had a formal program. And this is the point of my earlier reply to objection II.

Suppose we knew that the robot's behavior was entirely accounted for by the fact that a man inside it was receiving uninterpreted formal symbols from the robot's sensory receptors and sending out uninterpreted formal symbols to its motor mechanisms, and the man was doing this symbol manipulation in accordance with a bunch of rules. Furthermore, suppose the man knows none of these facts about the robot; all he knows is which operations to perform on which meaningless symbols. In such a case we would regard the robot as an ingenious mechanical dummy. The hypothesis that the dummy has a mind would now be unwarranted and unnecessary, for there is now no longer any reason to ascribe intentionality to the robot or to the system of which it is a part (except of course for the man's intentionality in manipulating the symbols). The formal symbol manipulations go on, the input and output are correctly matched, but the only real locus of intentionality is the man, and he doesn't know any of the relevant intentional states; he doesn't, for example, *see* what comes into the robot's eyes, he doesn't *intend* to move the robot's arm, and he doesn't *understand* any of the remarks made to or by the robot. Nor, for the reasons stated earlier, does the system of which man and robot are a part.

To see the point contrast this case with cases where we find it completely natural to ascribe intentionality to members of certain other primate species, such as apes and monkeys, and to domestic animals, such as dogs. The reasons we find it natural are, roughly, two: we can't make sense of the animal's behavior without the ascription of intentionality, and we can see that the beasts are made of stuff similar to our own — an eye, a nose, its skin, etc. Given the coherence of the animal's behavior and the assumption of the same causal stuff underlying it, we assume both that the animal must have mental states underlying its behavior, and the mental states must be produced by mechanisms made out of the stuff that is like our stuff. We would certainly make similar assumptions about the robot unless we had some reason not to, but as soon as we knew that the behavior was the result of a formal program, and that the actual causal properties of the physical substance were irrelevant, we would abandon the assumption of intentionality.

There are two other responses to my example which come up frequently (and so are worth discussing) but really miss the point.

V. *The Other Minds Reply* (Yale): 'How do you know that other people understand Chinese or anything else? Only by their behavior. Now the computer can pass the behavioral tests as well as they can (in principle), so if you are going to attribute cognition to other people, you must in principle also attribute it to computers.'

The objection is worth only a short reply. The problem in this discussion is not about how I know that other people have cognitive states, but rather what it is that I am attributing to them when I attribute cognitive states to them. The thrust of the argument is that it couldn't be just computational processes and their output because there can be computational processes and their output without the cognitive state. It is no answer to this argument to feign anesthesia. In 'cognitive sciences' one presupposes the reality and knowability of the mental in the same way that in physical sciences one has to presuppose the reality and knowability of physical objects.

VI. *The Many Mansions Reply* (Berkeley): 'Your whole argument presupposes that AI is only about analogue and digital computers. But that just happens to be the present state of technology. Whatever these causal processes are that you say are essential for intentionality (assuming you are right), eventually we will be able to build devices that have these causal processes and that will be artificial intelligence. So your arguments are in no way directed at the ability of artificial intelligence to produce and explain cognition.'

I have no objection to this reply except to say that it in effect trivializes the project of strong artificial intelligence by redefining it as whatever artificially produces and explains cognition. The interest of the original claims made on behalf of artificial intelligence is that it was a precise, well defined thesis: mental processes are computational processes over formally defined elements. I have been concerned to challenge that thesis. If the claim is redefined so that it is no longer that thesis, my objections no longer apply, because there is no longer a testable hypothesis for them to apply to.

Let us now return to the questions I promised I would try to answer: Granted that in my original example I understand the English and I do not understand the Chinese, and granted therefore that the machine doesn't understand either English or Chinese; still there must be something about me that makes it the case that I understand English and a corresponding something lacking in me which makes it the case that I fail to understand Chinese. Now why couldn't we give those somethings, whatever they are, to a machine?

I see no reason in principle why we couldn't give a machine the capacity to understand English or Chinese, since in an important sense our bodies with our brains are precisely such machines. But I do see very strong arguments for saying that we could not give such a thing to a machine where the operation of the machine is defined solely in terms of computational processes over formally defined elements; that is, where the operation of the machine is defined as an instantiation of a computer program. It is not because I am the instantiation of a computer program that I am able to understand English and have other forms of intentionality (I am, I suppose, the instantiation of any number of computer programs), but as far as we know it is because I am a certain sort of organism with a certain biological (i.e. chemical and physical) structure, and this structure under certain conditions is causally capable of producing perception, action, understanding, learning and other intentional phenomena. And part of the point of the present argument is that only something that had those causal powers could have that intentionality. Perhaps other physical and chemical processes could produce exactly these effects; perhaps, for example, Martians also have intentionality, but their brains are made of different stuff. That is an empirical question, rather like the question whether photosynthesis can be done by something with a chemistry different from that of chlorophyl.

But the main point of the present argument is that no purely formal model will ever be by itself sufficient for intentionality, because the formal properties are not by themselves constitutive of intentionality, and they have by themselves no causal powers except the power, when instantiated, to produce the next stage of the formalism when the machine is running. And any other causal properties which particular realizations of the formal model have are irrelevant to the formal model because we can always put the same formal model in a different realization where those causal properties are obviously absent. Even if by some miracle Chinese speakers exactly realize Schank's program, we can put the same program in English speakers, water pipes, or computers, none of which understand Chinese, the program notwithstanding.

What matters about brain operation is not the formal shadow cast by the sequence of synapses but rather the actual properties of the sequences. All the arguments for the strong version of artificial intelligence that I have seen insist on drawing an outline around the shadows cast by cognition and then claiming that the shadows are the real thing.

By way of concluding I want to state some of the general philosophical points implicit in the argument. For clarity I will try to do it in a question-and-answer fashion, and I begin with that old chestnut:

'Could a machine think?'

The answer is, obviously, yes. We are precisely such machines.

'Yes, but could an artifact, a man-made machine, think?'

Assuming it is possible to produce artificially a machine with a nervous system, neurons with axons and dendrites, and all the rest of it, sufficiently like ours, again the answer to the question seems to be obviously 'yes'. If you can exactly duplicate the causes, you could duplicate the effects. And indeed it might be possible to produce consciousness, intentionality and all the rest of it using chemical principles different from those human beings use. It is, as I said, an empirical question.

'OK, but could a digital computer think?'

If by 'digital computer' we mean anything at all which has a level of description where it can correctly be described as the instantiation of a computer program, then again the answer is, of course, yes, since we are the instantiations of any number of computer programs and we can think.

'But could something think, understand, etc. *solely* by virtue of being a computer with the right sort of program? Could instantiating a program, the right program of course, by itself be a sufficient condition of understanding?'

This I think is the right question to ask, though it is usually confused with one or more of the earlier questions, and the answer to it is 'no'.

'Why not?'

Because the formal symbol manipulations by themselves don't have any intentionality: they are meaningless; they aren't even *symbol* manipulations, since the symbols don't symbolize anything. In the linguistic jargon they have only a syntax but no semantics. Such intentionality as computers appear to have is solely in the minds of those who program them and those who use them, those who send in the input and who interpret the output.

The aim of the Chinese room example was to try to show this by showing that as soon as we put something into the system which really does have intentionality, a man, and we program the man with the formal program, you can see that the formal program carries no additional intentionality. It adds nothing, for example, to a man's ability to understand Chinese.

Precisely that feature of AI which seemed so appealing — the distinction between the program and the realization — proves fatal to the claim that simulation could be duplication. The distinction between the program and its realization in the hardware seems to be parallel to the distinction between the level of mental operations and the level of brain operations. And if we could describe the level of mental operations as a formal program, it seems we could describe what was essential about the mind without doing either introspective psychology or neurophysiology of the brain. But the equation 'Mind is to brain as program is to hardware' breaks down at several points, among them the following three.

First, the distinction between program and realization has the consequence that the same program could have all sorts of crazy realizations which had no form of intentionality. Weizenbaum (1976), for example, shows in detail how to construct a computer using a roll of toilet paper and a pile of small stones. Similarly, the Chinese story-understanding program can be programmed into a sequence of water pipes, a set of wind machines, or a monolingual English speaker, none of which thereby acquires an understanding of Chinese. Stones, toilet paper, wind and water pipes are the wrong kind of stuff to have intentionality in the first place (only something that has the same causal powers as brains can have intentionality), and though the English speaker has the right kind of stuff for intentionality, you can easily see that he doesn't get any extra intentionality by memorizing the program, since memorizing it won't teach him Chinese.

Second, the program is purely formal, but the intentional states are not in that way formal. They are defined in terms of their content, not their form. The belief that it is raining, for example, is defined not as a certain formal shape, but as a certain mental content, with conditions of satisfaction, a direction of fit (cf. Searle, 1979), etc. Indeed, the belief as such hasn't even got a formal shape in this syntactical sense, since one and the same belief can be given an indefinite number of different syntactical expressions in different linguistic systems.

Third, as I mentioned before, mental states and events are a product of the operation of the brain, but the program is not in that way a product of the computer.

'Well if programs are in no way constitutive of mental processes, then why have so many people believed the converse? That at least needs some explanation.'

I don't know the answer to that. The idea that computer simulations could be the real thing ought to have seemed suspicious in the first place because the computer isn't confined to simulating mental operations, by any means. No one supposes that computer simulations of a five-alarm fire will burn the neighborhood down or that a computer simulation of a rainstorm will leave us all drenched. Why on earth would anyone suppose that a computer simulation of understanding actually understood anything? It is sometimes said that it would be frightfully hard to get computers to feel pain or fall in love, but love and pain are neither harder nor easier than cognition or anything else. For simulation, all you need is the right input and output and a program in the middle that transforms the former into the latter. That is all the computer has for anything it does. To confuse simulation with duplication is the same mistake, whether it is pain, love, cognition, fires or rainstorms.

Still, there are several reasons why AI must have seemed and to many people perhaps still does seem in some way to reproduce and thereby explain mental phenomena, and I believe we will not succeed in removing these illusions until we have fully exposed the reasons that give rise to them.

First, and perhaps most important, is a confusion about the notion of 'information processing'. Many people in cognitive science believe that the human brain with its mind does something called 'information processing', and analogously the computer with its program does information processing, but fires and rainstorms on the other hand don't do information processing at all. Thus, though the computer can simulate the formal features of any process whatever, it stands in a special relation to the mind and brain because when the computer is properly programmed, ideally with the same program as the brain, the information processing is identical in the two cases, and this information processing is really the essence of the mental. But the trouble with this argument is that it rests on an ambiguity in the notion of 'information'. In the sense in which people 'process information' when they reflect, say, on problems in arithmetic or when they read and answer questions about stories, the programmed computer does not do 'information processing'. Rather, what it does is manipulate formal symbols. The fact that the programmer and the interpreter of the computer output use the symbols to stand for objects in the world is totally beyond the scope of the computer. The computer, to repeat, has a syntax but no semantics. Thus, if you type into the computer '2 plus 2 equals?' it will type out '4'. But it has no idea that '4' means

4 or that it means anything at all. And the point is not that it lacks some second-order information about the interpretation of its first-order symbols, but rather that its first-order symbols don't have any interpretations as far as the computer is concerned. All the computer has is more symbols. The introduction of the notion of 'information processing' therefore produces a dilemma: either we construe the notion of 'information processing' in such a way that it implies intentionality as part of the process or we don't. If the former, then the programmed computer does not do information processing, it only manipulates formal symbols. If the latter, then although the computer does information procesing, it is only in the sense in which adding machines, typewriters, stomachs, thermostats, rainstorms and hurricanes do information processing — namely, they have a level of description where we can describe them as taking information in at one end, transforming it, and producing information as output. But in this case it is up to outside observers to interpret the input and output as information in the ordinary sense. And no similarity is established between the computer and the brain in terms of any similarity of information processing in the two cases.

Secondly, in much of AI there is a residual behaviorism or operationalism. Since appropriately programmed computers can have input/output patterns similar to human beings, we are tempted to postulate mental states in the computer similar to human mental states. But once we see that it is both conceptually and empirically possible for a system to have human capacities in some realm without having any intentionality at all, we should be able to overcome this impulse. My desk adding machine has calculating capacities but no intentionality, and in this paper I have tried to show that a system could have input and output capabilities which duplicated those of a native Chinese speaker and still not understand Chinese, regardless of how it was programmed. The Turing test is typical of the tradition in being unashamedly behavioristic and operationalistic, and I believe that if AI workers totally repudiated behaviorism and operationalism, much of the confusion between simulation and duplication would be eliminated.

Thirdly, this residual operationalism is joined to a residual form of dualism; indeed, strong AI only makes sense given the dualistic assumption that where the mind is concerned the brain doesn't matter. In strong AI (and in functionalism, as well) what matters are programs, and programs are independent of their realization in machines; indeed, as far as AI is concerned, the same program could be realized by an electronic machine, a Cartesian mental substance, or a Hegelian world spirit. The single most surprising discovery that I have made in discussing these issues is that many AI workers are shocked by my idea that actual human mental phenomena might be dependent on actual physical-chemical properties of actual human brains. But I should not have been surprised; for unless you accept some form of dualism, the strong AI project hasn't got a chance. The project is to reproduce and explain the mental by designing programs; but unless the mind is not only conceptually but empirically independent of the brain, you cannot carry out the project, for the program is completely independent of any realization. Unless you believe that the mind is separable from the brain both conceptually and empirically — dualism in a strong form — you cannot hope to reproduce the mental by writing and running programs since programs must be independent of brains or any other particular forms of instantiation. If mental operations consist of computational operations on formal symbols, it follows that they have no interesting connection with the brain, and the only connection would be that the brain just happens to be one of the indefinitely many types of machines capable of instantiating the program. This form of dualism is not the traditional Cartesian variety that claims there are two sorts of *substances*, but it is Cartesian in the sense that it insists that what is specifically mental about the mind has no intrinsic connection with the actual properties of the brain. This underlying dualism is masked from us by the fact that AI literature contains frequent fulminations against 'dualism'; what the authors seem to be unaware of is that their position presupposes a strong version of dualism.

'Could a machine think?' My own view is that *only* a machine could think, and indeed only very special kinds of machines, namely brains and machines that had the *same causal powers* as brains. And that is the main reason why strong AI has had little to tell us about thinking: it has nothing to tell us about machines. By its own definition it is about programs, and programs are not machines. Whatever else intentionality is, it is a biological phenomenon and it is as likely to be as causally dependent on the specific biochemistry of its origins as lactation, photosynthesis, or any other biological phenomena. No one would suppose that we could produce milk and sugar by running a computer simulation of the formal sequences in lactation and photosynthesis; but where the mind is concerned, many people are willing to believe in such a miracle, because of a deep and abiding dualism: the mind they suppose is a matter of formal processes and is independent of specific material causes in the way that milk and sugar are not.

In defense of this dualism, the hope is often expressed that the brain is a digital computer (early computers, by the way, were often called 'electronic brains'). But that is no help. Of course the brain is a digital computer. Since everything is a digital computer, brains are too. The point is that the brain's causal capacity to produce intentionality cannot consist in its instantiating a computer program, since for any program you like it is possible for something to instantiate that program and still not have any mental states. Whatever it is that the brain does to produce intentionality, it cannot consist of instantiating a program, since no program by itself is sufficient for intentionality.

## Acknowledgements

I am indebted to a rather large number of people for discussion of these matters and for their patient attempts to overcome my ignorance of artificial intelligence. I would especially like to thank Ned Block, Hubert Dreyfus, John Haugeland, Roger Schank, Robert Wilensky and Terry Winograd.

## Notes

1. I am not saying, of course, that Schank himself is committed to these claims.

2. Also, 'understanding' implies both the possession of mental (intentional) states and the truth (validity, success) of these states. For the purposes of this discussion, we are concerned only with the possession of the states.

3. Intentionality is by definition that feature of certain mental states by which they are directed at or about objects and states of affairs in the world. Thus beliefs, desires, and intentions are intentional states; undirected forms of anxiety and depression are not. For further discussion, see Searle (1979).

# 3   MISREPRESENTING HUMAN INTELLIGENCE

Hubert L. Dreyfus

In *What Computers Can't Do*[1] I argued that research in Artificial Intelligence (AI) was based upon mistaken assumptions about the nature of human knowledge and understanding. In the first part of this essay I will review that argument briefly. In spite of the noisy protestations from AI researchers, most of my critical claims and negative predictions have not only been borne out by subsequent research and developments in the field, but have even come to be acknowledged as accurate indications of major problems by AI workers themselves. In the years since the revised edition of my book was published, what I have come to see is not only that my early pessimism was well founded, but also that some of my assessments for the future of AI were overly optimistic. In the second part of this essay I will explain why I now believe that even the cautious and guarded optimism which I once had with respect to certain isolated areas of AI research was unjustified and, ultimately, mistaken.

## I

The early stages of AI research were characterized by overly ambitious goals, wishful rhetoric and outlandish predictions. The goal, in general, was to equal or exceed the capacities of human beings in every area of intelligent behavior. The rhetoric turned failure after failure into partial and promising success. And the predictions had computers doing everything an intelligent human brain could do, within a decade or so at most. The terms on these predictions have all expired with none of the miraculous feats accomplished, and most researchers have begun to face the hard facts about the real limits of artificial intelligence.

The basic project of AI research is to produce genuine intelligence by means of a programmed digital computer. This requires, in effect, that human knowledge and understanding be reconstructed out of bits of isolated and meaningless data and sequences of rule-governed operations. The problems facing this approach can be put quite simply: human knowledge and understanding do not consist of such data, rules and operations; and nothing which does consist essentially of these things will ever duplicate any interesting range of intelligent human behavior.

Early research projects in artificial intelligence tried to meet head-on the task of duplicating human mentality. Major areas of emphasis included natural language understanding, pattern recognition and general problem-solving. Problems in each of these areas were seen initially as problems of size — organizing and using a very large quantity of data. In order to understand even a small and ordinary sample of natural language, for example, a very large mass of background facts seemed to be required; and this massive collection of facts seemed in turn to require some kind of organization in terms of relevance so that not every fact required explicit consideration in every exercise of linguistic understanding. Pattern-recognition research ran into similar problems. The number of possibly relevant features was immense, and rules for separating those features actually relevant to recognition of a given shape or figure from all the others proved incredibly difficult to formulate. More general problem-solving faced exactly the same difficulties, only several orders of magnitude larger due to the increased generality of the task.

In the first edition of *What Computers Can't Do* I argued that the problems encountered by AI workers in these research areas were not just a matter of size, and would not succumb to more efficient programs and programming languages or to dramatic increases in computing speed and storage capacity. None of the available empirical evidence suggested that human beings function in the manner required by then current AI models, and much of the evidence suggested an entirely different and incompatible view of human mentality — but this view emerges only after some long-standing psychological and philosophical assumptions are discarded. Those assumptions lie at the very heart of the information processing model of the mind. Put generally, there is only one assumption — that human mental processes are essentially identical to those of a digital computer. Put more specifically, the crucial assumptions are these: (i) that mental processes are sequences of rule-governed operations, and (ii) that these operations are carried out on determinate bits of data (symbols) which represent features of or facts about the world (information, but only in a technical sense of that term). I can best explain why those specific assumptions are implausible by looking at the problems encountered in each area of AI research.

The main problem for programs whose aim was to understand natural language was the need to do so either without any context to determine or disambiguate meaning, or else with a context completely spelled out in terms of explicit facts, features and rules for relating them. Even the meanings of individual terms are context- or situation-determined. Whether the word 'pen' refers to a writing implement, a place for infants to play, a place in which pigs or other animals are kept, the area of a baseball field in which pitchers warm up, or a place for confining criminals, is determined by the context in which the term appears within a story or conversation. It is even clearer that context determines the meaning of whole sentences. 'The book is in the pen' could mean that the child's story book is in the playpen, that the pigs' enclosure is where the paperback fell out of the farmer's pocket, that the microfilm of the diary is cleverly concealed in the compartment containing the ink cartridge, and so on. We human beings don't seem to need to explicitly consider all the alternatives: and, in fact, it's not even clear that there could be an exhaustive list of all the alternative meanings for typical samples of natural language. We are always involved in a situation or context which seems to restrict the range of possible meanings without requiring explicit or exhaustive consideration of the range of context-free alternatives.

The obvious solution from the standpoint of AI would be to give the computer the situation. The attempt to do this in a general way has been unsuccessful, and begs some important questions. The most important question begged is whether or not our command of the situation is just a matter of a number of facts which we accept, that is, a system of beliefs which could be made explicit. If it is, then it could, at least in principle, be given to a computer, and the only problems would be practical, problems of size and structure for the belief system. If our command of the situation cannot be represented as such a belief system, however, then there will be no way to get the computer into the situation or the situation into the computer so as to duplicate general human understanding. I believe that this is the real impasse which AI faces.

Influenced by philosophers such as Heidegger and Merleau-Ponty, it seems to me that the evidence points toward the following picture of the relation between facts and situations. Our sense of the situation we are in determines how we interpret things, what significance we place on the facts, and even what counts as facts for us at any given time. But our sense of the situation we are in is not just our belief in a set of facts, nor is it a product of independent facts or context-free features of our environment. The aspects of our surroundings which somehow give us our sense of our current situation are themselves products of a situation we were already in, so that situations grow out of situations without recourse to situation-neutral facts and features at any point. We never get into a situation from outside any situation whatsoever, nor do we do so by means of context-free data. But the computer has only such data to work with and must start completely unsituated. From the standpoint of the programmer, our natural situatedness consists of an indefinite regress of situations with no way to break in from the outside, no way to start from nothing. And this is only part of the problem for AI. Not only can the situation not be constructed out of context-free facts and features, but in fact the situation as it figures in intelligent human behavior is not primarily a matter of facts and features of any kind. It is much more like an implicit and very general sense of appropriateness, and seems to be triggered by global similarities to previously experienced situations rather than by any number of individual facts and features. I will try to make clear just how I think this works in the second part of this essay. Here, I will simply observe that, lacking access to anything very like the human situation, it is not surprising that digital computers also lack access to anything very like human understanding.

Pattern-recognition programs encountered similarly instructive difficulties. Whether it is a matter of recognizing perceived figures and shapes or the similarity of board positions or sequences of moves in a game of chess, the context seems to guide human pattern recognition in ways that cannot be duplicated by the computer using context-free features and precise rules for relating them. Our sense of our situation seems to allow us to zero in on just those features that are relevant to the task at hand and to virtually ignore an indefinite number of further features. Moreover, a great deal of human pattern recognition seems to be based on the perception of global similarity and not to involve any feature by feature comparison at all.

The expert chess player sees the board in terms of fields of force rather than precise positions of each of the individual pieces, recognizes intuitively the similarity to situations encountered in previous games, even though none of the individual positions of pieces and few of the objective relations among individual pieces are the same, and selects a move after explicitly examining relatively few alternatives. The computer, on the other hand, analyzes the board in terms of the position of each of the pieces and then either has recourse to heuristic rules which connect that information to precise moves or else uses brute computing force to examine every possible course of action to as great a depth as time will allow. The latter strategy has been more successful, but the moves selected by this technique are still inferior to those chosen by the human expert, in spite of the fact that the computer examines thousands of times as many future positions in its selection process. I will explain exactly why this is so in the second part of this essay.

Human beings also recognize people they know or familiar surroundings without noticing, much less carefully comparing, the individual features of the persons or things recognized. Duplicating this kind of ordinary recognition has proven impossible for AI. The reason, I think, is the same as in the case of the expert chess player, but more on this later.

Programs designed to duplicate the general human ability to solve problems achieved results only by restricting the task in such a way that general human problem solving was never at issue. Programs typically solved word puzzles which were restricted so as to include only relevant information and which contained explicit cues to invoke the correct heuristic rule as needed. The human ability to identify the kind of problem faced, to sort information in terms of relevance, and to find the correct method of solution on the basis of similarity to previously solved problems — that is, full-fledged human problem-solving — was simply bypassed, supplied, in effect, by the human 'processing' of the problems to be 'solved'.

In the late 1960s and early 70s, the difficulties described above were taken seriously by workers in AI. Instead of trying to duplicate in one giant step general human understanding of the world, attention turned to producing understanding in very restricted 'worlds'. These artificially restricted domains were called 'micro-worlds'. Impressive micro-world successes included Terry Winograd's SHRDLU, Thomas Evans' Analogy Problem Program, David Waltz's Scene Analysis Program, and Patrick Winston's program for learning concepts from examples. The micro-worlds were restricted in such a way that the problems of context-restricted relevance and context-determined meaning seemed to be manageable. The hope was that micro-world techniques could be extended to more general domains, the micro-worlds made increasingly more realistic and combined to produce eventually the everyday world, and the computer's capacity to cope with these micro-worlds thereby transformed into genuine artificial intelligence.

The subsequent failure of every attempt to generalize micro-world techniques beyond the artificially restricted domains for which they were invented has put an end to the hopes inspired by early micro-world successes and brought AI to a virtual standstill. Some researchers, including Winograd, have given up on AI entirely. The micro-world strategy failures have been instructive, however, focusing attention in the direction I had argued was crucial for more than a decade, namely, toward the nature of everyday human understanding and know-how. The problem encountered in the attempt to move from micro-worlds to any aspect of the everyday world is that micro-worlds aren't worlds at all, or, from the other side, domains within the everyday world aren't anything like micro-worlds. This insight emerged in the attempt to program children's story understanding. It was soon discovered that the 'world' of even a single child's story, unlike a micro-world, is not a self-contained domain and cannot be treated independently of the larger everyday world onto which it opens. Everyday understanding is presupposed in every real domain, no matter how small. The everyday world is not composed of smaller independent worlds at all, is not like a building which can be built up of tiny bricks — but is rather a whole somehow present in each of its parts. Once this was realized, micro-world research and its successes were recognized for what they really were, not small steps toward the programming of everyday or common-sense know-how and understanding, but clever evasions of the real need to program such general competence and understanding. And the prospects for programming a digital computer to display our everyday understanding of the world were looking less bright all the time. Cognitive scientists were discovering the importance of images and prototypes in human understanding. Gradually, most researchers were becoming convinced that human beings form images and compare them by means of holistic processes very different from the logical operations which computers perform on symbolic descriptions.[2]

A recent *Scientific American* article echoed my earlier assessment of AI:

> Probably the most telling criticism of current work in artificial intelligence is that it has not yet been successful in modeling what is called common sense . . . Substantially better models of human cognition must be developed before systems can be desgined that will carry out even simplified versions of commonsense tasks.[3]

## II

For the reasons discussed in the preceding section, I concluded in 1979[4] that AI would remain at a standstill in areas that required common-sense understanding of the everyday world, that there would be no major breakthroughs in interpreting ordinary samples of natural language, in recognizing ordinary objects or patterns in everyday contexts, or in everyday problem solving of any kind within a natural rather than artificially constrained setting. The evidence to date indicates that I was correct in my assessment of AI's prospects in these areas. However, I also predicted success for AI in certain isolated tasks, cut off from the everyday world and seemingly self-contained, tasks such as medical diagnosis and spectrograph analysis. It appeared to me at the time that ordinary common sense played no role in such tasks and that the computer, with its massive data storage capacity and ability to perform large numbers of inferences almost instantaneously and with unerring accuracy, might well equal or exceed the performance of human experts. It has turned out that I was mistaken about this. In a book that we have just finished,[5] my brother Stuart and I attempt to explain this surprising result. Here I can give only a brief account of that explanation.

The attempt to give computers human expertise in these special domains has come to be referred to as 'expert systems' research. It works as follows. Human experts in the domain are interviewed to ascertain the rules or principles which they employ. These are then programmed into the computer. The idea seems simple and uncontroversial. Human experts and computers work from the same facts with the same inference rules. Since the computer can't forget or overlook any of the facts, can't make any faulty inferences, and can make correct inferences much more swiftly than the human expert, the expertise of the computer should be superior. And yet in study after study the computer proves inferior to the human experts who provide its working principles. To understand how this is possible, we need to look closely at the process by which human beings acquire expertise.

The following model of the stages of skill acquisition emerged from our study of that process among airplane pilots, chess players, automobile drivers, and adult learners of a second language. We later found that our model fit almost perfectly data which had been gathered independently on the acquisition of nursing skills.[6] The model consists of five stages of increasing skill which I will summarize briefly in terms of the chess players. For more mundane skills such as automobile driving, you may be able to check much of the model against your own past experience.

*Stage 1: Novice*

During this first stage of skill acquisition through instruction, the novice is taught to recognize various objective facts and features relevant to the skill, and acquires rules for determining what to do based upon these facts and features. Relevant elements of the situation are defined so clearly and objectively for the novice that recognition of them requires no reference to the overall situation in which they occur. Such elements are, in this sense, context free. The novice's rules are also context free in the sense that they are simply to be applied to these context-free elements regardless of anything else that may be going on in the overall situation. For example, the novice chess player is given a formula for assigning point values to pieces independent of their position, and the rule, 'always exchange your pieces for the opponent's if the total value of pieces captured exceeds that of pieces lost.' The novice is generally not taught that there are situations in which this rule should be violated.

The novice typically lacks a coherent sense of his overall task, and judges his performance primarily in terms of how well he has followed the rules he has learned. After he acquires more than just a few such rules, the exercise of this skill requires such concentration that his capacity to talk or listen to advice becomes very limited.

The mental processes of the novice are easily imitated by the digital computer. Since it can use more rules and consider more context-free elements in a given amount of time, the computer typically outperforms the novice.

*Stage 2: Advanced Beginner*

Performance reaches a barely acceptable level only after the novice has considerable experience in coping with real situations. In addition to the ability to handle more context-free facts and more sophisticated rules for dealing with them, this experience has the more important effect of enlarging the learner's conception of the world of the skill. Through practical experience in concrete situations with meaningful elements which neither instructor nor learner can define in terms of objectively recognizable context-free features, the advanced beginner learns to recognize when these elements are present. This recognition is based entirely on perceived similarity to previously experienced examples. These new features are situational rather than context free. Rules for acting may now refer to situational as well as context-free elements. For example, the advanced chess beginner learns to recognize and avoid over-extended positions, and to respond to such situational aspects of board positions as a weakened king's side or a strong pawn structure even though he lacks precise objective definitional rules for their identification.

Because the advanced beginner has no context-free rules for identifying situational elements, he can communicate this ability to others only by the use of examples. Thus, the capacity to identify such features, as well as the ability to use rules which refer to them, is beyond the reach of the computer. The use of concrete examples and the ability to learn context-determined features from them, easy for human beings but impossible for the computer, represents a severe limitation on computer intelligence.

*Stage 3: Competence*

As a result of increased' experience, the number of recognizable elements present in concrete situations, both context free and situational, eventually becomes overwhelming. To cope with this the competent performer learns or is taught to view the process of decision-making in a hierarchical manner. By choosing a plan and examining only the relatively small number of facts and features which are most important, given the choice of plan, he can both simplify and improve his performance. A competent chess player,[7] for example, may decide, after studying his position and weighing alternatives, that he can attack his opponent's king. He would then ignore certain weaknesses in his own position and personal losses created by his attack, and the removal of pieces defending the enemy king would become salient.

The choice of a plan, although necessary, is no simple matter for the competent performer. It is not governed by an objective procedure like the context-free feature recognition of the novice. But performance at this level requires the choice of an organizing plan. And this choice radically alters the relation between the performer and his environment. For the novice and the advanced beginner, performance is entirely a matter of recognizing learned facts and features and then applying learned rules and procedures for dealing with them. Success and failure can be viewed as products of these learned elements and principles, of their adequacy or inadequacy. But the competent performer, after wrestling with the choice of a plan, feels personally responsible for, and thus emotionally involved in, the outcome of that choice. While he both understands his initial situation and decides upon a particular plan in a detached manner, he finds himself deeply involved in what transpires thereafter. A successful outcome will be very satisfying and leave a vivid memory of the chosen plan and the situation as organized in terms of that plan. Failure, also, will not be easily forgotten.

*Stage 4: Proficiency*

The novice and advanced beginner simply follow rules. The competent performer makes conscious choices of goals and plans for achieving them after reflecting upon various alternatives. This actual decision-making is detached and deliberative in nature, even though the competent performer may agonize over the selection because of his involvement in its outcome.

The proficient performer is usually very involved in his task and experiences it from a particular perspective as a result of recent previous events. As a result of having this perspective, certain features of the situation will stand out as salient and others will recede into the background and be ignored. As further events modify these salient features, there will be a gradual change in plans, expectations, and even which features stand out as salient or important. No detached choice or deliberation is involved in this process. It seems to just happen, presumably because the proficient performer has been in similar situations in the past and memory of them triggers plans similar to those which worked in the past and expectations of further events similar to those which occurred previously.

The proficient performer's understanding and organizing of his task is intuitive, triggered naturally and without explicit thought by his prior experience. But he will still find himself thinking analytically about what to do. During this reasoning, elements that present themselves as salient due to the performer's intuitive understanding will be evaluated and combined by rule to yield decisions about the best way to manipulate the environment. The spell of involvement in the world of the skill is temporarily broken by this detached and rule-governed thinking. For example, the proficient chess player[8] can recognize a very large repertoire of types of positions. Recognizing almost immediately, and without conscious effort, the sense of a position, he sets about calculating a move that best achieves his intuitively recognized plan. He may, for example, know that he should attack, but he must deliberate about how best to do so.

*Stage 5: Expertise*

The expert performer knows how to proceed without any detached deliberation about his situation or actions, and without any conscious contemplation of alternatives. While deeply involved in coping with his environment, he does not see problems in a detached way, does not work at solving them, and does not worry about the future or devise plans. The expert's skill has become so much a part of him that he need be no more aware of it than he is of his own body in ordinary motor activity. In fact, tools or instruments become like extensions of the expert's body. Chess grandmasters,[9] for example, when engrossed in a game, can lose entirely the awareness that they are manipulating pieces on a board, and see themselves as involved participants in a world of opportunities, threats, strengths, weaknesses, hopes and fears. When playing rapidly they sidestep dangers in the same automatic way that a child, himself an expert, avoids missiles in a familiar video game. In general, experts neither solve problems nor make decisions; they simply do what works. The performance of the expert is fluid, and his involvement in his task unbroken by detached deliberation or analysis.

The fluid performance of the expert is a natural extension of the skill of the proficient performer. The proficient performer, as a result of concrete experience, develops an intuitive understanding of a large number of situations. The expert recognizes an even larger number along with the associated successful tactic or decision. When a situation is recognized, the associated course of action simultaneously presents itself to the mind of the expert performer. It has been estimated that a master chess player can distinguish roughly 50,000 types of positions. We doubtless store far more typical situations in our memories than words in our vocabularies. Consequently, these reference situations, unlike the situational elements learned by the advanced beginner, bear no names and defy complete verbal description.

The grandmaster chess player recognizes a vast repertoire of types of positions for which the desirable tactic or move becomes immediately obvious. Excellent chess players can play at a rate of speed at which they must depend almost entirely on intuition, and hardly at all upon analysis and the comparison of alternatives, without any serious degradation in their performance. In a recent experiment International Master Julio Kaplan was required rapidly to add numbers presented to him audibly at the rate of about one number per second, while at the same time playing five-seconds-a-move chess against a slightly weaker, but master-level player. Even with his analytical mind completely occupied with the addition, Kaplan more than held his own against the master in a series of games. Deprived of the time necessary to see problems or construct plans, Kaplan still produced fluid and co-ordinated play.

What emerges from this model of human skill acquisition is a progression from the analytic, rule-governed behavior of a detached subject who consciously breaks down his environment into recognizable elements, to the skilled behavior of an involved subject based on an accumulation of concrete experiences and the unconscious recognition of new situations as similar to remembered ones. The innate human ability to recognize whole current situations as similar to past ones facilitates our acquisition of high levels of skill, and separates us dramatically from the artificially intelligent digital computer endowed only with context-free fact and feature-recognition devices and with inference-making power.

This model provided Stuart and me with an explanation of the failure of the expert-systems approach which also connects it with the failure of previous work in AI. When the interviewer elicits rules and principles from the human expert, he forces him, in effect, to revert to a much lower skill level at which rules were actually operative in determining his actions and decisions. This is why experts frequently have a great deal of trouble 'recalling' the rules they use even when pressed by the interviewer. They seem more naturally to think of their field of expertise as a huge set of special cases.[10] It is no wonder that systems based on principles abstracted from experts do not capture those experts' expertise, and hence do not perform as well as the experts themselves.

In terms of skill level, the computer is stuck somewhere between the novice and advanced beginner level and, if our model of skill acquisition is accurate, has no way of advancing beyond this stage. What has obscured this fact for so long is the tremendous memory of the computer, in terms of numbers of facts and features which can be stored, and the tremendous number of rules and principles which it can utilize with superhuman speed and accuracy. Although its skill is of a kind which would place it below the level of the advanced beginner, its computing power makes its performance vastly superior to that of a human being at the same skill level. But power of this kind alone is not sufficient to duplicate the ability, the intuitive expertise, of the human expert.

This model of human skill levels also explains the failure of AI researchers to duplicate human language understanding, pattern recognition, and problem-solving. In each of these areas we are, for the most part, experts. We are expert perceivers, expert speakers, hearers and readers of our native language, and expert problem-solvers in most areas of everyday life. That doesn't mean that we don't make mistakes, but it does mean that our performance is entirely different in kind from that of the programmed digital computer. In each of these areas the computer is, at best, a very powerful and sophisticated beginner, competent in artificial micro-worlds where situational understanding and intuitive expertise have no part to play, but incompetent in the real world of human expertise.

I still believe, as I did in 1965,[11] that computers may someday be intelligent. Real computer intelligence will be achieved, however, only after researchers abandon the idea of finding a symbolic representation of the everyday world and a rule-governed equivalent of common-sense know-how, and turn to something like a neural-net modeling of the brain instead. If such modeling turns out to be the direction that AI should follow, it will be aided by the massively parallel computing machines on the horizon — not because parallel machines can make millions of inferences per second, but because faster, more parallel architecture can better implement the kind of pattern processing that does not use representations of rules and features at all.

## Notes

1. Hubert Dreyfus, *What Computers Can't Do*, revised edition, Harper & Row, 1979.

2. For an account of the experiments which show how human beings actually use images, and the unsuccessful attempts to understand this capacity in terms of programs which use features and rules, see *Imagery*, ed. Ned Block, MIT Press, 1981. Also Ned Block, 'Mental Pictures and Cognitive Science,' *The Philosophical Review*, 1983, 499-541.

3. *Scientific American*, Oct. 1982, 133.

4. *What Computers Can't Do*.

5. Hubert Dreyfus and Stuart Dreyfus, *Mind over Machine*, Macmillan, 1986. My brother Stuart has played an essential part in all of the critical study of machine intelligence in which I have been involved. It was Stuart, working then at RAND as a programmer in the new field of operations research, who was responsible for RAND's hiring me in 1964 as a consultant to study their pioneering work in what was then called Cognitive Simulation. And it is Stuart's intuitions about the nature of human skill acquisition, and his working out of those intuitions, which are summarized in the remainder of this essay.

6. See Patricia Benner, *From Novice to Expert: Excellence and Power in Clinical Nursing Practices*, Addison-Wesley, 1984.

7. Such a player would have a rating of approximately Class A, which would rank him in the top 20% of tournament players.

8. Such players are termed masters, and the roughly 400 American masters rank in the top 1% of all serious players.

9. There are about two dozen players holding this rank in the US and they, as well as about four dozen slightly less strong players called International Masters, qualify as what we call experts.

10. Edward Feigenbaum and Pamela McCorduck, *The Fifth Generation. Artificial Intelligence and Japan's Computer Challenge to the World*, Addison-Wesley, 1983, 82.

11. The year of publication of my initial RAND report, 'Alchemy and Artificial Intelligence'.

*Note*: A Bibliography is included in Further Reading.

# 4 PARAMETERS OF COGNITIVE EFFICIENCY — A NEW APPROACH TO MEASURING HUMAN INTELLIGENCE

Friedhart Klix

Measuring intelligence is indeed a classical task of psychology. But so far psychologists have not succeeded in separating exactly high degrees of general intelligence from major variants of specific talent, e.g. for mathematics.

The classical approach to assessing intelligence is based upon the correlative analysis of test results. But in spite of all the mathematics involved, it has remained basically intuitive. The ascending order of difficulties, by which intelligence is measured, is derived from the position strategies which are likely to be used in solving them within a certain distribution of performances mapped on score values. The actual process of problem-solving is of no importance although it includes most certainly the characteristics of any intelligence-based performance. The resulting shortcomings have often been subject to criticism concerning the measuring of intelligence by means of tests. Critical contributions were directed at the low validity, the ambiguity of the factors which leaves much scope for interpretation, the arbitrariness in system design (e.g. Guilford, 1a) and other shortcomings.

Over many years our research team (Sydow, van der Meer, Krause, Sprung and others) has investigated cognitive performance in the formation of concepts, in problem-solving, in the recognition of semantic relations, in aspects of knowledge representation, etc. Therefore, it was only natural to examine if the inter-individual variability in these processes justifies to identify a relationship to the intellectual potentials of the persons involved.

In our investigation we were naturally faced with the necessity of defining the nature of human intelligence. The axiom we started from has led us to a definition of the essence of human intelligence and talent. It implies the idea that mental efficiency and intelligence are synonymous concepts in so far as intelligence is reflected in the efficiency of any mental activity. The relationship between effort and result is governed by the degree of efficiency. A teacher will consider that pupil more intelligent for whom a given problem is 'easier', 'simpler' than for others and who will therefore solve it' more easily. It may sound a trivial statement but it is correct. What is this difference in handling a problem due to? Why is it easier for some persons to understand and solve a problem? We assume that there are information-processing procedures by means of which complex requirements are reduced to an extent which is essential for decision-making.

This consequence of our axiom leads to an evolutionary validation of the phenomenon of human intelligence. In order to understand the essential core of this phenomenon, we ask the question why in the evolutionary development of the organisms it was increasingly living creatures with a superior intellectual potential that have survived.

Seeing the subject from this angle, we have to consider the advantage of intelligence or mental efficiency, which is basically the same, in natural selection. In my book *Erwachendes Denken*, which is due to be published under the title *On the Origin of Human Intelligence* by Cambridge University Press in 1985, I have explained that one of the great advantages of cognitive processes in natural selection is due to their value in predicting forthcoming events. This implies that they reduce the degree of insecurity in connection with the obscure future. In order to understand this function we must be aware that, strictly speaking, we are unable to look, just one minute, into the future. Nobody knows whether he or she will survive the next day, which important news he or she will receive soon, or what kind of misfortune is going to happen to him or her before very long. Prediction of the future becomes feasible indirectly by means of our memory. Recurring events or regularities in general are recorded in the memory and thus generate expectations. Observation of the tides is necessary in order to predict the incoming tide. The succession of the seasons must be studied in order to be able to predict the next one at any point. The registration of the fact that Sirius rises over Memphis every 365 days makes it possible to predict precisely its return. At any rate, predictability reduces uncertainty and insecurity. Both uncertainty and insecurity have an utterly negative touch in our motivational system. That is why all processes counteracting insecurity are stimulated, and therefore cognitive performance is of particular importance.

The predictability of events in the environment is impeded by the fact that the environment is extremely complex, considering the respective capacity of our nervous system. The relations between causes and effects are easily comprehensible only in the simplest situations. And in the simplest situations conditioned responses are developed in the nervous system. In the great majority of cases, however, extremely complex inter-relationships are involved. The inadequate predictability of the weather is a striking example in this context. This almost natural insecurity, due to the high degree of complexity of the events has always remained, seen in an evolutionary context, a most powerful stimulus in the efforts aimed at reducing complexity by means of pre-processing incoming information. In fact information pre-processing reduces the complexity and thus makes it comprehensible. (The generation of star images in our minds facilitates a certain degree of transparency in the otherwise rather irregular complexity. The country sayings concerning the development of the weather could be mentioned here as an example, because the sophisticated network of inter-relationships has been replaced by simplified relations between causes and effects at major points of decision.) Thus, pre-processing of information produces a simplified representation of a problem, which reduces the amount of mental effort in solving complex problems. This in turn is an essential characteristic of human intelligence with regard to both the individual and the historical development of mankind. As I said before: if two persons are given a problem to solve, that person who is capable of mapping the problem in more simplified terms and who for this reason invests less effort in the solution will be the more intelligent of them. The same phenomenon can be proved also in connection with intellectual advances in the historical development, e.g. in the numerical systems. (Compare, for example, the representation of numerals in ancient Egypt or Rome with the one we are familiar with now, which has been extremely simplified as a result of the digital system.)

We now know that phylogenetic advantages in the selection processes are the actual source of cognitive processes, and these advantages are obtained by the capacity to predict events in the environment. We also know the criterion by which cognitive processes can be measured, i.e. the degree to which complexity can be reduced. The latter point is of particular importance in the following because we are now in a position to define a number of cognitive phenomena in their function as components of information pre-processing.

**Example 1**

Pre-processing of information starts with the formation of perceptive structures. If subjects are shown, for the very short time of approximately 100 ms, patterns as in Figure 4.1a, and then asked to sketch them on paper from their memory, they will produce structures similar to the ones in Figure 4.1b. In each case they will

**Figure 4.1. Simplification Trends in Perception Manifesting *Gestalt* Laws**

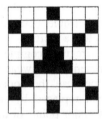 

If the pattern on the left is exposed for a very short time, this will lead to impressions of structural simplifications of the kind shown by the picture on the right. The recognition of the type of pattern is nevertheless ensured, as a result.

be simplified versions of the actual pattern, a kind of schema based on the perceptive pattern formation (*gestalt* laws of perception) in which the complexity of the real object is reduced.

**Example 2**

Pre-processing of information can also be brought about by way of comparing structural properties of perception. And as a result, relations between structure are recognized. Figure 4.2 provides some examples. The relations include vertical, horizontal and diagonal mirrorings. They are identified by comparing perceptive cues.

**Example 3**

This example illustrates a process which is superordinate to the

**Figure 4.2**

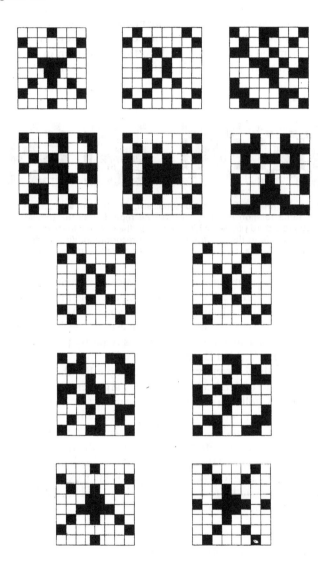

Top: Chessboard patterns of the kind used in the experiments.
Bottom: Three kinds of relation between two patterns: reflecting along the
vertical, the horizontal, and the diagonal line.

recognition of relations. It is based upon the comparison of relations, by means of which it can be decided whether or not relations between structures are identical. This cognitive process, which consists of a number of componental factors involved in the recognition of relations, leads to the recognition of analogies between structures (Figure 4.3). Before I proceed to an exact analysis

**Figure 4.3**

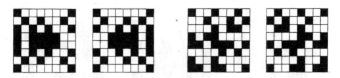

Transfer of a relation $R_i$ to a second pattern, which then, as a pair, is linked by the same relation $R_i$. This, too, can be regarded as the transfer of an operation to a third pattern, which generates the relation. In structural terms, this corresponds to the process of analogy recognition. VI(  ) indicate four kinds of pre-information given immediately before the analogy-problem.

of the process let us have a look at the chart describing analogy recognition within the framework of genuine cognitive processes. Figure 4.4 shows how Thales of Miletus at about 650 BC (according to Herodotus) is supposed to have measured the height of the pyramids. The analogous structure of this cognitive performance is quite obvious (A : A' or B : B') (Figure 4.5).

A seemingly completely different example has the same basic structure. In the *Discorsi* Galileo's arguments against the contemporary followers of Aristotle were in fact analogy-based deductions. He refuted the argument that as the earth rotates (Copernicus' assumption) a falling object would hit the ground at a point not directly opposite the point at which the free fall started. Galileo compares the stationary relation A—A' with that governing a closed moving system (B—B'). Many similar examples of this structural type can be found in the works of Euclid, Archimedes, Gauss, Polya and many others.

**Analysis of an Analogy Recognition Process**

On the basis of the efficiency criterion for any cognitive performance as we defined it above, specifically intelligent and

Figure 4.4

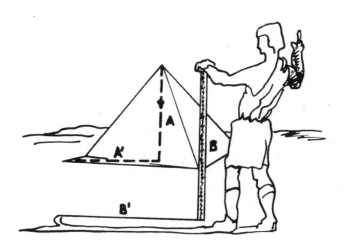

It is shown how Thales of Miletus at about 650 BC is supposed to have measured the height of the pyramids.

Figure 4.5. General Scheme of Analogy Recognition

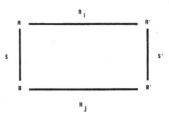

A or A' respectively correspond to a pattern (or concept) pair. $R_i$ denotes the relation existing between the two structures. The same has been shown for the pair of B and B'. If $R_i$ equals $R_{jr}$ then the analogy condition has been met. Distance S denotes the distance between structures or the degree of their difference. It influences the degree of difficulty in the process of recognition and plays a part in creative processes.

particularly persons with a special talent for mathematics were expected to recognize analogies more efficiently than persons with a more general intelligence. With this idea in mind we compared a group of pupils who because of their special mathematical talent are given specialized teaching in mathematics at the Humboldt University in Berlin with a group of first-year students of the University's Psychology Department. In the experiment both groups were given the task of recognizing analogies between structures as shown in Figure 4.3.

*Organization of the Experiment*

Sitting in a dark room, subjects are given four kinds of pre-information concerning the immediately following analogy problem: either an empty square (VI(0)) or the first pattern (VI(1)) or the first pattern pair (VI(2)) or the first pattern triple (VI(3)). Subsequently, the two pairs whose relation identity has to be examined will be presented. The subjects were instructed (i) to look at the pre-information in as briefly as possible time, and (ii) to decide the analogy problem by answering either 'yes' or 'no' in the shortest possible time (with 'yes' indicating identity and 'no' indicating non-identity of relations). Time, including the time actually needed for a response to the given problem, was measured. The main results are shown in Figure 4.6.

The time needed to process the preliminary information offered was shorter in the extreme group (i.e. the talented mathematical pupils). Nevertheless, the recognition process was faster. And the rate of correctness (+ or − decisions) was equally good.

What is this result due to? Do the members of the extreme group just work faster? Do they have a more efficient strategy? The question of speed can be examined easily. We compared the time expenditure rates of the two groups at pre-information stage 2 when the relations between the structures had to be discovered (VI(2)). The results are given in Figure 4.7. It says that relations are recognized by means of scanning processes. Time expenditure was fairly constant at a rate of almost precisely $\Delta t = 220$ ms.

Let us now have a look at the patterns drawn from the model structures. The experiment was interrupted after the presentation of the first 17 patterns, and the subjects were asked to draw into a grid what they had just seen in VI(1) = A. Figure 4.8 shows some of the drawings.

Significant differences were found (i) in the number of partial

## Figure 4.6. The Principal Results of the Basic Tests

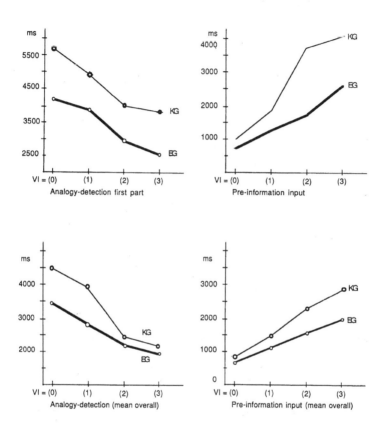

On the left there are the times needed for analogy recognition; and on the right there are those needed for the intake of preliminary information. At the top there are the average data of the first series; and at the bottom there are those for all stages of the test (first and second series).

structures ($\varphi$), and (ii) in the average size of the partial structures ($\nu$) as well as in the time needed, on average, to draw a partial structure ($\theta$). It is by means of these three parameters that the entire process can be reconstructed. Figure 4.9 (bottom) gives a schematic representation of the experiment, while Figure 4.9 (top) shows one of the strategies (strategy II) of our two groups. This

Figure 4.7. The Determination of a Time Constant in the Process of Relation Recognition

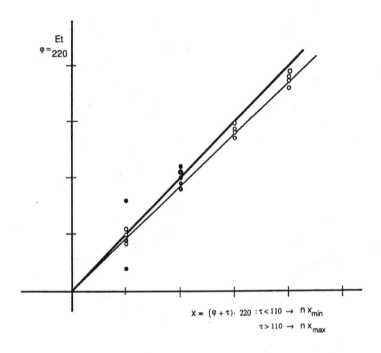

$$x = (\varphi + \tau) \cdot 220 : \tau < 110 \rightarrow n \, x_{min}$$
$$\tau > 110 \rightarrow n \, x_{max}$$

Ordinate: recognition time for the individual pattern divided by the assumed time constant of 220 ms. Abscissa: attribution of the ordinate datum to the next higher ($+ \tau$) or next lower ($- \tau$) whole-number multiple of 220 ($\varphi \pm \tau$) = n; n = $\theta$ mod 220. Among them are the degrees of regression for the extreme group and the control group.

process can be simulated by means of a computer. The results of the computer simulation can then be compared with the data obtained in the experiment.

In this context a third strategy, which tends to be characteristic of the extreme group rather than the control group, is of considerable significance. Figures 4.10a and 4.10b show the typical basic structure. It becomes evident, in comparison with Figure 4.9 at which points time savings have had their origin.

Figure 4.8. Subjective Representation of a Pattern Structure in Drawings Made by Subjects

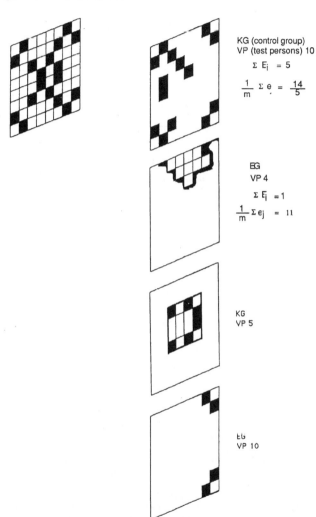

KG (control group)
VP (test persons) 10

$$\Sigma\ E_i\ =\ 5$$

$$\frac{1}{m}\ \Sigma\ e\ =\ \frac{14}{5}$$

EG
VP 4

$$\Sigma\ E_i\ =1$$

$$\frac{1}{m}\Sigma e_j\ =\ 11$$

KG
VP 5

EG
VP 10

They are different, (1), in the number of partial structures formed ($\Sigma E_i$) and, (2), the average areal size of the partial structures. ($\frac{1}{m} \Sigma\ e_j$), with $e_j$ being the areal unit. The average data of quantity (1) for all subjects are called $\varphi$, and those of quantity (2) are called $\nu$. The third personal parameter $\theta$ denotes the recognition time expenditure per unit of partial structure.

## Figure 4.9

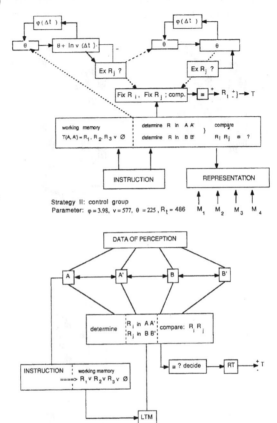

Bottom: Hypothetic representation of the analogy-deduction process.

Top: The course that the process takes is the same for the two groups. The difference in the parameter data are shown to lead to the recorded differences in time. The perceptive representation is marked as input (in the bottom right-hand corner). The instruction acts upon the mode of operation adopted by the working memory, which, in turn, controls the intake of information in accordance with the demand.

On the extreme left: encoding of structural parts of the first pattern. Then (with A') encoding and pattern search, retrograde comparison with the first pattern (without new encoding) until the fixing of a figure part specific to the transformation. Fixing of the recognized relation $R_i$ in working memory, encoding of B and B̂', comparison processes in accordance with ($\Delta t = 220$ ms) until the recognition of $\bar{R}_j$; comparison between $\bar{R}_j$ and $R_i$, and identity decision (3 or 4 times $\Delta t$) in the case of positive or negative agreement.

($M_i$ = pattern, T = transformation, $R_i$ = type of relation, $R_t$ = total time, $\varphi, \nu$ $\theta$ parameter data.)

One source is most certainly the distinct formation of structures, emphasizing particularly relation-relevant characteristics of the structures (parameter $\varphi$ ). This could be connected with the hypothesis-controlled mode of perception, which concentrates on relation-relevant components of structures. Another source can be seen in the hypothesis-controlled comparison of relations between B and B'. This implies that on the basis of one single pattern detail of the transformation model the pattern B was transformed according to the relation which was found to exist between A and A'. B' is then only checked as to whether or not it has the predicted property of the mode, while memory is relieved from action. There is no need for further comparative processes of recognition of relations. What is so exciting is that with regard to the time spent on the actual processes, it is the slowest group (conf. parameter   ). Nevertheless, it eventually had the shortest overall time expenditure. Figure 4.11 shows a computer diagram of the various strategies under consideration. On the basis of this diagram it seems justified to maintain that the processes involved in analogy-recognition have been cleared up to a large extent.

**Figures 4.10a and 4.10b. Extremely Effective Strategy Three
a: extreme group; b: control group**

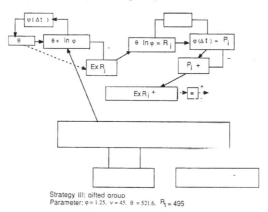

Strategy III: gifted group
Parameter: $\varphi = 1.25$, $v = 45$, $\theta = 521.6$, $R_t = 495$

The time saving (despite extremely slow encoding) is due to the criterion-related information intake (i.e. the information intake controlled by working memory) (pattern A'). Pattern B is recoded in accordance with the example set by the A—A' relation. The fourth pattern need not, as a result, be encoded, but only checked as to whether the anticipated figure criterion is present or not. This obviates the need for remembering and comparison processes.

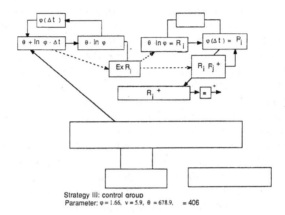

Strategy III: control group
Parameter: φ = 1.66, v = 5.9, θ = 678.9,  = 406

The process takes a similar course to that in 10a, the difference being that encoding is less purposive (criterion search by means of In $\varphi$ ($\Delta$t) ).

**Figure 4.11**

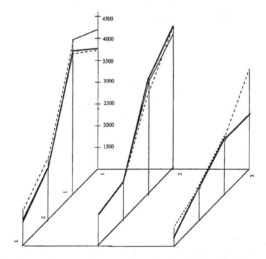

Computer chart for the comparison between a simulation program after Figures 4.9 & 4.10 on the one hand, and the empirical data, on the other. Both the data for the extreme group and those for the control group are well-adapted and statistically indistinguishable.

Finally, I should like to discuss the question of the mutual dependence of structure and dynamic elements within these relatively transparent processes, which have been established to be an essential part of cognitive performance and in which framework differences in talent appear to originate in the depths of elementary stages of cognition.

## Some Remarks on Intelligence and Talent

In our model we have not only simulated processes involved in any cognitive performance, but we have also reproduced classes of individual differences. Our findings suggest that the processes are based on the characteristic concatenation of componential

**Figure 4.12. The Partial Functions (Modules of the Process of Analogy Recognition)**

Process-module:

0.  Pure reaction time $\quad = \quad$ Rt

1.  Encoding (recognition) of partial structures:
    $$Enk \quad = \quad n \cdot \theta$$

2.  Encoding- (recognition-) rate at the change of partial structures:
    $$EA\,(TSW) \quad = \quad \theta \cdot \ln \varphi$$

3.  Efficiency rate of relation-recognition between partial structures:
    $$= \quad \varphi \cdot \Delta t; \quad \Delta t = 220 \text{ ms}$$

4.  Efficiency rate at the change of partial structures:
    $$SA\,(WS) \quad = \quad \ln v \cdot \Delta t \text{ (unspecific)}$$
    $$= \quad \ln \varphi \cdot \Delta t \text{ (specific)}$$

5.  Analogy identification as relation identity:
    $$= \quad \Delta t = 3 \cdot \Delta t$$

The favourable adaptations that arise from the logarithmization of structural elements and patterns areas, point to a processing performance in perception that is based on processes of pattern recognition, as far as details are concerned. It has not as yet been possible to provide a satisfactory simulation of this part of the process.

cognitive functions which can be regarded as subprocedures or modules of the problem-solving process. A survey of these modules is given in Figure 4.12. Their specific concatenation and interaction has a crucial impact on the efficiency of the problem-solving process.

Thus, the different strategies pursued by different groups of subjects can be regarded as different ways of concatenating these modules, i.e. as different dynamic structures. What had *a priori* been identified as a mathematical talent was found to be a specific concatenation of componential cognitive functions (in the sense of a modular architecture) in the course of the investigations. The modules function as combinable tools and their respective concatenation determines the efficiency rate of the reasoning process.

From this point of view, intelligence can be considered as the ability to organize modules, i.e. componential structures, involved in any cognitive process in such a way that given problems can be solved with a highest degree of efficiency. The effort needed to solve a problem can be reduced and the efficiency increased to the degree to which the concatenation of modules is adequate to the given type of problem.

Talent, or giftedness in this framework, appears to be a nonconsciously preferred form of modular organization which results in an individual kind of cognitive functioning. It is manifested in a kind of complementary relationship between a certain class of problems and an appropriate organization of the multitude of processes involved in information processing. This specific organization or concatenation fits specific classes of problems just as the key fits the lock. With a growing appropriateness of the modular organization, the effort can be reduced whereas the efficiency will be increased.

This complementary relationship between requirements and inherent patterns of problem-solving also has an emotional aspect which is evident in the affinity of a talented person for certain types of problems which fit the individual predisposition. It appears as if a profound sympathy for a particular type of requirement propels the constant desire to solve difficult problems.

As for the predisposition for solving mathematical problem classes, we found that it is determined by an adaptive dynamics of information-processing structures, especially in the construction and dismantling of cognitive structures and their concatenation, and in selecting, comparing, identifying and extrapolating informational entities.

Fluent and dynamic structures of this kind (including sensomotor co-ordinations) are required

- in mathematics and theoretical physics,
- in music, and
- in language comprehension, especially in the easy grasp of grammatical structures.

These are in fact areas and requirements in which talents can be found at a very early age. Such talents are hardly found in disciples as, for example, geography, history or philosophy, which is certainly due to the heterogeneity of the cognitive requirements made, but also to the enormous range of knowledge that has to be acquired before major achievements can be produced. A young and talented mathematician can come to entirely new insights on a very limited basis of knowledge.

Summing up I should like to say:

(1) I set out to explain the phenomenon of human intelligence within the evolutionary development. Integrated in the advantage of cognitive processes in natural selection and signifying their efficiency, it proved to be that predisposition by which the future becomes predictable. Within the relevant processes, complexity is reduced to the essentials required in decision-making.
(2) We have analysed a mathematically talented extreme group and found

- distinct procedures for reducing the amount of information,
- as a consequence, a more distinct ability to anticipate.

What had been deduced from the historical development was proved *in vitro* in the experiment.

One of the great authorities in physics, Heinrich Hertz, said, in the nineteenth century:

It is the next and foremost task in our discovery of nature to enable ourselves to foresee future experience and to adjust our present-day activities to that foresight . . . The possibility of achieving this aim probably represents the very origin of natural science in general.

It was my intention to demonstrate that inter-individual analysis and the description of the parameters of cognitive processes are closely related to the discovery of the nature of human intelligence.

# 5 THE DECLINE AND FALL OF THE MECHANIST METAPHOR[1]

## S.G. Shanker

### Philosophy Versus Science

The 'philosophy versus science' confrontation which has so dominated discussions of Artificial Intelligence (hereafter AI) has increasingly become a source of unnecessary and fruitless conflict. Where philosophers and scientists should be striving to serve a common purpose they all too often meet each other instead in open hostility. The key to resolving this undeclared state of war rests, however, on a purely internal philosophical affair. For until the 'philosophy versus science' controversy which rages *within* philosophy has been settled, there can be little hope of scientists and philosophers joining in a concerted attack on the conceptual problems which plague AI.

The very manner of describing the philosophical controversy over the nature of *philosophy* in terms of a 'philosophy versus science' confrontation has itself been the source, not of unnecessary, but rather of inconclusive conflict. What was originally intended as a means of clarifying the conceptual nature of a philosophical investigation — by distinguishing it from scientific inquiry — has led to a state of affairs where, inside philosophy itself, allegiances have been divided between two opposed camps which view the tactics of the other as diversionary, if not completely abortive. A considerable amount of time is thus devoted solely to the task of countering the offensives launched by the enemy (otherwise known as scholarly 'in-fighting'). But a large part of the trouble is that the 'philosophy versus science' dichotomy is far too crude to perform the role originally intended.

Russell quite rightly argued that philosophy should serve the same interests as science: viz. a better understanding of the world we inhabit. Where he went disastrously wrong was in his conception of the nature of this understanding. For Russell believed that philosophy, like science, endeavours to attain a 'theoretical understanding of the world'.[2] Hence he concluded that if philosophy was to contribute to scientific progress, it could only do so by modelling itself on the methods which characterize a scientific discipline. Wittgenstein, of course, devoted a considerable amount of effort to overthrowing this picture by clarifying the nature of the logical demarcation between an empirical and a conceptual investigation: i.e. between theory-construction versus the removal of philosophical confusions which are engendered by transgressions of logical grammar. But having said that, Wittgenstein was by no means intent on employing his attack on the 'scientistic' conception of philosophy as part of a larger campaign to consolidate a 'two cultures' division. On the contrary, he emphasized that the role of modern philosophy will (or at least should) become increasingly bound up with the interpretation of scientific discoveries.[3] Thus, the Wittgensteinian no less than the Russellian conception of philosophy is intent on contributing to the needs of science; where the crucial difference lies is in the perception of the manner in which this is to be accomplished.

Neither lesson has as yet been fully absorbed. The 'scientistic' philosophers have, I believe, contributed to the actual retardation of scientific progress in many areas, usually by the development of armchair theories which either create or sustain scientific confusions which can seriously hamper genuine empirical investigations. Conversely, Wittgensteinian philosophers have tended to concentrate primarily on the importance of exposing chimeras; armed with the subtle tools of conceptual clarification, they reveal the confusions which predominate in scientific prose for what they are: the muddled result of trying to transgress logical boundaries governing the employment of concepts lying in disparate grammatical systems. To be sure, the significance of this task should in no way be minimized: for such broad confusions can themselves be the source of considerable scientific muddle. Yet this need not necessarily be the case: a fact that Wittgensteinian philosophers have, perhaps, been all too loathe to confront. For the fact remains that, despite the confusions which might riddle scientific prose, the theories themselves might continue to develop *ventre à terre*.[4] The disturbing question which this raises, therefore, is whether scientific prose is entirely irrelevant to scientific progress, and *a fortiori*, whether 'philosophy is an idleness' in science. If not, it is incumbent on the aspiring Wittgensteinian philosopher to address this issue, and consequently set about to remedy the attitudes which have allowed such a question to arise in the first place.

The first step to correcting this situation is to abandon the crude 'philosophy versus science' conflict. For the role which philosophy plays in science highlights the importance of conceptual clarification alongside theory-construction. But then, if the philosopher really wants to serve science in this capacity he must shed his amateur status in matters scientific. For where philosophers and scientists share a similar goal, the philosopher must take considerable pains to make his contribution relevant and constructive if he expects scientists to recognize the benefits of a philosophical critique. There is a general feeling amongst scientists that philosophers amuse themselves with superficialities whilst ignoring the complex arguments which support and substantiate theoretical conclusions. Moreover, there is a widespread conviction that philosophers tend to underestimate the extent to which scientists have anticipated — and sought to resolve — the objections subsequently voiced by philosophers. Both complaints may not be without some merit. It is a failing which understandably exacerbates tensions; for not least of the dangers which it leads to is the philosopher's peremptory verdict that the scientist is uttering *nonsense*, full-stop. Unfortunately, such an uncompromising position is frequently vitiated by the philosopher's refusal to consider the actual theories which lie beneath the prose.

No better example of this conflict could be found than in the controversies that have raged over the mechanist theories espoused by AI scientists. In a fundamental sense — viz. the manner in which the (strong) AI scientist *intends* his argument to be interpreted — it is indeed generally the case that his claims are unintelligible. Yet that does not entail that such scientists are engaged in purely fanciful pursuits, or are seriously unable to communicate with one another. A case in point is provided by the widespread discussions of 'intelligent' — i.e. *learning* — systems. It is certainly unintelligible to suggest that a machine can *learn* in the sense in which this concept is commonly employed (for reasons of logical grammar, not empirical limitations). It is equally clear, however, that when AI scientists employ this concept in their technical discussions they are not talking nonsense *per se*. For they all understand what — at the technical level — is meant by a 'learning' system, even if their interpretations fail to render this perspicuous. Our task, then, is two-fold: to clarify the source of the confusion that a computer can be said to *learn* in the accepted meaning of the term, and conversely, to clarify exactly what scientists do *mean* when they refer to 'learning' systems.

Philosophical approaches to AI have hitherto tended to concentrate on the dangerous implications of AI for our conception of man and his place in society. Hence, advocates of the Mechanist Thesis have struggled to satisfy the objections of their critics, first, by applying some version of the Turing Test to demonstrate that there is nothing paradoxical involved in the claim that machines 'think', and then, to satisfy the qualms of the many humanists who worry about the consequences of such a conceptual revolution for our attitudes towards human autonomy by pointing to the manner in which these remarkable technological achievements have only served to heighten the potential fulfilment of *homo faber*. I have attempted elsewhere to clarify the myriad confusions involved in the Mechanist Thesis — all of which trade upon a confused apprehension of the Turing Test, or else commit some version of the homunculus fallacy — and to indicate the full significance of the conceptual revolution involved in the Mechanist Thesis in terms which may be far from immediately evident.[5] These are serious matters, and they should be carefully and meticulously examined. But having said that, there remains a no less vital area of philosophical concern in the field of AI which, because of the attention devoted to the former issues, has been strikingly neglected. For the philosopher should not rest with merely attacking the confusions embedded in the prose of AI scientists while the need remains to clarify exactly what *is* going on in AI research. This is not only a matter of furthering our understanding of the above issues, but equally important, it provides a crucial means of participating in the advance of AI. For the prose of AI scientists is no mere indulgence in scientific hyperbole or futuristic planning: it is, in fact, a vital medium in which scientists seek to interpret the results of their own achievements, and thence shape the future of AI research. Thus, the philosopher should certainly investigate the goals of the Fifth Generation project in order to assess its social and conceptual implications, but at a deeper level he should scrutinize the arguments underlying the presentation of the project with an eye to evaluating and perhaps contributing to the further chances of the project's success. If he focuses solely on the former and ignores the latter issue, however, the philosopher can hardly be surprised to find that a great many scientists remain hostile to the presence of philosophical intruders in their field.

The great irony in all this is that the philosopher is in a unique position to provide a bridge between the 'two cultures'; yet instead, because of the internecine conflict described above, philosophers have only served to consolidate this great divide. On the one hand, those 'scientistic' philosophers who merely popularize or encourage the scientist's conceptual confusions may well be trying to bridge the gap between the 'two cultures', yet by seizing hold of the wrong end of the stick they have become the agents of technological obscurantism. Conversely, those Wittgensteinian philosophers who have disdained to delve into the technical details of the scientist's work have not only fostered the attitude that philosophy's interest in science is purely negative, but they have also neglected an area where their services might well be instrumental. For a common feature of scientific progress is the extent to which discoveries hinge on the ability to view a problem from some totally novel point of view; i.e. to construct a new grammatical system in which an 'unsolvable' problem is in effect given an entirely new meaning and thence a solution. Yet it is then obviously crucial that the conceptual implications of this grammatical revolution be fully appreciated for what they are in order to maximize the empirical possibilities inherent in this new system. Such a pattern is particularly evident in the largely mathematical sciences; it is thus no surprise to find that it plays what is perhaps the central role in the development of AI.

**Prose**

The term 'prose' in the context of scientific discussion refers to the use which scientists make of ordinary descriptive or metaphorical expressions in order to interpret or describe their theories. It is meant to signify the fact that the expression plays no legitimate role within the construction of the theory. Rather, it is drawn from an external — and usually (although not necessarily) a less abstract — level of discourse. The distinctly pejorative overtones of the term are largely due to the fact that the prose attached to a theory can be the source of considerable confusion in regards to understanding the mechanics and/or significance of that theory. The more that scientific theories are constructed in some highly abstruse and technical language, the greater this danger becomes.

The results of such confusions — which arise only at the level of the *interpretation* of the theory — can range anywhere from the proliferation of scientific goals which are strictly unintelligible, to the creation of ingenious theories which are of no conceivable practical (or scientific) importance.

Perhaps the basic question which this raises is: What is the point of introducing scientific prose — as a vehicle for the communication of ideas amongst scientists — in the first place? For example, why should AI scientists even bother to introduce the term 'learning' when what they really refer to are self-modifying programs? After all, if the prose were removed entirely none of these hazards would arise. Yet as obvious as this point may seem, it is clear that the prose serves more than an incidental role in scientific communication. For there is more involved here than the simple use of the vernacular as a form of shorthand; the choice of the metaphor which governs the early stages in the evolution of a scientific theory can be a matter of prodigious significance. For it is clear that the metaphor which is adopted is selected essentially for its value as an illuminating or heuristic picture. Traditionally, poetry has been regarded as the vehicle for 'flights of the imagination'; in science this role is performed by prose. In a manner which no technical description could possibly equal, it manages to stimulate interest as well as point research in a definite — as opposed to random — direction. One repeatedly hears the theme that pure scientific research is conducted solely as a matter of satisfying innate curiosity. Yet this is clearly far from being all that is involved. In fact, problems are explored precisely because of the type of discovery which the scientist hopes to achieve, however inchoate the goals involved might be. Moreover, despite his alienation from the community of laymen, the scientist remains very much a member of society, interested perhaps in gaining recognition for his efforts, if not in pursuing his research in order to serve the needs of society. At any rate, whatever his attitudes to the communal welfare, the scientist is generally eager to ensure that at least his scientific colleagues understand the nature and significance of his results: a matter which might be far from straightforward in the technical presentation of his argument.

This raises a further point in regard to the essential role of prose terms or metaphors in keeping track of what is going on in a long and complex argument which, because of its very intricacy, might surpass the bounds of ordinary human comprehension. A particu-

particularly relevant example of this can be found in the brief history of computer programming. Given the limits of human comprehension, it was clear from the start that some form of symbolic assembly language was essential if computer science was to make any progress. For only a limited number of technicians were capable of reading a program written in machine code, let alone keeping track of the structure and direction of the program. Hence the design of higher-level languages was immediately identified as a crucial step in the evolution of AI: a process which will culminate, if the Fifth Generation project is successful, in the virtual obliteration of the distinction between high-level and ordinary language.

We might distinguish in principle between two broad species of scientific prose: that which is employed for scientific communication and that which is intended for non-specialist consumption. The importance of such a distinction lies in the fact that, while the use of a prose term might be unintelligible at one level of discourse (invariably, the non-specialist), it might none the less be significant at the scientific level. For example, the term 'machine learning' is perfectly intelligible on the scientific level of prose, but entirely meaningless in the context of the ordinary use of the concept of 'learning'. That is, 'machine learning' is a prose term whereby AI scientists refer to a species of self-modifying algorithms (cf. 'Learning Systems' below). The term thus performs the functions listed above: it is, in fact, superfluous, yet it serves to focus attention in the construction of Expert Systems. When we shift, however, to the concept of *learning* as this is ordinarily understood, the scientist's prose begins to idle.

With respect to the latter, it is clear that in order for scientists to communicate their results to the general public, it is essential that some form of simplified verbal description be deployed for the purpose. It is clearly in the interests of the latter, therefore — if not always of the former — that these descriptions should be intelligible. For the inescapable fact of scientific existence is that major research efforts will only be viable to the extent to which public or private support can be mobilized. Hence, the appropriate public or private authority must be educated in the general purpose and significance of the research in question. And prose provides the crucial, and it might be said, highly convenient medium whereby this is to be accomplished. For the fact is that the grammatical confusions involved in e.g. the unqualified claim that computers can 'learn' can be used to disguise the technical complexities involved in the actual scientific tasks involved. However, that is not to say that these confusions must *ipso facto* render the project impossible because unintelligible. For, as we have already seen, at the intra-scientific level of discourse the term 'computer learning' has acquired a perfectly legitimate (if misleading) connotation. But then the problem is that what the AI scientist really means by 'learning' conceals far more complexity than that which applies in the ordinary application of the term.

The Fifth Generation project[6] provides an excellent case in point of the potential dangers involved here. Before sanctioning the ten-year project the Japanese Ministry of International Trade and Industry (MITI) was certainly intent on understanding as clearly as possible precisely what was involved in the enterprise. But then the conceptual confusions which are enshrined in the Mechanist Thesis could have become a serious obstacle to the soundness of their judgement. When described in these terms the Fifth Generation project sounds exciting, adventurous, bold, and most important of all, *feasible* (within the cost/time parameters which MITI envisaged). However, were this all that was involved, then a philosophical critique would have sufficed to establish that the Fifth Generation project is doomed to failure: on the purely *a priori* grounds that the goals as stated in 1.3.1 of 'Challenge for Knowledge Information Processing Systems' are unintelligible.[7] But at this level of the report we are floating solely in the realm of the public-directed prose, where the conceptual confusions are both glaring and — as far as the technical feasibility of the project is concerned — relatively unimportant. (Although this is a point which the vast majority of AI scientists would still vigorously contest.) It is only when we delve into the depths of the report — particularly as outlined in the fourth chapter of 'Challenge for Knowledge Information Processing Systems' — that we begin to see precisely what is involved in the Fifth Generation project, and thus, to assess the team's chances of success.

Whether or not an informed decision could be made about the implementation of the Fifth Generation project on the basis of this later section of the report is a difficult question. But one thing is clear: a decision that was formed solely on the basis of the arguments outlined in 1.3.1 would be singularly uninformed, thereby increasing the possibility of a ruinously expensive exercise in futility (an experience certainly common enough amongst those

Western nations that have been persuaded to subsidize mega-scientific projects). For the history of science is littered with examples of the 'ashtray' syndrome: viz. after countless false starts and wasted resources, the end result of a once grand design is reduced to a caricature of what was originally envisaged. The pictures which are contained in the scientist's prose may be the great motivating force behind technological progress, but they can also be the source of the great scientific disasters. It is thus as important for the scientist to know exactly what it is that he is proposing as it is for the general public when judging the merits of the scientist's case. (By the same token, however, science is also littered with examples of the 'America' syndrome! Columbus' picture might have been seriously mistaken, yet none the less remarkably fruitful.)

There is still another way in which the prose can be pernicious: it can interfere with our ability to exploit the undisclosed potential of a tool or theory which we are constructing. For example, the overall direction of the Fifth Generation project is very much based on the goal of adapting the machines to meet general skills; but there is a genuine practical question here whether this is the wisest way to proceed at this stage. That is not to question the wisdom of the Fifth Generation project, but rather, to clarify the fact that, in adopting their particular research goals, the AI scientists were forced to make a decision: viz. what is more important, to extend the use of computers so that an ever larger section of society can utilize a tool which only a minority is currently exploiting, or to pursue the purely technical/mechanical potential of computers in a manner which might make them even more inaccessible to the general public than is currently the case. The problem here is essentially that, if you decide to concentrate (as the Fifth Generation project is doing) on developing natural language input systems, you might actually be moving away from the technical capacity of the machine. (i.e. the basic issue here is whether you can best maximize the computer's potential by staying as closely as possible to the actual mechanical level as represented in the machine code, so that machine time and potential is not wasted.) Thus, the Fifth Generation project was forced to make quite a serious decision at the outset, the consequences of which — in either direction — could be enormous. Yet at the general level of prose (where the Mechanist Thesis flourishes) the full dimensions of this decision are completely obscured. (This in turn leads to a further question: given that an analogy may in some sense be necessary to the initial stages of scientific research, did the pioneers in AI choose the most suitable analogy, or was there a less misleading metaphor available than that of 'Artificial Intelligence'? Fortunately, the question is largely academic, as the discipline seems to be fast approaching the point where no analogy will any longer be necessary or useful, cf. 'Concluding Remarks' below.)

The criticisms of a scientific theory can take any number of different forms; e.g. empirical falsification, lack of explanatory power, the demonstration of an inconsistency, or of a straight-forward error. But a considerable part of scientific criticism is presented in prose: by necessity, rather than choice. A large part of scientific research is intended not so much to *solve* an empirical problem as to further our understanding of some phenomenon. The scientist thus sees his work as part of an ongoing effort to penetrate some enigma; a successful explanation/theory is simply one which advances matters. The problem is that in such frontier areas as the development of AI the scientist is essentially groping in the dark. In which case the difficulty arises: how do you (con-structively) criticize the parts of a theory which clearly fail to accom-plish (or identify) the ultimate goals of this research? Without the final answer from whence to spot the errors in a theory, the scientist often has no choice but to resort to prose in order to articulate what he thinks has gone wrong; particularly if the point of such a critical exercise is to glean some idea of where to proceed from there. It should be evident, therefore, that a prose criticism which is based on a conceptual confusion will point the discussion in the wrong (or no) direction. My purpose in this chapter, therefore, is to contribute — from a purely philosophical point of view — to the process of setting these criticisms on the right track.

## High-level Language

One of the first questions which we must address is: what exactly is meant by describing a high-level language as a *language*?[8] Significantly, this is a question which has received little attention, despite the obviously crucial role which the concept of a 'high-level language' plays in the Mechanist Thesis. The dangers in describing high-level languages as languages *simpliciter* are evident: the natural consequence is to treat programs as a series of *instructions* which we *communicate* to the machine. Hence, at this level of the argument all of the prose unreflectingly describes the various operations in terms of the communication network of concepts. AI scientists speak of the 'hierarchy of languages' involved in computer programming, ranging from the 'machine language' to the high-level language with the reductions from a higher to a lower-level language performed by 'symbolic assemblers', 'compilers' (which convert the high-level language program into machine code and then execute the program), or the line-by-line type of compilers which significantly are known as 'interpreters'. The compilers convert the 'instructions' recorded in the high-level language into a binary form, which in turn can be encoded by electrical impulses. But the *machine* is not executing the instructions encoded in these electrical impulses; rather, it is still *we* who are executing the instructions, albeit with the aid of this sophisticated electro-mechanical tool (cf. 'Computer Programs' below). What the machine is doing can only be intelligibly described in terms of its electro-mechanical operations (viz. in terms of the computer's 'clock' which generates at a constant rate the electrical pulses which are used to transport the 'bits' around the computer).

A somewhat simpler case might help to clarify this point. Consider, for example, pebbles or beads which are arranged in columns of ten and then used to calculate sums. It is not the abacus which calculates the various sums; rather, it is the agent who calculates with the aid of the abacus. Nor does it make sense to say that the abacus 'executes' or 'follows' the rules of arithmetic. Again, it is the agent who performs these feats; the proper description of the manipulation of the beads — at the mechanical level — is solely in those terms: viz. the manipulation of beads. (NB Why not say that the abacus is an 'intelligent' machine, since it can simulate remarkably sophisticated arithmetical operations — as in e.g. the case of the saroban — and there is no empirical obstacle to our designing abaci which could store arithmetical information? Babbage's Differential Engine, for example, might be one such suitable example.)

The first point to establish, therefore, is that a high-level language is not a language for communicating with the machine. But having disposed of this preliminary problem, we have still to clarify in what sense a high-level language is a language. One way to approach this question is to consider the evolution of high-level languages. It was clear from the start that the viability of computer science rested on the development of less cumbersome programming 'languages' than the original machine codes. Once the first crude high-level language had been developed (FORTRAN), AI scientists quickly learnt how to create high-level languages which were better-suited to a given problem-domain.[9] (For example, if you are writing a program to solve algebraic problems it is extremely useful if you can employ a high-level language which adapts familiar algebraic terms, such as ALGOL). So for obvious reasons it would be considerably easier to write a word-processing program in a high-level language which employed a large number of familiar text-editing terms. But here there arises both a potential source of considerable confusion, and of the remarkable discoveries that are continually made in computer programming (and frequently misleadingly classed as examples of the computer's putative ability to learn).

Suppose that you are writing a mathematical program in ALGOL: the temptation is overwhelming to regard the various terms of the high-level language selected as meaning the same as their mathematical 'equivalents'. But the meaning of a mathematical term is determined by the rules governing its use in a given mathematical system. (For example, although there are considerable parallels between '2' and '+2', the two numerals do not mean the same. The very presence of the positive affix in the latter indicates that it is intelligible to subtract such a number from another smaller than itself, whereas any attempt to perform a similar operation with the former number is unintelligible.) Thus, the symbol '2' could only mean the same in this high-level language as it does in ordinary arithmetic if all of the same rules apply. For example, to take Wittgenstein's case of a primitive community which employs a counting system of '1,2,3,4,5,many', we can see that there are important parallels between their use of '1,2,3,4,5' and ours (e.g. they say '1 | 1 + 2 = 2 + 2'); yet the symbols in each case do not *mean the same* (e.g. in their system '4 + 3 − 5 + 3').

This last example suggests still another important demarcation. In the case of arithmetic, we are comparing the meaning of terms which operate in autonomous calculi; but does the same point apply in the comparison of high-level languages to natural languages? To suppose that such is the case is to assume, either that high-level languages are *not* calculi, or that natural languages are. It is clearly the latter assumption which is primarily operative in AI (although that does not exclude the former as well). This betrays the profound influence which modern linguistic theory has had on the development of AI. It would be far too time consuming an issue to examine here all of the major confusions embodied in the theory that natural languages are calculi.[10] What is important for our purposes is to recognize that AI scientists are perfectly right to regard their high-level languages as formal systems: the design of a high-level language involves the construction of a complex calculus in which the terms of the language are given a precise definition, and the various rules of inference and syntax are explicitly laid out. Moreover, high-level languages are *complete*: if a question is intelligible in a high-level language, there must exist a method of answering it (i.e. we cannot understand an expression in a high-level language unless it is well formed; but if it is well formed — i.e. if it is intelligible — then there exists a method for answering it). But then, this opens up a problem of a different order. For just as you must not confuse the meaning of parallel terms drawn from autonomous mathematical calculi, it is even more problematic to confuse the terms from formal calculi which have been designed to simulate some ordinary language game with the terms employed in that language game. Thus, we must be particularly wary about the idea of 'translating' from a natural language into a high-level language. For you can only translate (in the ordinary sense) between two natural languages; i.e. it is only in such contexts that it makes sense to say that two terms 'mean the same'. In the case of high-level language/natural language parallels — as the study of formal languages over the past few decades has made only too clear — we have, not a translation, but rather, a *formal analogue* for a natural language expression. Hence, the questions asked in a formal language can at best be a formal analogue of a question asked in a natural language.

Still another complication closely related to this is that many computer programmers introduce operations into their programs which yield expressions that are strictly meaningless within the high-level language, yet meaningful in a natural language (as in, e.g. word processing programs, where the instructions may read: 'If *1X write "Mr"/If *1Y write "Mrs"') but in the high-level language itself the expressions 'Mr' and 'Mrs' are simply meaningless marks. The net result is to further the illusion that the operator is communicating with the program (or vice versa!).

It is thus essential that we clarify the nature of high-level languages as *calculi* before we can consider the question of their relationship to languages. But it is no less important that we consider the bearing which this point has on the question whether it makes sense to describe the expressions of a program as *meaningful*. But then, this obviously bears importantly on one of the more familiar arguments against the intelligibility of the Mechanist Thesis, which is based on the idea that 'the rules which the computer performs are purely syntactical, not semantic.'[11] Not surprisingly, the argument has failed to win many converts amongst the advocates of the Mechanist Thesis. Without entering into the matter of what exactly this 'syntactic/semantic' distinction amounts to, it is clear that, although this argument is based on the important principle that it is unintelligible to describe the electro-mechanical operations of a computer in the same normative/intentional terms which underpin the notion of *understanding*, the argument breaks down because of the syntactic/semantic gloss which is introduced; for by yoking the former important point to the theme that the computer can only follow syntactic, not semantic rules, the argument offends in two different directions.

To begin with, a computer can no more follow 'syntactic' than it can follow 'semantic' rules. After all, the AI scientist may quite rightly question why, if the computer can be developed to follow 'syntactic' rules, it cannot some day become clever enough to follow 'semantic' rules. (This is very much the standard response which advocates of the Mechanist Thesis have adopted towards Searle's argument. Thus, for example, they point to the use of sophisticated 'semantic networks' in computational linguistics.) But the problem here lies solely in the muddled attempt to ascribe normative concepts to computers, and not with any such 'syntax/semantics' distinction.[12] The second problem with this argument is that it simply ignores the basic AI claim that the Mechanist Thesis is based on the nature of computer *programs*, and one would hardly want to claim that programs consist of well-formed but meaningless strings of symbols without examining the use which computer scientists and users make of programs. Nor does one want to be forced into the paradoxical position of claiming that the program is *meaningful* for the user but *meaningless* for the computer without clarifying the role of the program in the execution of the programmer's tasks. In the following section on computer programs we shall consider precisely what it means to describe programs as a 'set of instructions'. For the moment our task must be to clarify in what sense the instructions written in a high-level language are *meaningful*, and thus, how high-level languages relate to natural languages.

An important key to this issue lies in the familiar theme that not even the programmer can predict with any certainty how his program will 'answer' a question. But then, as we have already seen, high-level languages are complete; so how, then, could this possibly be the case? The first step to disentangling this problem is to recognize that the application of a term in a high-level language is strictly determined by the rules which have been laid down for its use. For a high-level language is a calculus, in which the rules governing the use of the various terms are strictly defined. Hence, the programmer is involved in the application of these formal rules in the construction of a system designed to perform some identifiable task. His failure to predict how the program will 'behave' in certain situations is a direct consequence, not only of the complexity of programming, but also of the fact that, by failing to understand the nature of a high-level language as a calculus, he can easily slip into regarding one of its terms as synonymous with some natural language homonym.

There are two different points to notice here. The first is that the fact that a high-level language is a calculus does not entail that the expressions constructed in this system are 'meaningless marks' (any more than in the case of mathematical calculi). The second point is a direct consequence of this: in order to ascertain the meaning of a high-level language expression, you must look at the rules of the high-level language and disregard the meaning which that sign might have in a natural language (particularly if there are important parallels between the rules of these two signs). But it is by no means straightforward to clarify the meaning of the formal term: especially when there is such a temptation to conflate it with its homophonic relative. Of course, the easiest way to bypass such problems is simply to use some artificial notation in the construction of a high-level language, so as to minimize the chance of slipping unconsciously into such grammatical confusions. But then, that would only serve to defeat the basic purpose of high-level languages as discussed above. Hence, the programmer tends to proceed by trial and error. Indeed, one of the great benefits of computer programming is that we are presented with an immediate and concrete manifestation of the inferential relations which have been established in a calculus, which may otherwise be far from obvious (not the least of our difficulties being this tendency to read the meaning of a natural language expression into a formal term). The result of misusing these rules are program 'bugs', which are not necessarily — despite the common apprehension — errors in the program, but might also arise from errors in our understanding of the high-level language. Hence the first step to eliminating a 'bug' is invariably to scrutinize the rules of the high level language.

Having said that there is a widespread tendency to confuse the terms of a high-level language with natural language 'equivalents', it must immediately be added that this is far from being an incidental matter. For the whole essence of computer programming — at least, in terms of the directions in which AI research is currently moving — rests on the deliberate attempt to construct calculi which will simulate language games. Hence the dangers of grammatical confusion are doubly present, for where it is inevitable that 'formal translations' of natural language expressions will create 'bugs' if we try to use the former in the same manner as the latter, so too it must be remarked that it is equally possible to arrive at 'bugs' solely at the level of a natural language. Y.A. Wilks argues that the fact that water freezes to form ice is not part of the meaning of 'water', in so far as people in southern climates mean the same substance as we do by 'water'.[13] But this confusion (which is born here from a referential theory of meaning) is simply an example of supposing that Wittgenstein's primitive culture means the same as we do by '1'. The real point is that the two cultures in Wilks's argument do not mean exactly the same thing by 'water'; but that there are enough overlaps to allow communication. However, when the conversation turns to some aspect of the meaning of a term not covered in the other speaker's lexicon, the result is in effect a 'bug'. (We can communicate without difficulty with the primitive builders provided our demands keep within the limit of five units. But if we try to go beyond this the conversation begins to 'idle'.)

The real problem here, however, is that the significance of the distinctions between high-level languages/calculi and natural languages, and thence program simulations/language games, has not been fully grasped. For one thing, it is clear that, bearing in mind the restrictions imposed by this conceptual demarcation, certain linguistic activities will be more amenable to 'modelling' than others (e.g. computer programs are well suited to employing the methods of projective geometry in order to identify the size or shape of objects; but that in no way serves as a model of what *we* are doing — i.e. at the neurophysiological level — when we see that something is a cube). It is important to enter a note of caution here, however, for the task of the philosopher is not to clarify what every term means in the context of its calculus; that is the responsibility of the relevant AI scientist or mathematician. The philosopher's sole concern is with the resolution of philosophical problems. However, the philosopher's clarifications should serve an important role in the scientist's/mathematician's efforts to elucidate the meaning of a given term. (E.g. it is only in light of the philosopher's clarification of such concepts as *number, set,* and *infinity* that the mathematician is in any position to clarify the meaning of aleph$_0$ and its relation to the natural numbers.) There is, moreover, a further point involved, for the scientist's/ mathematician's efforts to elucidate the meaning of a given term might well proceed from and emulate the methods employed by philosophers: viz. by clarifying the rules of logical grammar governing the use of the terms in his theory. Hence, the point of what might be called the philosophical dimension of the scientist's/ mathematician's work, as evidenced in the ongoing interpretation of his theories.[14]

**Computer Programs**

Without minimizing the importance of removing the cluster of conceptual confusions which inspire the Mechanist Thesis, there is a more fundamental problem which needs to be addressed, both in order to cut off one of the main roots of the Mechanist Thesis, and also as a direct means of attacking one of the primary sources of the AI scientist's confusions as they occur in his prose. This deeper issue is quite simply: What is a computer program? It is an extraordinary fact that this question has received so little critical attention (particularly when you bear in mind the emphasis in mechanist writings that it is not the computer *per se* which thinks, but more properly, the computer program, or perhaps, the entire system comprising computer plus program). The standard definition presented in introductory texts is invariably along the lines: 'A program is an ordered list of instructions directing a computer to perform a desired sequence of operations.'[15] What is perhaps the key concept, which is not fully spelt out by this definition, is that this 'set of instructions' must constitute an effective procedure (such that the instructions can be 'carried out by a machine processor built in such a way as to accept these rules as determining its operations'.[16] The metaphors most frequently cited to elucidate the nature of programs *qua* ordered set of instructions are musical scores, knitting patterns and cookbook recipes. Or perhaps, one might say that this cluster of metaphors is commonly cited, since each analogy serves to highlight a different aspect of a computer program (i.e. a recipe suggests a list of instructions; a knitting pattern adds onto this the idea of reiterated coded operations; and a musical score adds still further the idea of the notes symbolising the sounds which the musician is thus instructed to produce).

As it stands, this conception of computer programs is deeply troubling. The basic problem which it raises is: what exactly does it mean to speak of issuing instructions to a machine? But before attempting to answer this we should first bear in mind that it is unintelligible to speak of a machine following a rule. I have already discussed this topic in some detail in 'The Nature of Philosophy', and have no wish to reproduce those arguments here. I will, however, try to summarize the main points of that argument which relate to the present discussion, all of which arise from a basic misconception about the nature of algorithms.

The main point that must be considered is what it means to say that an algorithm is the precise formulation of a (potentially vague) rule, such that, by being broken down into a number of completely meaningless sub-rules each of which can be performed mechanically, algorithms are machine-computable. Each of the main three themes contained in this definition are misguided. First, it makes no sense to describe a machine as 'following a rule', however precise the rule-formulation in question might be, simply because of the fundamental demarcation which exists in our logical grammar separating the concepts of a *normative action* from a *mechanical operation*. In other words, the nature of this division is entirely conceptual, not empirical: a distinction which is highlighted rather than undermined by the Turing Test. Secondly, it makes no sense to speak of a 'meaningless sub-rule', simply because it is unintelligible to speak of following a rule — no matter how simple or complex — without *understanding* that rule. To follow a rule is *ipso facto* a normative practice, and in those cases where someone has performed a rule so often that he begins to execute the task mechanically, he is no longer following the rule. For to say that he is behaving mechanically is to say just that, due to the constant repetition or simplicity of the task, he is no longer conscious of his actions. (To behave like an automaton is to cease functioning as a rule-following agent, capable of explaining, justifying, correcting etc. one's actions.) Thirdly, an algorithm is not a *precise formulation* of a rule; rather, it is a *different* rule from the original which it is intended to supplant. To elucidate this last point, consider the case of the algorithm which Andrew Colin presents in *Fundamentals of Computer Science* which is purportedly designed to perform multiplication 'mechanically' by storing the results of repeated simple operations of addition.[17] But then, someone who was following the instructions outlined in Colin's algorithm would not be multiplying: rather, he would be adding. That is, the algorithm is not a 'more precise' formulation of multiplication; it is completely different from multiplication, for it uses addition to bypass the need for multiplication. To be sure, the result of this algorithm corresponds to the results yielded by multiplication, but the two systems of rules are none the less different. (What is really involved here is simply the fact that one set of rules is far more efficient than another in one context, yet in different circumstances the exact opposite might be the case.)

Given that it is unintelligible to speak of a machine following rules, the question which now arises is: Is it any more intelligible to speak of issuing instructions to a machine? Such a suggestion gives rise to the distinctly uncomfortable feeling that the Mechanist Thesis is only able to get started in the first place by assuming from the outset what is, in fact, the basic theme which the arguments for the Mechanist Thesis are intended to establish. However, although pursuing this line of argument may dispose of the Mechanist Thesis, it does not dispose of the central problem which concerns us here. For the crucial questions which remain are: first, what aspect of computer programs gave rise to this confusion, and second, how *should* we describe computer programs?

The initial step to resolving these questions is to clarify where computer programs stand in the chain of operations involved in computer applications. The brief answer to this is: roughly midway between the machine code and the program user's proposed applications of the system. The program is separated from the former by the compiler and from the latter by the program specifications (which instruct the user on how to employ the software system). The first problem to note with all such definitions of 'computer program' as the above is that they tend to collapse these operations together.

The basic question which this division raises is: should the program be seen as a *bi-directional* set of instructions, i.e. a set of directions moving downwards to the level of the machine code operator, and upwards to the program user? Some such assumption is clearly present in the Mechanist Thesis, but it is based on a subtle conceptual confusion, which might well have arisen because of the actual evolution of computer programming. For there is some truth to the idea that a computer program was originally a set of instructions moving downwards to the machine operator, telling him which binary signals to input into the machine. Thus, when the role of the machine operator was displaced by the compiler/ interpreter, it seemed only natural to conclude that the program was now issuing its set of instructions directly to the computer. But such an assumption is completely misguided; what should have been concluded was that, with the demise of the machine operator there correspondingly disappeared the program's function as a downwards set of instructions. For now what had happened was that, as far as the downwards process was concerned, the program had become part of the complex cryptanalytic process whereby the programmer's instructions were converted into electronic signals. As far as its position in the downwards chain is concerned, therefore, the program no longer serves as a 'set of instructions', but rather, as a set of ciphers which, by means of cryptanalytic techniques, trigger the various electronic signals intended by the programmer.

The question remains, however, of who exactly is the recipient of the upwards instructions contained in the program. And the answer to this is, of course, the program user. For the program specifications are the programmer's instructions on which moves in the calculus must be followed if such-and-such results are to be obtained. Hence by constantly upgrading the original machine operator's task by developing intermediary 'languages' designed to carry the program ever closer to the level of natural language, and by bridging the remaining gap between the high-level language and natural language with program specifications, the programmer introduces a set of rules instructing the program user on which sequences to follow. Thus, the program user is, in effect, performing the original function of the machine operator: he converts the programmer's instructions into a form which, by the various reduction methods involved, triggers off the electronic signals intended by the programmer.

The upshot of all this is that, perhaps as a direct result of the history of computer programming, the term 'computer program' is currently used to convey two quite distinct meanings. On the one hand, it is used to refer to the strictly mechanical aspect of the program's role in the chain of the computer's operations; on the other hand, it is used to refer to the set of instructions which the program user follows. To bring out the nature of this two-fold meaning of 'computer program', we might consider the role of computer programs in the solution of chess problems. The first thing to notice is that each line in the program actually activates an electronic process (like depressing the keys on a keyboard). It is no coincidence that programs are generally written in two columns, with the mechanical code on the left-hand side and the specifications on the right. The specifications can in turn be seen in either of two different contexts: as descriptions or as instructions, depending on the manner in which they are employed. (Cf. the two possible uses of 'knight to bishop three' as spoken by a player to a steward or by a match commentator.) The programmer who is merely describing the nature of the steps he has just executed writes down the specifications according to the rules laid down in the high-level language. (For the 'specifications' you can also substitute the 'flowchart'.) Conversely, an operator who is using a program according to a set of specifications treats the specifications as instructions which tell him, again on the basis of the rules laid down in the high-level language, which characters to register. For an illustration of the manner in which these points operate in practice we might turn to the example of computer chess.

**Computer Chess**

Computer scientists are often criticized for devoting too much time to the investigation of a problem-domain that is, after all, merely a game. AI scientists have thus endeavoured to explain why the refinement of chess programs is of overriding importance to the development of AI. No one who genuinely understands the role of computer chess in the advancement of general problem-solving techniques could seriously deny the force of these arguments. Indeed, the evolution of chess programming can justly be seen as both crystallizing and epitomizing the evolution of AI itself.

Nevertheless, the warnings of the dangers inherent in the devotion of so much attention to a game may not be entirely unfounded. The trouble is that the advancement of chess-programming is intimately bound up with the success of chess programs in actual game situations, and the danger here is that the mere issue of winning versus losing — i.e. of raising the chess program's USCF rating — may increasingly come to dominate AI objectives to the detriment of AI research. A case in point might well be the Greenblatt-Holloway-Missouris CHEOPS device, where all of the attention is focused on improving the hardware with the sole aim of raising the system's USCF performance in order to ascertain just how much play-improvement results from an increase of 2-3 ply in the program's look-ahead depth.[18] Of course, that is not to say that there can be no justification for exploring problem-specific circuitry in addition to software refinements, just as there may well be a strong case for the Japanese decision to devote a large portion of the Fifth Generation budget to the investigation of methods for increasing LIPS dramatically. Moreover, there is as yet no straightforward distinction to be drawn between game-playing success and programming progress. But then, that is all the more reason why AI scientists must be careful that they do not squander resources on comparatively minor advances as far as the power of the theory is concerned.

Neither of these points touches, however, on what is perhaps the central theme in the established AI defence of the importance of computer chess: the claim that games provide an excellent vehicle for 'studying methods of simulating certain behaviour'.[19] This in itself raises an intriguing point in so far as scientific rationale is concerned: not so much whether such simulations are feasible, as why they are desirable. It is even more important to note, however, that the standard interpretation of this theme is framed in orthodox mechanist terms. For example, in their influential paper, 'Chess-playing Programs and the Problems of Complexity', Newell, Shaw and Simon argue that the basic goal underlying this enterprise is to develop 'principles of play similar to those used by human players. Partly, this trend represents . . . a deliberate attempt to simulate human thought processes.'[20] Significantly, this argument relies primarily on Adriann de Groot's seminal work, *Thought and Choice in Chess*, in which the chess master's 'principles of play' are charted in meticulous detail.[21] This has naturally led (strong) AI scientists to argue that the success of their mechanist ambitions could best be realized by developing program simulations of the techniques recorded by de Groot. Ironically, the actual progress of chess programming has so far tended to be in the exact opposite direction: viz. the further programmers have moved away from a brute-force approach, the less successfully their programs have performed. (Largely as a result of the increased number of 'bugs' which occur with mounting program complexity.) Apart from any such contingent factors, however, there is a stronger reason why de Groot's work poses more of an embarrassment to the Mechanist Thesis than is commonly recognized.

De Groot's main thesis is that players' strengths vary primarily in accordance with their ability to associate playing strategies with board configurations. The key, he felt, lies in the player's knowledge-base, which is closely tied to his past experience. The chess master possesses a vast repertoire of what de Groot describes as 'strategic goals and means, standard procedures in certain types of position, [and] combinatorial gimmicks'.[22] Because of his experience, the master literally 'sees' a given position differently than a weaker player (just as an accomplished musician reads a score differently than a tyro). For his knowledge-base enables him to classify a given configuration according to a pre-established category of response. He is thus able to perceive possibilities and dangers contained in a given position which a weaker player can at best arrive at by laborious calculation.

If this was all there were to the matter one might reasonably feel that the programmer need only simulate the master's knowledge-base in order to improve the quality of computer play. In fact, in purely technical terms this is by no means an easy task; with a base of between 10,000 and 100,000 patterns, together with all their permutations, the combinatorial complexity involved is formidable. But even more important is the fact that, after identifying the major principles which the chess master employs, de Groot immediately goes on to emphasize that 'we must take care to distinguish between *knowledge* and *intuitive experience.*'[23] The difference, according to de Groot, amounts to the fact that the former can be verbalized whereas the latter cannot. Of course, the boundary between these two fields is constantly shifting, but the crucial point to bear in mind is that, according to de Groot, the brunt of the chess master's ability to recognize patterns is 'largely intuitive'. In other words, in the majority of cases the master is unable to provide any justification or explanation for the move or strategy he has chosen. There are even countless cases to suggest that, when conflicts between knowledge and intuition arise, the master does well to follow the dictates of intuition.

There is, in fact, a tension suffusing de Groot's own argument on this important issue. He argues repeatedly that both knowledge and intuition are largely acquired through learning. But he virtually passes over this point when he discusses the case of chess prodigies.[24] In a fleeting aside he remarks that it is not yet known whether their extraordinary abilities are due to 'nature or nurture'. Yet such a phenomenon is surely crucial to the thesis that intuitive experience is in direct proportion to learning experience. For it would certainly seem to be the case that the more we move down the age curve the less relevant experience becomes. To be sure, experience tends to increase the prodigy's knowledge-base and his intuitive resources; none the less, the fact remains that there is an enormous gap in de Groot's analysis of chess abilities: a gap which creates a formidable obstacle to AI ambitions to construct sophisticated simulations of chess-playing behaviour. Moreover, on de Groot's own account, it is not at all clear that this is the correct manner to interpret the development of chess programs. De Groot raises in passing an extremely relevant point when he mentions the fact that the importance of intuition to chess may stem largely from the fact that the game has nothing to do with verbalization; that chess is similar, in this respect, to a skill, such as playing tennis, which depends primarily on motor abilities.[25] But then, a chess program is something which operates entirely at the level of verbalization: a distinction which should immediately set us to thinking, not how the gap between computer chess and grand-master play might be closed, but rather, how such a gap should be *described!*

The naïve approach to computer chess is to suppose that unmediated brute force — e.g. in the form of having the computer run through all possible permutations at every step of the game — is all that is required to construct a successful chess program. Shannon demonstrated the absurdity of such an idea in his 1950 paper 'Programming a Computer for Playing Chess' simply by recording that 'a machine operating at the rate of one variation per micro-microsecond would require over $10^{90}$ years to calculate its first move!' But although no one may be guilty of this particular naïvety today, there is a similar problem underlying proposals to improve the quality of the 'brute-force' approach with more powerful main-frames. Apart from the fact that AI scientists appear to have reached the point of diminishing returns in this direction, there is the far more important matter that, by concentrating too much attention on this element they threaten to undermine developments in the far more exciting area of problem-solving techniques.

It was obvious from the start that the viability of chess programming hinged on the introduction of some form of a look-ahead approach together with pruning devices designed to keep the program manageable. To appreciate what is actually going on in current attempts to refine formal chess strategies, we must first consider the basic drawback of the Turing-Good/Shannon approach. The obvious problem with a look-ahead strategy is that the player is, in effect, locked into the formal routine he is following. Thus, a player using an algorithm who has embarked on a 2-10 ply look-ahead strategy designed to capture some minor piece will frequently be forced to watch hopelessly as his system bypasses what are quite clearly far more advantageous opportunities opening up before it.[26] There is, of course, also the converse point that one of the chess master's major advantages against chess programs lies simply in the exploitation of this rigidity. In essence, therefore, the major obstacles now are to devise some means of enabling the program to select the most promising move from the myriad possibilities, to vary the search depth according to the requirements of a given situation, and finally, to abandon and upgrade strategies, given the shifting developments in comparative board strengths.

The next question we must address is, how exactly did the Mechanist Thesis get bound up in this problem? Here, as in so many places, Turing's thought seems to have had a pronounced effect on subsequent attitudes to AI. Not surprisingly, when Turing began to consider the problem of formalizing chess (in the early 1940s) he saw the construction of a definite method for playing chess in terms which were completely analogous to those which he had earlier applied to his 'automatic machines': viz. a set of rules such that they could be followed by a 'slave player' (a euphemism for Turing's conception of a set of 'mechanical rules' such that they could be followed by a 'mindless player'). Turing thus saw his initial attempts together with Jack Good to devise a chess program based on a minimax approach as a first step towards 'mechanizing a fairly sophisticated thought process'. Thus, the driving force behind Turing's involvement with chess programming was his belief in the Mechanist Thesis; his primary interest in the problem lay in what he perceived as the construction of a 'model of thought'.[27]

Indeed, it is primarily this theme which accounts for the obvious importance of computer chess to those AI scientists whose essential motivation is to establish the Mechanist Thesis. One of the first problems which the advocate of the Mechanist Thesis must confront is the simple fact that the concept of *thought* is so amorphous, covering an array of mental activities which range from local deduction to the creation of poetry. But chess seems to offer the advocate of the Mechanist Thesis an ideal problem-domain: a species of thought concerned with the application of a set of rules which can be formalized, yielding a system which is both complete and consistent. Moreover, the formal system in question contains a considerable degree of computational complexity: so much so that a good deal of work has already been done on systematizing game strategies and quantifying chess abilities, thus providing a host of documented theory and a ready-made scale to measure the power and improvements realized in the chain of program evolution. Finally, from a programming point of view chess offers what is perhaps the ultimate benefit: the game is composed of a myriad of subsystems, allowing the scientist to focus on localized problems as well as considering the thorny issue of long-range strategies. What all this means is, first, that it was relatively clear how to proceed at the beginning in the construction of chess programs, and second that this in turn created a perspicuous problem for AI: for the type of chess programs which seemed to offer the obvious route to programming 'success' contrasted markedly with ordinary chess techniques, and even more significantly, quickly proved to be inferior to (expert) chess-playing abilities.

The importance of this last point cannot be emphasized too highly. Perhaps the most interesting aspect of the Turing-Good/Shannon 'brute-force' approach (the 'look-ahead/evaluate/minimax' paradigm which is now capable of beating the vast majority of chess players) is that it should have stopped just short of beating the minority of players at the expert level and higher, and that these brute-force techniques appear to have very nearly reached their performance limits. But far from being a 'failure', this has been an enormous stroke of good fortune for AI. Had the Turing-Good/Shannon approach proved to be invincible, it would no doubt have strengthened the Mechanist Thesis immeasurably (perhaps in the form of asserting that not only do machines think, but that in the realm of chess, they can do so far more effectively than the best of their human competitors, *pace* the claim that they can 'calculate' far more efficiently than humans). It would also have lost the tremendous impetus which has consequently been enjoyed in the perception of the present limitations and thence the development of heuristics and Expert Systems. From a philosophical point of view, however, perhaps the most interesting consequence of these developments has been the effect which it has had on the Mechanist Thesis.

One might naturally have expected that the obvious shortcomings of the Turing-Good/Shannon approach would have proved a serious embarrassment to the Mechanist Thesis; but such has not yet proved to be the case. To be sure, the advocates of the Mechanist Thesis find themselves in a curious position, but then, that has been the case from the start. Indeed, the mere fact that CHESS 4.6 can already play consistently at the USCF 2000 level should surely have satisfied the performance demands of a crude conception of the Turing Test. (After all, it is hardly a necessary condition of *playing chess* that one must be able to play at this level.) Yet AI scientists themselves are the first to acknowledge that the brute-force approach fails to provide a satisfactory vehicle for the Mechanist Thesis. But far from pursuing the basis for the anomaly which arises here, they conclude instead that the problem remains entirely empirical. Indeed, if anything, this obstacle has only served to further strengthen the grip of the Mechanist Thesis. For AI scientists have now set themselves two further goals: to improve current ratings, and to do so by developing alternative approaches which are based on the 'actual techniques' which chess masters seem to employ. Their feeling now is that even the most strident critic of the chess version of the Mechanist Thesis must be silenced in the face of a twin success in this latest venture.

As a direct result of the mechanist confusions which are embedded in this issue, therefore, the task of improving chess programs continues to be seen in terms of a thoroughly misleading 'man versus machine' conflict. In the beginning this was interpreted as a straightforward confrontation between the machine's brute force and the human's 'concept-driven' approaches. When the limits of the former were realized the issue was still perceived in the same mechanist terms: viz. how to overcome the human adversary's advantage by mechanizing his techniques. Before we consider this latter issue, we would do well to reconsider first what was actually involved in the initial 'brute-force' versus 'concept-driven' approaches. For this very way of stating the matter is misleading, in as much as it obscures the true nature of the conflict here: viz. that between formal and unverbalized methods of playing chess. The crucial point is to avoid phrasing the problem in such a way that we unknowingly build in as a premiss the very mechanist conclusion which the argument is purportedly designed to establish. The basic question to consider is whether *formalizing* chess (i.e. developing a 'direct method' for playing chess) amounts to the same thing as *mechanizing* chess playing. Simply to assume the cogency of such an assumption is to build the Mechanist Thesis into the argument as a premiss. What exactly does it mean, then, to speak of 'mechanizing' chess playing in the Turing-Good/ Shannon manner?

What lends so much plausibility to the chess version of the Mechanist Thesis is simply the fact that it seems to make sense to say that the computer system is playing chess unaided by human intervention, which should surely mean that chess playing can be mechanized. But such an argument is seriously misguided. It is here where the problem can be traced directly back to Turing's exposition of his 'automatic machines'. There is a somewhat puzzling reference to Turing's argument in Manuscript 229 in which Wittgenstein says: 'Turing's "machines". These machines are in fact human beings who calculate.' (1763) Once again Wittgenstein manages in his usual oblique way to put his finger on the heart of the problem: the assumption that Turing Machines (and chess 'slave' players) are *machines* rests on the premiss that formalizing chess results in the reduction of chess playing to the execution of a complex task composed of a set of 'meaningless' sub-rules, each of which can be performed mechanically (*supra*). And such an assumption is precisely what is unwarranted; for on the one hand, the execution of a rule, no matter how simple that might be, does not in the least entail that the rule is meaningless, while conversely, it is unintelligible to describe the operations of a mechanical device with normative or intentional concepts. (Cf. the mechanism of a clock with even the most primitive of games.) The basic conceptual — as opposed to empirical — conflict involved here, therefore, is simply that between the logical grammar of mechanical operations versus that of normative activities.

Unfortunately, we are still locked in the stage where advocates of the Mechanist Thesis will dismiss such an objection as dogmatic, and insist that the system is no less intent on 'winning' the game than its human opponent. The strict answer to this is that they confuse a normative concept — the programmer's goal — with an electrical operation. Short of reiterating all of the arguments which I have covered elsewhere to expose the numerous transgressions of logical grammar involved in this argument, I now feel that perhaps the only satisfactory way to dispose of this unnecessarily futile debate is simply to consider exactly what is going on here; and the key to this issue clearly lies in the role of the programmer's ability to store information — whether in the hardware or in the software — which is subsequently executed by the system. To adapt a comment of Lady Lovelace's, it is the programmer who designs the pattern and the machine which weaves the design. That is, it is the *programmer* — not the machine or the system — who is playing chess against the master; and he is compensating for his comparative lack of chess expertise (e.g. for his inferior number of remembered chess patterns) by relying on the mechanical powers provided by the computer's processing capacity and the computational power of his formal theory.

Of course, this point is likely to meet considerable resistance from supporters of the Mechanist Thesis, most likely on the grounds that such an argument overlooks the ability of an Expert System to make 'intelligible decisions' in a specialized domain, and that it ignores the role of 'learning' programs in the evolution of computer chess (e.g. by storing all the board positions of a given game together with their computational scores, thereby providing an important resource for future reference). I shall deal with the general themes involved in this argument in the following two sections; for the moment I would simply point out that the same arguments apply to these latter objections as to the above argument: viz. it makes no sense to speak of the system as 'making decisions', and the program no more takes on a life of its own than any other mechanical device which has been designed to improve its performance in subsequent operations. For it is the programmer who is setting the course of these subsequent 'learning' developments. To be sure, this is an argument which has long been familiar to proponents of the Mechanist Thesis. Turing sought to deflate it on the grounds that the 'intelligent' ('learning') machine would be one that was capable of performing tasks which the programmer had never envisaged.[28] The problem with this objection, however, is that it imposes a false (quasi-deistic) interpretation on the theme that it is the programmer who sets the course of the program's development. The point is not that the program may perform tasks which may far outstrip the programmer's 'explicit' intentions, but rather, that the programmer may be far from aware of the consequences of the course which he has programmed (cf, 'Prose' above).

To return to the heart of the issue, therefore, what is really going on in the formalization of chess-playing is the development of a new technique. Thus, the battle we are witnessing is between chess masters versus computer scientists: between the highly intuitive skill of the chess master, and the massed forces of sophisticated algorithms and heuristics backed up by advanced computer hardware. What is really going on here is thus that the two opponents (one *in absentia*, as it were) are playing the same game, but using vastly different techniques. (Cf. the gambler who relies on 'lady luck' or his 'feel' of the game versus the one who possesses 'a system'.) At the 'brute-force' stage of chess programming this difference is relatively perspicuous; where the issue has tended to become clouded is in the development of data structures as a direct result of the 'failure' of the look-ahead approach to surpass the USCF 2,200 level.

It was clear from the start that the chess prodigy employs a host of techniques which are *toto caelo* different from the brute-force 'look-ahead' approach. Chief amongst these, as we have seen, are his remarkable abilities to conceptualize problems, to recognize patterns, and to intuit consequences. (It is not without good reason that what is one of the chess master's most important talents — his ability to perceive and exploit the weaknesses of his opponents — so often goes without mention in mechanist discussions.) However, where it might have been thought that this distinction would have forced home the *conceptual* as opposed to the empirical gulf between the two techniques, quite the reverse has been the case. For the prevailing feeling today is, that by the twinned forces of advanced heuristics and the development of Expert Systems, the gulf between these two methods of play — which, of course, are perceived as the gulf between mechanized and informal play — will be increasingly narrowed, and it is to be hoped, obliterated.

It seems inevitable that the levels of performance between these two methods will eventually diminish. But to seek to narrow the categorical distinction between these two methods is a logical, not an empirical impossibility. For the gulf here is simply that between formal and ordinary chess playing; current attempts to devise a plan on the basis of a given configuration and then decide on the move best suited to advancing that plan will only result in the refinement of the formal method. There are two prongs to the argument that future advances in chess programming will ultimately close the gap between human and 'mechanical' chess players; the first falls victim to the homunculus fallacy,[29] while the second commits a variant of the mechanist confusion we have been considering throughout.

The first argument lies in the 'codification' of the techniques which chess masters employ; i.e. the development of Expert chess-playing Systems. But this argument is based on the fallacy that, if you can develop complex sets of rules which can be mapped onto the master's activities, then the master must actually have been following those rules; either tacitly, or else, that his 'brain' was following those rules. The latter is clearly an example of the homunculus fallacy, while the former lands us squarely in the host of paradoxes connected with the nebulous concept of 'tacit knowledge' (which inevitably leads into the homunculus fallacy that such tacit knowledge is contained in the brain). But while it may not make sense to say that chess masters tacitly follow — or that their brains follow — complex sets of rules, there is still the counter-argument that you can at any rate construct complex sets of rules which *simulate* the master's abilities. Apart from the practical difficulties involved with the simulation argument mentioned at the outset of this section, the basic conceptual issue remains that, even if such simulations did prove feasible, they would in no way enhance the Mechanist Thesis. For it is one thing to speak of the simulation of the chess master's ability to recognize chess patterns, but quite another to speak of the chess program itself 'recognizing' patterns. (A flight simulator does not itself fly!)

The greatest mistake we could make here, however, would be to conclude that this argument in any way threatens the prestige of AI scientists' achievements in the realm of computer chess. If anything, the situation is quite the reverse; it is the incoherent claims of the Mechanist Thesis which distort the true significance of what has so far been accomplished by provoking a controversy which only serves to deflect attention from the great advances which have so far been realized. For while adversaries dispute whether machines have yet reached a 'primitive level of thought' the enormous significance of what has so far been accomplished goes unmentioned. And as far as the familiar AI objection that resistance is in direct proportion to self-interest, the point is that the damage has already been done. To be sure, the expert in any given field might possess certain skills which it would be particularly difficult to replace with formal methods. (The problem has already become fully apparent in the field of computer programs in psychiatry; indeed, just as the psychiatrist may depend to a considerable extent on non-verbal clues to emotional stress, so too the chess master might exploit non-verbal signs, either as signs of weakness, or — as in the case of Fisher's tactics — to create alternative forms of strategic advantage.) Nevertheless, we have already seen enough to convince us of the extraordinary potential contained in formalized computer-assisted methods. It may be discomfiting, to say the least, to observe the continuing march of mathematics/-science, as they continue to batter at what have long been regarded as the bastions of human expertise. Nowhere is this more clear than in the development of Learning Systems.

## Learning Systems

The evolution of the concept of 'machine learning' serves as an important warning of the ease with which prose confusions can become entrenched in scientific discourse. At first the AI intention seems merely to have been to develop systems which would *simulate* human learning (under the general impression that this would be an effective means of improving algorithmic efficiency); but in light of the Turing Test this was soon equated with the conclusion that such a system would itself be learning. Indeed, Turing himself articulated such an argument in his address to the London Mathematical Society (on 20 February 1947). Turing insisted that, given the possibility of programming a machine with self-modifying rules such that after a period of time its rules would have 'altered out of recognition', we would have no choice but to describe its operations as examples of learning *simpliciter*:

> In such a case one would have to admit that the progress of the machine had not been foreseen when its original instructions were put in. It would be like a pupil who had learnt much from his master, but had added much more by his own work. When this happens I feel that one is obliged to regard the machine as showing intelligence.[30]

Following Turing's lead all talk of *merely* simulating learning quickly disappeared; there is now no hesitation whatsoever — even by those with no direct interest in the Mechanist Thesis — to speak of 'learning programs'.

There are several different elements involved in the development of learning systems *vis à vis* human learning which advocates of the Mechanist Thesis believe license the ascription of the notion of 'machine learning'. The most important of these are the development of programs which provide:

    (i)   the introduction of new information (e.g. the discovery of new facts or theories)
    (ii)  the reorganization of previous information
    (iii) the acquisition of new methods for processing information
    (iv) an ability to deal with an increased range of problems
    (v)  greater accuracy in analyses or predictions
    (vi) the development of induction algorithms

The basic idea behind the 'machine learning' argument is that the above items all belong to the wider category of learning *per se*. That is, these are simply computer examples within the wider family of learning methods. The fundamental properties of *learning* are identified as the acquisition of new knowledge and skills or the attainment of a greater level of conceptual abstraction. 'Human' learning methods are identified as only a subspecies in the family of possible methods of learning. The driving force behind research into 'machine learning' is thus to investigate the possibility of extending the family of learning methods in the direction of artificial techniques: to discover or develop new mechanical learning methods (which might even conceivably be simulated by human learners at a subsequent date).

The basic foundation of this argument — as articulated, for example, in Herbert A. Simon's putatively sceptical paper, 'Why Should Machines Learn?' — lies in a definition of learning which rests on the crucial point that:

learning is any change in a system that allows it to perform better the second time on repetition of the same task or on another task drawn from the same population . . . *Learning denotes changes in the system that are adaptive in the sense that they enable the system to do the same task or tasks drawn from the same population more efficiently and more effectively the next time.*[31]

Given the prior demands of the Mechanist Thesis it is no surprise that the definition is framed in such a way that it makes sense *ab initio* to speak of 'machine learning'. But if we can ignore the mechanist overtones contained in such a definition, the question we should be asking ourselves is: what is the underlying theme operating in such a conception?

The point that stands out foremost is that the above definition does not discriminate between evolutionary or mechanical changes and so-called 'machine learning'. For the fundamental picture here is one of modification or adjustment; hence, any organism which adapts to its environment or any device which improves on its efficiency would *ipso facto* be said to be learning. Obviously, there is something seriously amiss with a definition which would include somatic or cybernetic change within the class of learning methods. To be sure, the concept of learning is ambiguous, ranging from conditioned responses through the acquisition of motor and cognitive skills to the mastery of abstract theories. But we are *ex hypothesi* only considering learning within the context of concept-acquisition. Admittedly, even here the concept remains ambiguous, ranging from rote learning to abstract theory-construction. But it is clear that the above definition is trying to pull learning in a direction which totally undermines the thrust of the concept *qua* cognitive ability. To see why this is so, we need only consider what is *left out* of the above definition. For there is absolutely no mention made of the concepts of *understanding* or *mastery of a rule*. Of course, in one sense that is entirely as it should be, in so far as the latter concepts cannot be intelligibly applied to mechanical operations. But the inevitable strategy of the mechanist argument is to shift from some version of the above definition of 'machine learning' to the conclusion that, by virtue of its belonging to the larger genus of *learning* it must after all be equally true to say that, *qua* artificial learning system, computers must also be capable of understanding, mastering a rule, etc. As a vicious circle the argument is both compact and, so it would seem, compelling to a great many AI scientists.

The philosophical objections to this version of the Turing Test are precisely the same as those we have examined throughout: the notion of learning — in terms of concept-acquisition (which is the essence of Turing's position) — is underpinned by the notions of understanding, explaining, mastering a rule, correcting etc., and the obstacles to transgressing the grammatical divide separating this cluster of normative concepts from mechanical operations is entirely logico-grammatical, not empirical. So too, the reason why it makes no sense to speak of a computer system as a 'learning program' is that such a notion is unintelligible, not that it is physically impossible. Yet, although it is strictly nonsensical to speak of a 'mechanical learning system', it is none the less clear that the term 'learning program' has taken on an entirely legitimate — technical — meaning which is perfectly obvious to all AI scientists who employ the term. (Cf. the use of Shannon's information-theoretic notion *vis à vis* 'information' as ordinarily understood.) Our task, then, is to elucidate the real nature of the type of systems designated by this term; a challenge which is hindered by the persistent mechanist intention to undermine any such distinction (for reasons which are, perhaps, not quite clear to its advocates). Moreover, the confusions here lie at a deeper level than may at first appear. There is a natural tendency to view program families in anthropomorphic terms at the various levels of program operations. The trouble starts almost as soon as one speaks of programs as 'problem-solvers' which are 'intent on answering certain questions'. Such a conception naturally leads one to describe the interactions between the various sub-routines in equally anthropomorphic terms; e.g. as 'requesting' information from one another, or 'reporting' certain facts, 'asking' for further 'instructions' etc.

If the premisses underlying the mechanist argument were permitted, we would soon find ourselves forced to accept a far more disparate number of processes as learning than even those envisaged by AI scientists. For example, if learning were reduced to the brute acquisition of new facts, we would be forced to conclude that the *Voyager* space craft is a learning system, since it is certainly engaged in the accumulation of new facts about the solar system. Not only is such a suggestion absurd, but even the suggestion that *Voyager* is acquiring new facts is potentially misleading. For it is the scientists who interpret the photographs relayed by *Voyager* who acquire new facts about the solar system. (Imagine the response of a primitive culture who stumbled across these photographs.) Indeed, the programs we are concerned with in this section are very much like *Voyager* in the sense that AI scientists set them on certain courses and then examine the data which they generate. But whether they acquire new facts from these data depends entirely on how they interpret their results. (Children who use chemical model kits as building blocks are not learning anything about chemistry, nor implicitly building molecular models.) There is a quasi-Platonist assumption (particularly evident in critical reactions to Lenat's AM system) that the data themselves contain the facts, regardless of how or even whether they are interpreted. (Hence the conclusion that the system is learning.) But whether we learn new facts from data depends entirely on how we use the data. Of course, the obvious mechanist riposte to this is that the same is no less true for the system: it is because the system uses the data in the same way that we would do (e.g. to make predictions, corrections, refinements etc.) that we should describe the system as 'learning'. Yet such an animist argument merely confuses the goals we have encoded in the rules of the system with putatively mechanical intentions.

Perhaps the best way to illustrate the confusions operating here is with a case study. The standard mechanist argument is that learning systems are classified according to the amount of inference that the system must perform in order to acquire new facts. At the bottom of the scale lies the fully programmed algorithm; at the opposite extreme is the system which 'independently discovers new theories' or 'invents new concepts'. But given that it makes no sense to interpret program operations as inferential operations in the first place, the question which remains is: What is the real criterion according to which such a classification is made? Or to put this another way, what do 'learning systems' actually 'learn'? Disregarding the numerous prose explanations which have been offered, what we discover when we look at the systems themselves are self-modifying programs which adjust the numerical parameters or coefficients in algebraic expressions; programs which develop decision trees to discriminate between formal networks; the induction of formal grammars from sequences of expressions; the development of various sorts of production rules; the implementation of graph-matching techniques to modify semantic networks; the development of hierarchic or taxonomic classifications; and the various procedural encodings involved in robotics. The real distinguishing feature in so far as the 'inferential hierarchy' of learning systems is concerned seems to be the recursive depth contained in the program. It is obviously impractical to investigate all of the various operations alluded to here, so I have chosen to concentrate on P.H. Winston's research into 'Learning Structural Descriptions from Examples', partly because it occupies a relatively high position on the hierarchy of machine-learning classification, and partly because Winston's program is a seemingly straightforward example of a basic learning situation.

It is instructive to approach our case example via the prose confusions which inspired its development in the first place. Winston describes the goals of his research in terms which are thoroughly redolent of an homunculus fallacy. He lists at the outset four 'key' questions:

How do we recognize examples of various concepts?
How do we learn to make such recognitions?
How can machines do these things?
How important is careful teaching?[32]

The tacit premiss which runs throughout his argument is that learning is an innate ability (e.g. to acquire facts, skills, and more abstract concepts), the mechanics of which have as yet only been partially clarified by cognitive psychology. The two-fold objective of machine learning is thus to simulate these methods, and in so doing, disclose the operations performed by the brain in learning situations. Indeed, Winston expresses the hope that his research will contribute to the ultimate development of machines that can learn from human teachers, and vice versa, where each will 'understand its environment' in precisely the same terms.[33] Thus, Winston does not see his own system in terms of a programmer-program relationship; rather, he makes it clear throughout that he regards his system as an example of an orthodox teacher-pupil relationship, on the grounds that *both* types of learning (machine and human) involve programming.[34] For Winston agrees with those 'who believe that the learning of children is better described by theories using the notions of programming and self-programming, rather than by theories advocating the idea of self-organization.[35]

The immediate goal of Winston's research is to create a 'running program that can learn to recognize structures'.[36] Needless to say, to those who seize on Winston's system for its importance to the

Mechanist Thesis this is precisely the theme which is paramount. Thus, Boden characterizes Winston's program as one 'which learns to recognize structures such as tables, arches, pedestals and arcades by being shown examples and counterexamples of them'.[37] The significance of the program derives, therefore, from its ability to 'learn what arches are'; and 'By "learning what arches are"' Boden means 'coming to be able to interpret correctly an infinite number of pictures of individual arches, not just those exactly like the specific examples encountered in the teaching process.'[38]

It is no coincidence that this account occupies a very general level of prose. There is a fine line to be drawn in the amount of detailed information which should be included in an interpretation. After all, the point of the exercise is to articulate the significance and/or mechanics of the theory as concisely as possible; add too much detail and you have simply recapitulated the original scientific presentation in a slightly generalized version. Yet the further one moves from these technical details the greater becomes the opportunity for prose confusions to infiltrate. In Boden's account we have the added problem of dealing with an interpretation which is deliberately written from a dogmatic standpoint. Hence, the argument is consistently couched in the very mechanist terms which Winston's learning system was purportedly devised to establish. And in order to lessen the impression of theory-begging it is precisely at those points where the most information is suppressed that the mechanist characterizations are most forcefully presented. Indeed, a reliable methodological maxim when considering the Mechanist Thesis is: look for the instances of anthropomorphic intrusion and begin your investigation of the absent technical apparatus at that point. Perhaps the main problem which one faces in such a task, however, is that when we abandon this prose level and descend into the depths of Winston's program we find ourselves in a foreboding domain of predicate logic in which even the prose confusions of the Mechanist Thesis begin to look somewhat appealing.

There are several instances in Boden's account where she slips effortlessly into the mechanist idiom, each of which clearly represents a crucial stage in our understanding of the program's operations. The first occurs when she describes how 'On first being shown a picture of an arch, Winston's program builds a structural description of it, in terms of objects.'[39] Almost as an afterthought she concedes that 'This obviously requires prior articulation of the picture into objects and relations, which is done by a series of programs.'[40] But let us be even more precise: what we are really dealing with here is the decomposition of the formal concept 'ARCH' into constituent elements, and the construction of the relations holding between these elements in predicate logic. The first step in the program is thus to develop a 'structural description' of the formal concept by defining the relations that subsist between these sub-components. In the resulting 'semantic network' constants stand for these sub-components, and thus are used to represent properties of objects; quantified variables range over the object-concepts; binary functions represent the relations between these sub-components; and type-ascending constants link the variables and constants of the network to one another — via the binary functions — into a hierarchical generalization. However, since Winston's program is purportedly concerned with the cognitive phase of scene analysis, the structural description is presented in terms of the decomposition of an 'object' — e.g. an arch — into its constituent objects — e.g. the bricks. The rationale behind this usage is clear: since we are dealing with the machine's 'perceptions', it would make no sense to speak of concepts here; i.e. what the machine 'sees' are the structural relations between sub-component objects. When purged of this mechanist premise what remains is simply the construction of formal concepts and networks.[41] The characterization of these networks in terms of the relations between objects is itself a heuristic device which — as in the use of line drawings in geometry — provides a useful method of clarifying the conceptual relations that are under construction.

In mechanist prose this initial construction is construed as an elementary learning encounter:

> On being shown an example, Winston's program builds a structural description of the scene in the form of a semantic network in which the nodes represent component objects and the lines represent their relations . . . On being told that this is an ARCH (the first time this concept has been mentioned) the program stores the description as its model of arches.[42]

There are two separate confusions operating here. The first is simply the familiar mechanist manoeuvre of treating the program as a surrogate agent (one which is 'told' things which it is capable of remembering). The second confusion, which is far less blatant, is that the semantic network represents a structural description of arches. It is interesting to see the role which this familiar confusion — which derives from the calculus conception of meaning — plays in the Mechanist Thesis. If what we were dealing with were a genuine learning situation we would still not be licensed to say that, by mastering the rules of the system the pupil had acquired the concept *arch*. Rather, he would have mastered a formal concept (which bears scant resemblance to our highly functional concept of an arch). Hence the confusion here is to describe the formal concept under construction as an 'arch' (cf. 'Computer Chess' above). We have to avoid two separate confusions here, therefore: the idea that such a formal training even remotely resembles — let alone mirrors — the actual manner in which we acquire the concept of arches, and the further supposition that this formal concept constitutes a model of our ordinary concept.

The chief interest of Winston's program lies in its gradual generalization of the initial structural description. In mechanist prose, this process

> requires decisions — or provision for subsequent decisions — about the importance, or conceptual salience, of the various features observed in the examples being compared. It is these decisions and comparisons that form the heart of Winston's program, and that give it whatever interest it has as a representation of intelligence in general, as opposed to a mere 'arch recognizer'.[43]

That is, by examining a series of pictures the program eliminates the contingent properties of arches, thereby identifying the essential properties of an arch; and it is precisely this 'ability' which constitutes the system's 'learning intelligence' as manifested (and measured) by its success-rate in identifying novel examples of relevant arch-structures. It goes without saying that the power of the program rests on the breadth of the 'relevance' alluded to here; like all calculi, Winston's program can only effectively identify an 'ARCH' if its structure conforms to the rules of the system.

Without succumbing to mechanist fantasies, it is safe to say that the primary significance of Winston's program lies in his develop-ment of conjunctive and discriminative rules which by a combined process of inclusion and exclusion gradually generalize the original semantic network. The fundamental purpose of such a program is thus to develop highly schematic 'structural descriptions' from elementary semantic networks on the basis of so-called 'learning' algorithms. In outline, these algorithms proceed by two stages: first, they compare the initial structural description to a new conceptual network, chiefly in order to generate a 'difference description'. The algorithm then processes this difference description in order to generate a revised structural description. But in mechanist prose this is the process which Boden refers to as the program's 'ability to make descriptions and comparisons'. On the mechanist reading the program 'recognizes' essential properties and 'excludes' contingent properties. (Or as Winston describes it, selects 'typical' and eliminates 'atypical objects' on the basis of shared relational attributes, thereby rendering a homogenous group.[44])

Obviously, such an extraordinary 'ability' requires some sort of explanation, and not surprisingly, this sticks resolutely to mechanist terms:

> 'Salience' for Winston's program relates not at all to its interests, for it has none: rather, it relates to categorizations made by its human teacher for human purposes.
>
> Even Winston's program, however, can economically capitalize on the structures exemplified in past experience. If shown an arcade . . . it can immediately recognize that the scene consists of three arches, since its network-matching module identifies substructures within the new description as corresponding to the schema of ARCH it already has.[45]

In actual program terms what this alludes to is the manner in which the difference description is produced by a graph-matching algorithm. The match, partial match, or mismatch between two cases is recorded in a sub-network. It should be noted that the program is only designed to deal with isolated changes, whether this be of the partial-match or mismatch order. Hence the succession of examples must be closely regulated. As Winston interprets this, 'Such carefully selected near misses can suggest to the machine the important qualities of a concept, can indicate what properties are never found, and permit the teacher to convey particular ideas quite directly.'[46] According to Boden, this reflects the well-known psychological fact that the human learner is unable to cope with too many new details in learning situations!

A generalized skeleton is then produced which contains those constants, variables, and predicates that matched, thereby providing the framework for the rest of the comparison description, to which the sub-networks are then attached. The crucial step in the program then comes down to the selection of 'salience', and as Boden rather hastily acknowledges, this is determined by the 'teacher's characterizations'. In mechanist prose one is given the impression that the program-pupil is provided with a series of heuristic maxims, on the basis of which it learns for itself how to identify salient features. In actual fact, the sub-networks generated are broken down into a series of types (depending on whether there was a match, partial match, or mismatch between the variables, constants, and predicates); the program then reverts to a table of categorizations (Winston's table of C-notes) specifying which generalizing operation to perform on each type of difference description. It is through a series of iterated operations and the storage of previous results that the program generalizes the initial structural description: strictly according to the recursive parameters which the programmer designs at the outset. The power of his 'learning' algorithm, therefore, is very much a function of the model-building responses which are devised together with the series of examples which are introduced into the program.[47]

As far as cybernetic mechanisms go, this type of self-modifying recursive program has several obvious drawbacks. Its chief virtue in computing terms is that, although it demands a considerable amount of machine 'memory', it can be processed fairly quickly. But the efficiency of the algorithm depends almost entirely on the nature of the examples — particularly the negative ones — that are chosen.[48] To be sure, there are far more sophisticated learning systems that we could have considered in this section, perhaps the most interesting of which is Lenat's EURISKO, where the research emphasis has shifted noticeably from developing complex induction algorithms to exploring the potential of the representation language. Yet whatever learning system we are considering, the basic philosophical confusions involved in describing these systems as 'learning' remain fundamentally the same. The key to avoiding the mechanist confusions which have proliferated in this area of AI is to shift from describing these operations in terms of concept acquisition (or discovery) to concept construction. For what these learning systems really amount to are the implementation of formal methods for constructing complex semantic networks which can be mapped onto physical objects and thence applied in sophisticated mechanical processes. In speaking of a 'learning system', therefore, what we are really dealing with is the transformation of a calculus (i.e. the generation of a network family) via the iteration of an algorithm. Whether such recursive structures can be used to program mechanical operations that will eventually outperform motor or cognitive skills is a perfectly legitimate and important empirical issue; but whether the conceptual gap between these two types of ability — mechanical versus cognitive — can be closed is a grammatical confusion which ultimately serves only to retard the comprehension — and perhaps thereby the development — of Expert Systems: an area which, as we shall see in the next section, is no less burdened by mechanist confusions than the programs touched on in the present section.

**Expert Systems**

To appreciate the full dimensions of AI — both its potential, and the manner in which this should be interpreted — we must look carefully at Expert Systems. For it is here that we can best see the direction in which AI is moving: viz. the formalization of complex reasoning techniques and the creation of 'knowledge systems'. What we are witnessing is the increasing ability of AI scientists to quantify and thence formalize bodies of knowledge which seem anything but arithmetical.[49] It is thus entirely understandable, perhaps, that so many AI scientists regard the developments which are occurring in this field as heralding a new Pythagorean revolution. They must be careful, however, that they do not fall victim to a similar confusion to that which ensnared the Pythagoreans (e.g. by assuming that the essence of ordinary 'knowledge systems' is that they rest on formal calculi). Rather, it is that they are learning how to develop formal systems which perform analogues of the operations which we currently apply in a comparatively unsystematic manner. While the development of Expert Systems clearly marks a watershed in computer science, however, it could also represent one of the greatest potential dangers yet posed by the Mechanist Thesis. For the language in which Expert Systems are to be described could easily become far more resolutely mechanist than anything that has yet been experienced. It is with this latter aspect of the issue that we shall be primarily concerned in this section.

What would seem to be the primary issue which concerns (strong) AI scientists involved in the development of Expert Systems (as opposed to the — highly significant — growing number of programmers who identify themselves as 'practical engineers'[50]) is the standard mechanist question: How can we make computers (or computer programs) reason in exactly the same way that we do? There are two different ways in which this question might be approached, as exemplified, for example, in the Fifth Generation project. The first lies solely on the side of hardware: e.g. the Fifth Generation project's proposed goal of achieving an enormous increase in the number of LIPS which a machine can perform. As far as I am aware, however, no one has actually seized on this side of the project as relevant to the issue (i.e. by suggesting that the chief obstacle to the Mechanist Thesis has so far lain in the brain's physiological advantage over the VLSP in regard to the number of LIPS it can perform). On the contrary, the emphasis seems to be very much towards the opposite conclusion: i.e. that the only way we can make the reasoning of a computer system resemble human reasoning is by compensating for the brain's physiological advantages over electronic circuitry, not simply by increasing the sheer number and speed of the inferential steps which the computer can perform, but more importantly, by developing selection procedures which enable the system to focus on the issues of prime importance and disregard the more tangential information contained in its memory base.

Thus, the heart of the AI scientist's mechanist vision lies at the software level. Interestingly, the primary picture underpinning this argument harks as much back to the early stages of psychology as it looks forward to a mechanized future. For the operative idea here springs straight out of the early empiricist theory of the 'association of ideas'. The predominant feeling seems to be that, where the brain can process information linearly and laterally ('horizontally' and 'synchronously') programmers have only been able to simulate the former operation; hence the ultimate success of the Mechanist Thesis hinges on the simulation of the latter type of reasoning. Both sides of such a picture are misguided, however, not simply in terms of the mechanist confusions we have been considering throughout, but more importantly in misconstruing the nature of the problems facing the 'knowledge engineer'. For what is essentially involved in the development of Expert Systems is the introduction of mathematical and statistical techniques in the formalization of complex skills based on sophisticated knowledge systems. What 'knowledge engineers' are gradually showing us is how areas of expertise which rely to a considerable extent on intuitive knowledge can, to a surprising degree, be verbalized and thence formalized. The development of Expert Systems is thus encouraging experts from various fields to think seriously about the techniques which they employ unreflectingly, and to articulate their methods.

It should be noted at the outset that the term 'knowledge engineer' is often used to refer to a team of experts each of whom specialises in one of the various operations involved in the complex process of constructing an Expert System, usually under the overall direction of a program supervisor (who perhaps unfairly is generally identified as the system's knowledge engineer). Otherwise, the term 'knowledge engineer' refers to the person whose primary responsibility is to codify the knowledge of a 'domain specialist'. The ultimate goal of an Expert System is to develop formalized problem-solving methods which will rival (and hopefully surpass) the skills of an expert. The power of an Expert System obviously rests, therefore, primarily on the size and quality of its knowledge-base. This in turn will largely depend upon the knowledge engineer's ability to verbalize and thence formalize the knowledge possessed by an expert in a selected field. But then — as we saw in the section on chess — this collides with the immediate problem that an expert's skill may be largely intuitive. The first step in the knowledge engineer's task, therefore, is to try to 'disclose' the expert's intuitive knowledge. Unfortunately, such a process offers the perfect foothold for the Mechanist Thesis: by treating the expert's intuitive knowledge as tacit knowledge of formal heuristics, the way is open to arguing that what the knowledge engineer is really doing is mechanically simulating the expert's thought processes. The first question we must address, therefore, is what is the relation between the expert's intuitive reactions and the system's formal heuristics?

Perhaps the best way to answer this question is by acquiring a better feel for the type of interaction which occurs between knowledge engineers and experts who are engaged in the joint effort to codify the expert's knowledge. (There is an obvious impatience with this phase in the development of Expert Systems in current AI writings, largely because of the inordinate amount of time and expense involved in this trial-and-error method. Hence, there is mounting pressure in the direction of developing formal methodologies and automatic induction programs (which employ 'meta-rules' to improve the quality of their heuristics). For the moment, however, it is more important to clarify the nature of knowledge engineering, and this issue is more perspicuous at the level of personal interaction. It bears remarking, however, that these trends are pulling in the opposite direction from the original mechanist conception that the knowledge engineer is engaged in mapping intuitive onto formal heuristics.) The first thing to notice is that the knowledge engineer is not, in fact, simply formalizing the expert's intuitive heuristics. If this were all that was involved, then the knowledge engineer would simply be producing a new textbook. The crucial point to bear in mind when considering the nature of knowledge engineering, therefore, is that the knowledge engineer is first and foremost a computer programmer.

H. Penny Nii has given the following highly illuminating account (as reported by Feigenbaum and McCorduck) of her method:

> Nii says that during interviews she is not necessarily listening to the facts the expert gives her so much as how he manipulates his knowledge. As he talks, she is systematically evaluating mentally the various AI knowledge representation and inference methods — object-oriented techniques, blackboard techniques, production rules, to name a few – seeing how well one or any of them matches the expert's behaviour. She asks questions. 'Would this make sense?' 'Can you do it that way?' These are not only to extract more knowledge from the expert, but also to test the model of his work she's building up in her own mind.[51]

In other words, Nii is not simply trying to verbalize the expert's intuitive knowledge: she is trying to articulate the expert's heuristics in light of pre-established formal systems. Thus, Nii listens closely to the expert while thinking to herself in terms of programming techniques. The expert in turn is called upon not simply to acknowledge whether she has captured what he intended, but more importantly, whether the manner in which she has constructed this will serve the same purpose as that which he had intended. Indeed, it is clear from this that we must be careful not to exaggerate the extent to which the knowledge engineer is verbalizing the expert's intuitive knowledge. Notoriously, experts find it far more difficult to articulate their intuitions than to criticize a working model.

Thus, in the majority of cases what really seems to be happening is that the expert provides a picture of what he intends, and *together* he and the knowledge engineer then try to develop a formal method on the basis of this inchoate information.

To bring out the complex nature of the task which the knowledge engineer is performing here, we might return to the example of the Jacquard looms. Suppose this time that the 'domain specialist' being interviewed is a master tapestry craftsman, skilled in the production of landscape scenes. The knowledge engineer must try to capture the rules whereby this artist designs his scenes, and he must do this in such a way that the same scene can be produced mechanically. So too in the development of Expert Systems, the resulting program is both Jacquard card and, as we shall see below, recursive proof. In other words, the knowledge engineer must operate at two distinct levels: formalization and conversion into the high-level language. Thus, the knowledge engineer constructs formal heuristics which can be suitably encoded in such a way that the end result of the mechanical process triggered by the machine code instructions will resemble the expert's own efforts or approximate his goals. (Because of the division of labour involved in knowledge engineering each of the specialists involved can concentrate on one particular area of the program while remaining aware, of course, of the constraints operating on the rest of the team.) To return to the nature of the relationship between the knowledge engineer's formal and the expert's intuitive approach, therefore, although there is no hard and fast rule, we can see that in general what is going on is either the adaptation of an existing technique (e.g. chess) or the construction of an entirely new theory on the basis of the expert's knowledge. Hence, knowledge engineers are performing a variety of roles: psychologist, theorist and programmer all in one.

The second major type of Expert System currently under development — alluded to above — are commonly referred to as 'simulation models' (either of motor or cognitive abilities). The general mechanist principle underlying this research rests on the basic Turingesque theme that if a machine can be designed to perform a task which would require intelligence when done by a human, then by parity of reasoning that system should be regarded as 'intelligent'. Perhaps the best-known example of these is Weizenbaum's ELIZA, a program which simulates the role of a Rogerian psychotherapist in an initial interview with a patient.[52]

The case of ELIZA provides an important example of how the prose confusions embodied in the Mechanist Thesis can set us off on entirely the wrong track. Because of the facility with which so many refer to the pictures underlying the Mechanist Thesis, a large number of subjects were predisposed to regard ELIZA as a substitute — if not a superior — psychotherapist. This in turn set off two equally undesirable reactions: one in which the Mechanist Thesis acquired an even greater currency (on the grounds that ELIZA provided a vindication of the Turing Thesis), and the opposite tendency to dismiss ELIZA as at best a sophisticated confidence trick, and at worst a dangerous threat to moral autonomy. With attention focused on this controversy, the more genuine area of psychological as well as AI interest escaped virtually untouched: viz. the very fact that so many people were prepared to regard ELIZA in such terms.[53]

Apart from such interesting considerations, the history of ELIZA raised the whole issue of the role of simulated models in areas where individual attention and skill supposedly constitute the essence of the practice. It is quite understandable for both patients and psychiatrists alike to be alarmed at the prospect of pre-programmed psychotherapy displacing the existing role of the analyst. In actual fact, the manner in which these programs are evolving should dispel any such anxieties (assuming, of course, the impending demise of the Mechanist Thesis and the gradual emergence of a more intelligible explanation of AI processes). For example, in the case of psychotherapy such systems might prove immensely serviceable in teaching situations, in providing the psychoanalyst with instant access to other methods of therapy which have proven successful in treating a similar set of symptoms, perhaps even in stimulating new forms of therapies which are a consequence – hitherto undetected — of certain principles embedded in a theory, or simply in helping to clarify the assumptions underlying a given theory; they might suggest a forward-backward method for identifying the relevant 'core' and their associated 'regnant' beliefs; and finally, they might provide facilities hitherto limited to a privileged minority on a universal scale. Perhaps even the worry of programs being used to supplant the role of the psychotherapist must be calmly addressed; for a large number of programs designed to reduce stress have already proved to be commercially successful.[54]

To be sure, there is the obvious danger in the spirit of the new

Pythagoreanism emanating from AI circles touched on above. In the case of psychotherapeutic programs there is the danger that we may begin to impose the formal patterns suggested by our programs onto human behaviour, thereby distorting the actual methods of decision-making which agents employ. For example, given the binary parameters of machine code, it might be tempting to structure the psychoanalytic program on the basis of a minimax strategy. The danger in this lies in the ease with which it might be overlooked that this structure has been *imposed* onto behaviour patterns, and hence to assume that humans actually do employ a minimax procedure in their decision-making (frequently expressed in that version of the homunculus fallacy which ascribes such a process to the brain). Such an assumption might, of course, suggest a hitherto undetected source of rationality in neurotic behaviour; the danger here is not that such a theory would be ludicrous, but rather that we might remain unaware that we have slipped into such theoretical assumptions.

There is, however, a far more immediate issue which has so far been ignored: the question whether it is even feasible that Expert Systems can be developed on the basis of 'fuzzy reasoning' techniques to the point where they could provide a valuable diagnostic tool.[55] But our concern here is neither with the long-range potential nor the present benefits of Expert Systems. Rather, our task is simply to clarify the nature of Expert Systems and knowledge engineering. For, without entering into any technical disputes about the potential of Expert Systems, we can safely accept that they have already reached the point where they constitute a significant philosophical issue, simply in virtue of the tremendous impetus which they have added to the Mechanist Thesis.

The one obvious objection to all of the arguments so far canvassed in this paper is that they are vitiated by the simple fact that I have only been dealing with a 'prehistoric' architecture (viz. data + algorithm = program) which has now been supplanted by the KIPS revolution (viz. knowledge + inference = Expert System). Such a counter-argument would maintain that, even if the objections raised do tell against data-processing, they have no bearing on 'knowledge-processing'. Indeed, the standard retort to the vast range of philosophical objections that have been raised against the Mechanist Thesis is that *all* are satisfied by the advent of the 'knowledge-information processing system'. For the popular mechanist image of the latter is that the 'inference engine' in a

KIPS can be thought of as a 'general purpose thinking machine', and the 'knowledge base' as 'that about which the engine shall think'. In other words, 'The former, if you like, is the equivalent of a "raw" human brain with the inbuilt capacity to do anything. Whereas the latter is the sum of all human experience in some particular field. Add the two together and you have the equivalent of a human expert.'[56]

Despite the obvious dangers contained in such a metaphor, it will be best to concede from the start that the confusions underlying the Mechanist Thesis are considerably more subtle when we shift from data-processing to knowledge-processing systems; and for that reason, the thesis itself becomes far more compelling. For the advent of Expert Systems does indeed mark a significant development in AI; the problem is to clarify its precise nature. Perhaps the simplest way to identify this is to draw attention to the shift in the domain of problems which are now being addressed. As Feigenbaum describes this, AI is beginning to go beyond the stage of solving 'toy' (i.e. game-theoretic) problems to addressing 'real-world' (i.e. scientific and commercial) issues.[57] Moreover, it is only on the basis of a significant change in programming techniques that such a shift has occurred. In seeking to deflate the Mechanist Thesis, therefore, we must be careful that we do not thereby underestimate the significance of the advances which have so far been realized in the development of Expert Systems.

It would be the most blatant type of superficiality to argue that an 'Expert System' *could not* exist, solely on the grounds that the notion of an Expert System as an *intelligent* (i.e. thinking) system is *stricto sensu* unintelligible. Obviously Expert Systems do exist, and what is more, their development represents one of the most exciting aspects of current research in AI. For despite the reservations expressed above, there are already several operational Expert Systems which seem to be providing excellent back-up services. Once again, then, our task is not to undermine, but rather to understand the processes involved in this revolutionary field. Unfortunately, the chances of bringing science fiction back down to the realm of science with a sobriquet such as 'knowledge engineer' waiting to prejudice critical reactions must be considerably reduced.

We might begin with the following definition of an Expert System, formulated by the British Computer Society's Specialist Group:

An expert system is regarded as the embodiment within a computer of a knowledge-based component, from an expert skill, in such a form that the system can offer intelligent advice or take an intelligent decision about a processing function. A desirable additional characteristic, which many would consider fundamental, is the capability of the system, on demand, to justify its own line of reasoning in a manner directly intelligible to the enquirer. The style adopted to attain these characteristics is rule-based programming.[58]

Here, as elsewhere, we must eschew these entrenched mechanist preconceptions and reconsider how the operations alluded to above should be properly assessed. The first step must be to try to clarify the main differences between a data-processing and a knowledge-processing system in order to ascertain the extent to which we are dealing with a categorical difference in computer systems. For the mainstay of current mechanist arguments is that the development of Expert Systems represents, not simply an enormous advance in computer technology, but more importantly, a quantum leap from the early days of 'number-crunching' to a fully intelligent, quasi-autonomous reasoning system.

The main difference most commonly cited by AI scientists between these two types of system is simply that between a database and a knowledge-base. The former is seen as essentially a static body of information, whereas the latter is regarded as a dynamic reservoir of information (i.e. capable of self-governed expansion). For unlike a data-base, a knowledge-base contains rules as well as assertions, and thus is constantly adding to its pool of information by storing the results of previous operations. Of course, if what we are thinking of are the actual bits which are literally contained in the memory, then there are neither assertions nor rules stored in the knowledge-base (any more than facts were previously stored in a data-base). Hence, in purely electronic terms, there has been no qualitative change at this technical level. Clearly, what is meant, however, is that the bits stored in the knowledge-base are correlated with two types of expression — assertions and rules — in order to write a completely different type of program than that which was possible with one-dimensional data-bases. The temptation to describe this change in intentional terms has, not surprisingly, proved to be irresistible. Thus, the knowledge-base is supposed to be capable, by following its own rules, of 'actively' seeking out missing information (purely, of course, on its own initiative). The steps to preventing such a line of argument before it can get started are essentially those already covered under the previous two headings of this chapter.

The second major difference lies in the KIPS' 'inference system' (or 'inference engine'). In simplest terms, the inference system is simply the methodological procedures built into the system (e.g. 'forward' or 'backward chaining'; i.e. posing a question and then drawing inferences from it, or else selecting a hypothesis from the knowledge-base and then looking for corroboration). With the introduction of increasingly sophisticated reasoning methods, we are witnessing a dramatic advance over the look-ahead GPS techniques introduced in the 1960s. Of course, one is reluctant to exaggerate the nature of these changes; to put this another way, it seems far more desirable to see the evolution of AI — at both the hardware and the software levels — over the past three decades as continuous rather than discrete. But there has clearly been a radical change in the manner in which programs are being written and applied. To elucidate the true significance of the above two developments, we should consider them in the light of the programmer's growing awareness of the needs and demands of the user.

One of the primary virtues of Expert Systems lies in the dynamic interaction between user and system which is rendered possible. The importance of such a facility is obvious: an expert using a diagnostic system, for example, will not feel comfortable with a given result (particularly if it disagrees with his own diagnosis) unless he can satisfy himself about the reliability of the reasoning which has led to it. To accomplish this, it is essential that he should be able to examine the cogency of the steps leading up to the diagnosis. Needless to say, it is precisely here where the mechanist pressures are most evident; for the temptation is to argue that the expert will not trust the system's judgement unless he can examine its reasoning (*supra*). The confusions which result from such a misconception lead to a picture of the user engaged in a dialogue with the system; e.g. of the user 'asking' the system to 'explain' the basis for its decision. Everywhere the mechanist steps here, there are temptations to slip into anthropomorphic metaphors which, unfortunately, are seldom seen as such. If necessary, we could simply rephrase this whole matter in the same terms used to describe the programmer's role in e.g. the performance of a chess program (cf. 'Computer Chess' above). Hence, if the user is asking questions, they are directed at the 'knowledge engineer'. But it is not at all clear why the matter should be phrased in these terms in the first place. Rather than speaking of the user 'asking' anything, it would be far more straightforward to refer to his actions as investigating the steps in the diagnosis. And the system is quite obviously not *answering* anything, although it is perfectly intelligible to speak of the system as *displaying* information.

The crucial point is to consider the manner in which this information is marshalled and presented; and it is here where the knowledge engineer's awareness of the user's responsiveness to a computer system has played a fundamental role in the evolution of Expert Systems. In the early type of program format, if a user called up the pattern which led to a given result he would have found himself provided with a straightforward list of operations. But an expert consulting a diagnostic tool does not want to be confronted with an algorithm! For he will not be satisfied with a mere demonstration of *how* a given conclusion was reached; he must also see why that conclusion was reached, and more importantly, he must be convinced that such a conclusion is licensed by the facts available. What better way for the knowledge engineer to accomplish this than to revert to the actual procedures already familiar to the expert: that is, to construct and display the program sequence as a recursive inferential structure? In other words, the knowledge engineer employs the rules and assertions stored in his knowledge-base together with the sophisticated methodological principles which constitute his inference system in order to construct *proofs*.

Such a mathematical concept is entirely apposite here. To begin with, the system can only respond to decidable questions (although it should also be noted that part of the charm of Expert Systems lies in the knowledge engineer's ability to work with ambiguous questions); hence, the power of the system rests squarely on the breadth of the rules contained in the system. Rather than simply constructing an algorithm for answering a given question, the programmer sets out to develop recursive structures for proving that some answer is correct (or probable) given the rules of his system together with any relevant facts stored in the knowledge-base or provided (on demand) by the user. The heart of the system thus lies in the programmer's ability to construct general recursive proofs; if a given piece of information is missing, the secret is to draw on the rules stored in the knowledge-base in order to revert to a recursive process designed to supply the missing fact. Thus, provided that the proof is valid/compelling, the system should be able to deal convincingly with any decidable question. When a user calls up the program steps, therefore, he is presented with the programmer's recursive proof. Of course, given the system's ability to store up the results obtained from any such recursive procedures, it is clear how the system can increase its knowledge-base; moreover, if the programmer constructs recursive proofs which use meta-rules as well as rules, it is equally clear how the system can augment its store of rules as well as facts. The great mistake here as elsewhere, however, is to confuse the programmer's intentions with the mechanical operations performed by the system. And what complicates matters tremendously is that the instructions/ descriptions of these programs are often written in a questionnaire format; partly because this facilitates use of the system, but largely, one suspects, because of the residual mechanist ambition to demonstrate that systems are capable of entering into 'intelligent dialogues' with their users.

It is thus little wonder, given the influence which the Mechanist Thesis continues to exert, that these important developments threaten to obscure the fundamental point that it is not the system which proves a given result: it is the *programmer*. By capitalizing on his ability to construct and store general recursive proofs the programmer is able to generate, not simply specific diagnostic proofs, but more importantly, proof-skeletons which can be applied in a wide range of cases (given the appropriate satisfaction of the variables in the conditional clauses of the production rules) and which are capable of storing previous results (whether in the form of facts or rules) which can increase both the speed and range of future applications. The knowledge engineer is thus called upon to perform a complex task: given its dual nature (cf. 'Computer Programs' above), the program must be well formed in two distinct ways; for the programmer must not only construct a cogent proof, but he must write this in his high-level language. Hence, the set of steps in his program must be arranged in such a way that the 'downward movement' (which can still be seen as an algorithm) activates the set of mechanical operations correlated to the instructions/descriptions recorded in the 'upward movement' of his program specifications (which are now arranged as a proof). Thus, the success of an Expert System rests on two very different types of criteria: its 'downward movement' must be well formed (i.e. debugged), and equally important, the corresponding program instructions/descriptions must be constructed in such a manner that the user will find the knowledge engineer's proof compelling.

This in turn raises an intriguing problem in regard to the future development of Expert Systems. Given the present understandable desire to preserve the expert's control over the ultimate decision-making process, the reasoning procedures must first be made perspicuous, and second congenial. That is, the system designer is constrained in his ability to devise sophisticated methodological approaches by the need to cater to the expert's own prejudices or limitations. For unless the expert can actually understand and follow the steps in a diagnosis, he will clearly be reluctant to sanction its diagnosis. (But, of course, the same point applies no less forcefully to proofs in general in mathematics.) Secondly, there is the wholly natural anxiety that if Expert Systems attain a high level of success this demand for user-control will be increasingly relaxed, and with it, the expert's role in the diagnostic process.[59] Hence, it is entirely conceivable that he will find his position reduced to virtually that of a technician, which in turn has raised fears of a society governed by machines. If not for the mechanical confusions involved here, this is certainly an issue which should be taken seriously. But what we have to keep in mind is that we are dealing, not with the creation of 'artificial forms of intelligence', but rather, with the inexorable march of mathematical science.

**Concluding Remarks**

In 'Heuristic Search' Donald Michie offers a simplified guide to the sociology of science. He distinguishes between three broad stages in the evolution of a scientific theory: 'First comes the phase of *ad hoc* innovation' in which the pioneers in a new field rely on their native skills and intuitions to lay the groundwork of the theory. 'Next comes the phase of formalisation. Enter the mathematicians, their curiosity provoked by the spectacle of unexplained achievements and clumsy contrivances lacking perceptible principles of rational design.' Finally, there comes the period of 'stabilisation and systematic development. The mathematician still holds the commanding position, but the type of mathematician has changed. The research mathematicians have moved on to virgin fields, either of abstraction or of newer application areas. In their place are practitioners.'[60] Obviously such a framework must not be taken too seriously as far as providing a formal theory in the sociology of science is concerned. But what principally concerns me is that this is how one of the leading exponents of the Mechanist Thesis within the serried ranks of AI scientists views the development of his own discipline. And in this respect, Michie's remarks are extremely illuminating.

Michie's argument ties in with the point which Philip Leith made in his article, 'A Real Expert'.[61] According to Leith,

> Current research in the sociology of science tells us that scientists frequently argue over what the content of their discoveries is and, in fact, over whether anything has been discovered at all. Now research is beginning to demonstrate that just the same thing is happening in computer science with expert systems.

Such, I would argue, is essentially the result of the prose confusions which, although to some extent they dog all phases of scientific evolution, are particularly rife in Michie's initial stage of '*ad hoc* innovation'. At any rate, whether or not we can legitimately draw any such sweeping conclusion, this certainly seems to have been the case in the development of AI. For the very presence of such contention is an important manifestation of the obstacles to communication brought about by prose confusions.

On Michie's interpretation, AI is currently undergoing the transition from the first to the second phase. I would certainly like to believe that this is the case, solely because, if this is so, it would herald the imminent collapse of the Mechanist Thesis as a serious philosophical issue. For metaphor plays only an instrumental role in the initial stages of the evolution of a new mathematical science. Perhaps more than any other device, it is the metaphor which generates enthusiasm and motivates research. Yet, as is so often the case, the metaphor may turn out to be far from intelligible, let alone relevant. But old metaphors never die, they just fade away as their presence increasingly begins to hinder informed discussion. And such, if Michie is right, should emerge as one of the most prominent characteristics of the stage which AI is now beginning to enter. To be sure, there is still a strong element of mechanist prose suffusing the latest crop of writings on the development of knowledge-information processing systems; but compared to the early writings on learning systems of the 1960s, their presence is becoming noticeably muted, if not token. To paraphrase Michie, one might say that the second phase in the evolution of AI belongs to the boffins, who notoriously have rarely had time for the prosaic.

Indeed, perhaps this chapter is itself a symptom of the internal pressures rapidly building to adjust our perceptions in order to suit the shift to the new phase in AI which is occurring. The situation here is becoming increasingly similar to that which exists in the philosophy of mathematics. The metaphysical themes which have for so long plagued the philosophy of mathematics are far less important today than was the case fifty years ago, even though when philosophizing mathematicians may continue to speak naïvely of abstract or ideal objects and platonic domains of mathematical discovery; for in practice they are more than happy to proceed on the basis of a tacit formalism. The main thing, as most practising mathematicians now seem to be aware, is to stick to the mathematics. So too the philosophizing AI scientist may revert to mechanist confusions, but in practice the field is becoming increasingly mathematical, and thus the prose is becoming increasingly isolated. Such an analogy may, in fact, be far more than that, for the two fields are moving much more closely together in the area of so-called 'creative intelligence' (as opposed to the merely 'intelligent behaviour' system discussed above under the heading 'Expert Systems'). In particular, Lenat's AM thesis (that given a basic set of pre-numeric mathematical concepts, it is possible to design formal methods for discovering mathematical systems such as Lenat claims to have accomplished with his AM system which purportedly 'rediscovered' large parts of number theory) raises the whole issue of mathematical discovery *vis à vis* computer autonomy. Here, then, is an excellent problem with which to pursue the various themes posed in this chapter. But will the desire to undertake such a challenge exist? Philosophers no less than scientists who insist on addressing the issues raised by the first phase of AI run the risk of finding their efforts dismissed as an idle if entertaining diversion. The most startling aspect of AI is the sheer speed at which it is progressing. It would be deeply reassuring if philosophy could match the pace.

# Notes

1. As always, my greatest debt in the present paper is to Dr Peter Hacker, whose assistance it gives me great pleasure to acknowledge. I would also like to thank Dr Philip Leith, who read a draft version of this paper, and provided me with several important comments.

2. Bertrand Russell, 'Mysticism and Logic', *Mysticism and Logic and Other Essays*, London, Longmans, Green & Co., 1918, p.17.

3. Cf. The unpublished 'Bouwsma Notes'; P.M.S. Hacker, 'Languages, Minds, and Brains', forthcoming; and S.G. Shanker, 'The Nature of Philosophy' in S.G. Shanker (ed.), *Ludwig Wittgenstein: Critical Assessments*, vol. IV, London, Croom Helm, 1986.

4. Cf. Hacker, 'Languages, Minds and Brains', Russell, 'Mysticism and Logic' and Shanker, 'The Nature of Philosophy'.

5. Cf. 'The Nature of Philosophy'.

6. Cf. Edward A. Feigenbaum and Pamela McCorduck, *The Fifth Generation*, London, Pan Books, 1984.

7. Cf. T. Moto-Oka *et al.*, 'Keynote Speech' in T. Moto-Oka (ed.), *Fifth Generation Computer Systems*, Amsterdam, North-Holland Publishing Company, 1982, pp.7,8.

8. A 'high-level language' is simply a programming language which employs a familiar notation. Perhaps there is no short answer to why the various HLLs are not languages, but the mistake here would be to try to decide this issue on the basis of the syntax of an HLL rather than considering how it is used *vis à vis* the logical grammar of 'language'. If you look at the various 'list processing languages' — e.g. LISP — which are direct offshoots of predicate logic (as opposed to FORTRAN or ALGOL, which are numerically oriented) you soon find yourself searching for some structural feature to distinguish them from (say) Esperanto. Maybe the words in LISP, like Esperanto, are 'cold, lacking in associations, and yet it plays at being a language', but then couldn't they none the less be used to communicate and hence be acknowledged as a 'language' of sorts, even if one which 'disgusts' us? But the real problem here lies precisely in what HLLs are used for. The problem with calling PASCAL a language is that this implicitly accepts that it is the vehicle whereby we communicate ideas to the computer. PASCAL may be constructed according to well-defined rules but these are not rules which the computer can follow. One can certainly conceive of people using PASCAL to communicate, just as you could conceive of a community using a pianola roll to communicate — compare the use of Braille — but its use in the pianola provides no basis to describe the rules for constructing a roll as a form of language. (And do not the pianola-roll manual and PASCAL share a striking structural similarity with basic 'notes' and rules for transforming a melody into 'machine code'?) But obviously, if a culture did use a pianola roll in this manner that still would not license the description of its use in the pianola as *linguistic*.

9. Or vice versa, as Philip Leith has wisely pointed out to me.

10. Cf. G.P. Baker and P.M.S. Hacker, *Language, Sense, and Nonsense*, Oxford, Basil Blackwell, 1984.

11. Cf. John Searle, 'Beer Cans and Meat Machines', 1984 Reith Lectures, 'Minds, Brains and Science', *The Listener* 15 November 1984.

12. Cf. 'The Nature of Philosophy'.

13. Cf. Margaret Boden, *Artificial Intelligence and Natural Man*, Brighton, Sussex, The Harvester Press, 1977, pp.171ff.

14. This, I believe, was one of the basic points that Wittgenstein was trying to make about the relationship between science and philosophy in the 'Bouwsma Notes'. An earlier manifestation of Wittgenstein's influence can be found in one of

Ramsey's posthumous papers, where he argues: 'Philosophy is not a science, but part of scientific activity; in science we discover facts, and at the same time analyse them and exhibit their logical relations. This last activity is simply philosophy.' (April 1928, 006-02-01 in the Ramsey Papers.)

15. Cf. A.J. Meadows, M. Gordon and A. Singleton, *Dictionary of Computing and New Information Technology*, London, Century Publishing, 1982, p.169.

16. Cf. Boden, *Artificial Intelligence*, p.7.

17. Cf. Andrew J.T. Colin, *Fundamentals of Computer Science*, London, The Macmillan Press Ltd, 1983, p.73.

18. Cf. R.D. Greenblatt, J. Holloway and J. Moussouris, 'CHEOPS: a Chess-oriented Processing System' in J.E. Hayes, D. Michie and L.I. Mikulich (eds), *Machine Intelligence 9*, New York, John Wiley, 1984.

19. Arthur L. Samuel, 'Programming Computers to Play Games' in F.L. Alt (ed.), *Advances in Computers*, New York, Academic Press, 1960, p.166.

20. 'Chess-Playing Programs and the Problem of Complexity', *IBM Journal of Research Development* 2, 320 (1959).

21. Adriann D. de Groot, *Thought and Choice in Chess*, The Hague, Mouton & Co., 1965.

22. Ibid., p.305.

23. Ibid., p.308.

24. Ibid., pp.353ff.

25. Cf. Ibid., p.309.

26. Andrew Hodges tells the story of Turing watching with considerable frustration while an algorithm he had devised missed the splendid chances offered it; and exasperation, no doubt, at the 'blindness' of his 'thinking system'. Cf. Andrew Hodges, *Alan Turing: The Enigma*, London, Burnett Books, 1983, p.440.

27. Cf. Ibid., pp.211ff, 349.

28. Ibid., p.359.

29. Cf. Anthony Kenny, 'The Homunculus Fallacy' in *The Legacy of Wittgenstein*, Oxford, Basil Blackwell, 1984.

30. Hodges *Alan Turing: The Enigma*, p.359.

31. Herbert A. Simon, 'Why Should Machines Learn?' in Ryszard S. Michalski, Jaime G. Carbonell and Tom M. Mitchell (eds), *Machine Learning: An Artificial Intelligence Approach*, Berlin, Springer-Verlag, 1984, p.28.

32. P.H. Winston, 'Learning Structural Descriptions from Examples' in P.H. Winston (ed.), *The Psychology of Computer Vision*, McGraw-Hill Book Company, 1975, p.157.

33. Cf. Ibid., p.160.

34. Cf. Ibid., p.186.

35. Ibid., p.187.

36. Ibid., p.159.

37. Boden, *Artificial Intelligence*, p.252.

38. Ibid., p.253.

39. Ibid.

40. Ibid.

41. Cf. Winston, 'Learning Structural Descriptions', p.171.

42. Boden, *Artificial Intelligence*, p.258.

43. Ibid.

44. Cf. Winston, 'Learning Structural Descriptions', p.172.

45. Boden, *Artificial Intelligence*, p.263.

46. Winston, 'Learning Structural Descriptions', p.186.

47. Cf. Ibid., pp.187ff.

48. For those more interested in the technical reactions to Winston's program, cf. J. Knapman's 'A Critical Review of Winston's Learning Structural Descriptions

From Examples', *AISB Quarterly*, vol. 31 (September 1976), and Thomas G. Dietterich and Ryszard S. Michalski's 'A Comparative Review of Selected Methods for Learning from Examples' in *Machine Learning: An Artificial Intelligence Approach*.

49. E.g. cf. K.M. Colby's 'Computer Simulation of a Neurotic Process', which in effect systematises a crude psychoanalytic theory by quantifying the relations which subsit between basic psychoanalytic terms; in S.S. Tomkins and S. Messick (eds), *Computer Simulation of Personality: Frontier of Psychological Research*, New York, Wiley, 1963.

50. Cf. Phil Cox, 'How We Built Micro Expert' in Richard Forsyth (ed.), *Expert Systems: Principles and Case Studies*, London, Chapman & Hall, 1984.

51. Cf. Feigenbaum and McCorduck, *The Fifth Generation*, p.110.

52. Cf. Joseph Weizenbaum, *Computer Power and Human Reason: From Judgment to Calculation*, San Francisco, Freeman, 1976.

53. There are various ways in which to account for this phenomenon. One might simply be to consider the malleability of human attitudes; but another quite serious possibility is that the reaction to ELIZA demonstrated some important fact about the individual's need for *self*-centred 'communication' in contemporary society; or indeed, of the modern individual's complete disregard for the actual content of the reactions which he encounters from others, and hence, of the individual's diminishing ability or desire to engage in genuine conversation.

54. Again, rather than blindly decrying such a development, we should seek to understand precisely why these programs have become so popular; and one possibility which immediately suggests itself is that their success is due to the fact that they do indeed fulfill what is clearly one of the therapist's primary roles in the alleviation of anxiety: they help the user to communicate with *himself*.

55. The inevitable response to such a question is to cite the successes of MYCIN or PROSPECTOR; for the opposite side of the picture — as seen by an insider — cf. Antony Stevens' 'How Shall We Judge an Expert System' in *Expert Systems*.

56. Chris Naylor, 'How to Build an Inferencing Engine', in *Expert Systems*.

57. Cf. Feigenbaum and McCorduck, *The Fifth Generation*, p.85.

58. Quoted in *Expert Systems*, p.10.

59. Just as some mathematicians fear the consequences of admitting 'computer proofs'; but cf. S.G. Shanker, 'The Appel-Haken Solution of the Four-Colour Problem' in *Ludwig Wittgenstein: Critical Assessments*, vol. 3.

60. Donald Michie, 'Heuristic Search' in *Machine Intelligence and Related Topics*, London, Gordon & Breach Science Publishers, 1982, p.44.

61. *Guardian*, Thursday 6 December 1984.

# 6 A WITTGENSTEINIAN VIEW OF ARTIFICIAL INTELLIGENCE[1]

Otto Neumaier

We do talk of artificial feet, but not of artificial pains in the foot.[2]

In this chapter I deal with some philosophical problems connected with research in the field of Artificial Intelligence (AI), in particular with problems arising from two central claims, namely that computers exhibit 'intelligence', 'consciousness' and other 'inner' processes[3] and that they 'simulate' human 'intelligence' and cognitive processes in general. More precisely, my main aim is to analyse the specific kind of mentalism underlying these claims, which are held by many psychologist and computer scientists working in the field of AI, and to discuss its importance for AI. My reflections are guided by Wittgenstein's analysis of psychological terms.

## Introduction

In the last two decades people have devoted much attention to and invested many hopes in AI, which not only promises better solutions to numerous technical problems, but also a better understanding of cognitive processes in general and, in particular, of the human mind. Although there is no doubt that AI provided us with a great deal of progress, practical *and* theoretical, from a philosophical point of view there is just as little doubt that a lot of assumptions in and implications inferred from AI are being overemphasized. In particular, cognitive scientists like Schank (1975) and Winograd (1972) maintain that 'programs already manifest intelligent behaviour in limited domains and are potentially able to deal with larger domains in due course' (cf. Obermeier 1983: 339), whereas philosophers like Dreyfus (1979) and Searle (1980) deny that programs will ever be able to 'simulate' (or to emulate) human 'intelligence'.

No one has been able to show the philosophical problems

underlying this dispute more clearly than Wittgenstein, whose considerations, on the other side, seem to have opened a door for the development of AI and cognitive science in general. Therefore, he is at the same time considered by some (e.g. Wilks, 1976a) as a forerunner to AI and by others (e.g. Dreyfus, 1979 and Obermeier, 1983) as a 'decidedly anthropocentric' philosopher whose reflections are not suitable to support claims of AI.[4] Yet these two views do not contradict one another; they are at most a challenge to investigate their common source *in* Wittgenstein. Therefore, they both offer good reasons for trying to outline the Wittgensteinian view of AI.

When Wittgenstein died in 1951, Artificial Intelligence had not yet been baptized by this name.[5] Despite the appeals to his philosophy mentioned above, it may therefore be surprising for some people to learn of a *Wittgensteinian* view of AI. Yet the discipline, although unnamed, was already born at that time. Let us remember the famous article by Alan Turing on 'Computing Machinery and Intelligence' (1950), or the eminent work on cybernetics by Wiener (1948). An earlier, decisive step to the 'simulation' of human cognitive processes by machines was made by Turing (1937) in his paper 'On Computable Numbers, With an Application to the *Entscheidungsproblem*', in which he demonstrated that any domain representable by effective procedures can be computed by machines; Turing even stressed that 'such a machine forms an abstract model of (certain attributes of) a human being' (cf. Cherry, 1978: 251n).

We do not know *exactly* how familiar Wittgenstein was with this kind of research. Yet we know that Turing, who was one of Wittgenstein's students in his lectures on the foundations of mathematics, emphasized Wittgenstein's remarkable influence on his own thoughts (cf. Nedò and Ranchetti, 1983: 309). We also know that Wittgenstein owned a copy of Turing's (1937) article and worked with it; furthermore, one of his remarks (from the year 1947) shows his realization that Turing's 'machines' represent *men* who calculate and that they amount to *games* of the sort he described (cf. *RPP* I 1096). Moreover, from the mid-1930s (*PG* and *BB*) until the end of his life (*PI, RPP* and *LWP*) Wittgenstein extensively dealt with the problem of whether machines can 'think' (cf. 'The "Intelligence" of Men and Machines' below). We may therefore speculate about a hidden connection between these data.

Wittgenstein's 'philosophy of psychology' (or, more exactly, his philosophical analysis of psychological terms) originated within a context which was steeped in behaviorist criticisms of traditional, introspectionist psychology. This is one reason why Wittgenstein was for a long time regarded as a behaviorist too. Additional reasons are that Wittgenstein occasionally referred to behaviorism (cf., e.g. *PI* I 307f., *RFM* II 61, *RPP* II 33); that he criticized introspection as well as mentalist assumptions; and finally that the critical character of his remarks on the grammatical features of such psychological terms like 'pain', 'understanding', 'consciousness' etc. invoked the impression that it is only the *uses* of these terms we are allowed to speak about (which at least *can* be understood in a behaviorist way).

Today it seems as if the assumption that Wittgenstein was a behaviorist is essentially mistaken.[6] This has been demonstrated by the remarks contained in *RPP* and *LWP* which have been published during recent years; in particular, the manuscripts which are to be published as the second part of *LWP* present impressive evidence for a specifically mentalist interpretation of Wittgenstein.[7] What he criticized is only *one* (other) kind of mentalism (to be characterized later in this chapter under the heading 'Wittgenstein's Philosophy of Psychology'), although the danger of this kind of mentalism has not been eliminated by his criticisms, since it developed its proper importance after Wittgenstein's death and is now widely represented within the framework of AI. We are therefore justified in applying Wittgenstein's reflections on psychological problems and his negative attitude towards that mistaken mentalism to some central assumptions of research in AI. We shall see later in his chapter how this criticism works. Let us first consider the main aims of AI.

### The Aims of AI

The aims of AI have been formulated in different ways, the most prominent being the one by Minsky (1968: v), who calls AI 'the science of making machines do things that would require intelligence if done by men'. Weizenbaum (1976: 202) even goes one step further. According to him, 'the overriding goal of AI is to create an artificial system which will equal or surpass a human being in intelligence'. Some variations of these definitions are presented by Winston (1977) and Boden (1977: 5), who defines AI as 'the use of computer programs and programming techniques to cast light on the principles of intelligence in general and human thought in particular', and — last, but not least — by Pylyshyn (1979: 25), according to whom AI 'attempts to understand the nature of intelligence by designing computational systems which exhibit it'. One can see the problem also from the other side of the coin and, like Haugeland (1981: 31), affirm 'that *intelligent beings are semantic engines* — in other words, automatic formal systems with interpretations under which they consistently make sense'.

Several claims are hidden in these definitions which can be reconstructed in the following way:

(1) If machines perform things which, if performed by men, would require 'intelligence', then we are justified in ascribing 'intelligence' (and other mental predicates) also to these machines; and machines surpass human beings in 'intelligence' (and other mental faculties) if they perform better than these.

(2) If we are not able to perceive a distinction between something performed by a machine and the action of a human being, then the machine *does* the same as the human being.

(3) If a machine performs in a way similar to a human being, then the program underlying its performance is an abstract *model* of the mental faculties underlying the human performance — or even a *theory* about (a specific part of) the human mind.

(4) The human mind itself is nothing but a formal automaton (which obviously *can* be modelled by computer programs). This idea, *pace* Haugeland (1981: 2), 'makes *artificial* intelligence seem not only possible, but also a central and pure form of *psychological* research'. Therefore:

(5) Computer programs are the most efficient means for explaining the nature of (human) 'intelligence'; they are the best psychological theories (if they provide performances of the kind mentioned above).

To be sure, this reconstruction should (and could) be refined in one respect or the other to do justice to AI. We ought, for example, to distinguish at least two versions with respect to the strength of psychological assumptions (cf. Searle, 1980; Weizenbaum, 1976). Some scientists defend a *weak* version of AI, according to which computers are 'only' tools to *perform* specific *tasks* (and to perform them more efficiently than men), whereas adherents of the *strong* view aim at programming computers in such a way that they (seem to) *'simulate'* certain human *abilities*. According to these scientists, if running a program results in the performance of some task which would require 'intelligence' if done by men, it is plausible to assume that the program provides us with a 'simulation' of the respective human ability.[8] Of course, the first assumption has little to do with AI, and it is the second one which is of interest here. If, however, the 'performative' approach is to be taken as a serious approach to AI, we shall discover stronger psychological implications than are admitted by its adherents. We can therefore neglect the difference between these two positions for our purposes and regard them as having similar philosophical implications.

### Some Philosophical Arguments Against AI

The claims mentioned in the previous section (which differ with respect to their scientific strength) are vague enough not only to cause enthusiasm in people who find their bearings with technical and economical success and regard meta-theoretical reflections as waste of time but also to provoke philosophical criticisms of different kinds. The most prominent argument against AI, which has been extensively discussed by philosophers, was introduced by Kurt Gödel a long time before the 'birth' of AI as a means to demonstrate the limits of formal logic and mathematics.

### The Gödel Argument

Gödel (1931) proved that in any consistent logical system which is rich enough to contain elementary arithmetic there is at least one meaningful sentence that would naturally be interpreted as *true* by logicians but can be neither proved nor refuted within the system.[9] Turing (1950: 15f.) himself realized that Gödel's argument has strong implications for the capacity of digital computers; he realized, in particular, that 'there are certain things that such a machine cannot do'. Turing thought, however, that this problem was of no importance with regard to the imitation game with which he tried to give the question of whether machines can 'think' a more precise form; since, in the context of this game, the only criterion for a machine 'being able to think' is that a spectator is unable to distinguish the performance of a computer from that of a human being. Consequently, there is no reason to deny the 'ability of thinking' to computers, and Gödel's argument seems to be of no importance. Boden (1977: 434f.), who discusses Gödel's argument in some detail, follows Turing, yet goes one step further in maintaining that it is irrelevant for AI, 'since even if Gödel's proof applies to programs as well as to logic, it still does not show that programs are essentially inferior to the human mind', and that, therefore, philosophers (like Lucas, 1961) 'who appeal to Gödel's theorem in rebutting mechanistic explanations of mind are . . . mistaken'. I agree with Boden in so far as Gödel's proof indeed does not show that computers are less 'intelligent' (or more 'stupid') than men, because the same problem holds for computers as well as for men trying to construct formal systems without the aid of computers. Yet was this the question Gödel tried to answer?

What Gödel proved is that in formal languages of a certain level (which are a *necessary* prerequisite for the *ability* to solve *some* scientific problems or, more precisely, to decide on the *existence* of a solution) there is at least one sentence Φ which can be recognized as true, but which is formally undecidable such that neither the logical formula φ(representing Φ) nor the formula ¬φ can be derived within the system. We might call this a (necessary) limit of our 'intelligence', although this use of language does not seem to be appropriate to me; we should rather speak of necessary limits of some kind of our scientific *knowledge*, i.e. that kind which is formally decidable. On the other hand, Gödel's proof is *a fortiori* valid (and therefore *not irrelevant*) for AI, because its generalization and reinterpretation for the special case of AI demonstrates that human thinking cannot be fully represented by *effective* procedures (which would be a necessary prerequisite to make human thinking fully computable). To my mind, Gödel's proof is the only strong argument against AI which is independent of Wittgenstein's line of thinking or, at least, needs no reformulation in Wittgensteinian terms to become more coherent and explicit.

*Some Further Arguments Against AI*

Boden (1977: 434ff.) discusses some further philosophical arguments designed 'to show that certain things done by people *could not be done* by computers'. Some of them are formulated in a misleading way, others fail to refute the criticized assumptions; and finally, some can be reconstructed and strengthened in Wittgensteinian terms. I shall therefore present those philosophical arguments against AI in the following paragraphs and discuss them in a preliminary way, and I shall come back to the central points after having presented an overview of Wittgenstein's analysis of psychological assumptions (later under the heading 'Wittgenstein's Philosophy of Psychology').

From a philosophical point of view, it seems first of all to be a mistake to call programs theories,[10] and it is not at all clear what is meant by the notion of 'intelligence', for what computers can 'do' up to now is scarcely comparable to the behavior of human beings. Even if we take all 'intelligent' programs together, the sum will not amount to what we call 'intelligent' in man. On the other hand, we are also careless in ascribing 'intelligence' to human beings; thus, the problem may not lie with the computer scientists but with the psychologists. I should like to neglect this problem for the time being (and come back to it later under the heading 'The "Intelligence" of Men and Machines' where some kind of a Wittgensteinian solution to it will be offered); for reasons of length the first point will not be discussed at all.

Most arguments against AI involve a misunderstanding which is connected with the assumption that computers cannot 'do' things done by people. No doubt, at the moment no computer is able to make an 'intelligent' performance similar to that of a human being (much less to perform *all* things people can do). However, we do not know the progress computer science will make in the near or far future. Yet that is not the misunderstanding I should like to speak about. The misunderstanding involved in Boden's discussion is much deeper.

To speak about something computers, unlike men, cannot 'do', we should be able to know (or describe or explain) what a human being (or a computer) actually *does*. For example, a description like 'X moves his hand at time t from A to B' does not yet explain that X has boxed another person's ear at time t. However, in saying that X does something, we do not mean that he moves his hand at time t from A to B, but that he boxes a person's ear. Whether a computer is able to 'do' so depends (in some sense) on our inclination to *explain* that a specific movement of such a robot could be a box on the ear. The problem (with computers *and* men) is whether we need such mentalistic assumptions; and I will deal with it later. What I should like to emphasize here is that it only makes sense to deny that computers can do specific things after we have made clear what we mean by 'doing something'. Therefore,

Dreyfus's (1979) critique of AI as well as Boden's (1977) is somehow in the air.

However, be that as it may: Boden (1977: 434ff.) also discusses the following two philosophical arguments against AI: 'the claim that digital computers could not achieve common kinds of "tacit knowledge", or cognitive information processing; and the view that computers could not simulate emotion even to the degree that they can simulate certain cognitive processes'. Both arguments appear unconvincing to Boden as well as to me, because they involve severe misunderstandings:

(1) The fact that our knowledge is (to some degree) always 'tacit' does not prohibit the construction of programs which may 'simulate' *some* behavioral features of ourselves (and, thereby, model some features of our minds). The argument may only show that we will never be able to 'simulate' *the* human mind (because a large part of our cognitive processes are 'tacit'), but for two reasons it misses the aim it is meant to refute. First, as I shall argue in the following, for principal reasons no theory can explain *the* so-and-so (e.g. *the* human mind) but only some important *aspects* of this or that (e.g. of what we call 'human mind'); therefore, the 'tacitness' of some (or even most) cognitive processes does not matter, because the psychological theories involved in AI do not aim to grasp 'the' human mind, but may neglect some 'tacit' aspects. Secondly, AI theories do not necessarily claim 'consciousness' for the phenomena they are to explain or to 'simulate'; they, rather, claim 'psychological reality' for some 'inner' processes (whether they are 'conscious' or not) which are assumed to underly specific observable phenomena exhibited by men as well as by machines. Thus, if such a theory is able to explain some observable *behavioral* phenomena (e.g. by 'simulating' it with a computer program), a set of 'inner' processes assumed by the theory is claimed to be 'psychologically real', but these may be 'conscious' as well as 'tacit'. Therefore, the existence of 'tacit knowledge' is in no way an obstacle for AI.[11]

(2) We cannot *prima facie* derive an argument against AI from a computer's inability to 'simulate' emotions, because computers are not designed to 'simulate' emotions but cognitive processes. However, AI faces another problem which is probably confused by some critics of AI with the argument mentioned above. Independent of the question whether AI should be able to 'simulate' emotions (as such) or not, it may be that cognitive processes may

not be adequately 'represented' without any reference to emotions; indeed, there is some evidence for this.[12] Moreover, it appears that 'there is nothing foolish about thinking that certain features of our minds, such as intentionality, consciousness, and the emotions, are in some essential way tied to the specific kind of organic machines we are'.[13] If this turns out to be true, it will set limits to AI which are much narrower than we would like; yet the discussion of this point is up to the moment inconclusive.

Another argument against AI which is just as unconvincing as those discussed in the preceding paragraphs is that computers are *digital* machines which, therefore, cannot process analog information. This 'argument', which is put forward, e.g. by Dreyfus (1967, 1979) and is even taken seriously by Turing (1950: 22), is far too weak, so that the discussion of it would be a waste of time.[14]

As I have already pointed out, one further argument is interwoven with those discussed so far, namely that computers can 'simulate' only specific *aspects* of cognitive processes. There are two points to mention here: the first is that the aspectual character of a computer 'simulation' is indeed a problem cognitive scientists should not neglect; they should at least be aware of this fact. The second is that this is not a specific problem of AI only but of any knowledge and any science. If, therefore, computer scientists *are* aware of the aspectual character of their programs designed for 'simulating' cognitive processes, they can go back to their everyday life. Under the next heading below I shall, however, discuss some problems connected with the aspectual character of our knowledge about psychological processes.

One philosophical argument still remains, namely that computers cannot 'think' because they do not share a *'form of life'*. This argument has been introduced with reference to Wittgenstein, who, in a famous remark, said: 'But a machine surely cannot think' (*PI* I 360). I shall neglect this argument for the moment, because I should first like to characterize Wittgenstein's philosophical analysis of psychological terms and then come back to his scepticism against the possibility of 'thinking' machines.

### Wittgenstein's Philosophy of Psychology

Wittgenstein's philosophy of psychology is generally best to be characterized as *explanatory mentalism*. Let me first explain this statement:

(1) Contrary to the prevailing interpretations of Wittgenstein he is here understood not as a behaviorist, but as (some kind of) a mentalist. As I have already remarked in my introduction, the impression of Wittgenstein's being a behaviorist is caused by different reasons and, despite all of them, mistaken. Wittgenstein emphasized that we have only observable phenomena as *evidence* for 'inner' processes, but this does not amount to denying that there is a possibility to speak about 'inner' processes in one way or another, i.e. that our language contains also psychological language games.

(2) Mentalism is not just one monolithic theory about psychological phenomena, but it is a bulk of different assumptions tied together by 'family resemblances' à la Wittgenstein. We can distinguish at least two radically different kinds of mentalism which have only one assumption in common, namely that it makes sense to conclude from the observation of 'outer' phenomena to the existence of 'inner' processes. However, whereas *descriptivistic* mentalists like Chomsky, Miller and Bresnan[15] maintain that a theory which can explain observable phenomena with reference to 'inner' processes can also be said to describe these 'inner' processes, this assumption is denied by explanatory mentalists. Even the best psychological explanations, they hold, are *theoretical constructs* which only allow the assumption of the existence of 'inner' processes, but never the description of 'inner' processes. The most important advocate of this position is, it seems to me, Wittgenstein.

(3) Explanatory mentalism is one facet of Wittgenstein's epistemological position which can best be called *explanatory realism*. According to this position, the value of theories generally lies in their explanation of some facts. This sounds quite trivial, but it has far-reaching consequences. If, according to Wittgenstein, we would like to characterize *globally* what is made valid by a theory, we can only point to the theory's explanatory power with respect to some universe of discourse; it does not make any sense to introduce truth (globally) as the one feature which makes a theory valuable. However, our evidence for a specific theory can differ from case to case. Therefore, *some* theories may rightly be called true. This, however, holds only *locally*, i.e. for special cases, and in these cases a theory can also be characterized as descriptive.

It does not hold, e.g. for psychological theories: in psychology we have only some outward evidence for 'inner' processes, and this evidence is always uncertain (cf., e.g. *RPP* I 137, II 682). Therefore, Wittgenstein's explanatory mentalism is in some sense a sceptical position; Wittgenstein does not say that there is no relation between a psychological theory and some psychological 'reality', but that it is impossible to prove such a relation because of the evidence for psychological theories. On the other hand, Wittgenstein was not a sceptic in any respect; it is even correct to call him a realist (i.e. an *explanatory* realist).

In his considerations about the use(s) of psychological terms Wittgenstein was mainly concerned with the following two questions: What justification is there for our assumption that somebody *follows* a specific *rule* (e.g. in mathematical operations or in language use)? And: What *criteria* have we for ascribing 'inner' processes (e.g. pain or the understanding of utterances) to somebody? In the following I should like to concentrate on the problem of criteria for 'inner' processes (because the problem of rule-following is based on this question). Before we can enter into the discussion, however, we have to clarify what Wittgenstein meant by criteria.[16]

## Wittgenstein's Uses of the Notion of Criterion

Beginning with *PG* I 10, Wittgenstein frequently uses the word 'criterion', so that this concept is regarded by many authors as a 'key word', as 'crucial' and as 'playing a fundamental role' in his so-called 'later' philosophy.[17] Wittgenstein doesn't use this term uniformly, as is acknowledged by almost all of his interpreters and critics. Nevertheless, some have tried to give precise definitions of what they think Wittgenstein meant with 'criterion'. For example, in the interpretation put forward by Oxford philosophers like Kenny (1967), Hacker (1972) and Baker (1974), criteria for a specific expression are interpreted as '*non-inductive grounds* for its application or use'. Such grounds are regarded as *defining* criteria, although there is not one *conclusive* criterion, but rather different ones, which may be *fixed* within different language games — according to *PI* I 164: 'In different circumstances we apply different criteria for a person's reading.' Hacker also holds that 'the criterial relation is clearly an evidential one'.[18]

The reason for this interpretation of criteria is that Oxford philosophers primarily consider passages in Wittgenstein's writings on which he speaks of the logical, or grammatical, status of criteria (cf., e.g. *BB* 51, 104; *PI* I 182; *Z* 437, 466). Criteria in this sense strictly determine the use of expressions; we go beyond the experience with a finite number of utterances and fix the meaning of an expression according to such a criterion. But this is not the only way to speak of criteria, as is shown by the approach of Wellman (1962) and Kripke (1982), who are both above all interested in Wittgenstein's philosophy of mind. The central section they quote is *PI* I 580: 'An "inner" process stands in need of outward criteria'.

With regard to this quote, it is by no means certain that for Wittgenstein outward criteria are 'non-inductive, logico-grammatical conditions for the application' of (sensation-) terms as is the Oxford interpretation.[19] This would contradict other passages in Wittgenstein's writings where he emphasizes that one 'can't give criteria which put the presence of the sensation beyond doubt; that is to say: there are no such criteria' (*RPP* I 137). A criterion in the first sense would by definition prove that some person *has* certain sensations (although the criteria may be different within different language games). Of course, the possibility that Wittgenstein contradicts himself is left open, but it seems to be more plausible to try to explain this apparent contradiction. The explanation which is nearest at hand is that Wittgenstein did not use the notion of 'criterion' in one sense only, but that, depending on the context, he used it in different ways which are only connected with one another by *family resemblance*.

With the notion of 'family resemblance' Wittgenstein wanted to illustrate that there is no uniform set of attributes which constitutes *the* meaning of a linguistic expression, but that there are only similarities between different uses of an expression (comparable to resemblances between different members of a family). Wittgenstein's use of language, however, is just the best demonstration of this view: there is no uniform set of features which constitutes *the* meaning of the terms he introduced into philosophy; rather, there are family resemblances between different uses of these terms, depending on the context in which they are used. This is also true of the notion 'criterion' which is used by Wittgenstein in many ways related to one another like the members of a big family.

In the context of the present considerations I do not want to list all members of the big 'family' of 'criterion', but only pick out two of them which can help us to explain the apparent contradiction mentioned above, i.e. the two uses of the notion 'criterion' which are suitable for a demonstration of the differences between the Oxford interpretation of Wittgenstein and the approaches of Wellman and Kripke:

(1) A criterion in the first sense offers decisive, **causal evidence** for the phenomenon for which 'the **criterial relation** holds' (cf. Hacker, 1972: 285). The identification of some **bacillus or virus**, for example, is the criterion for the existence of a specific illness, whereas the observation of some symptoms provides us with inductive grounds for a diagnosis only (which, therefore, is always uncertain). To speak of criteria in this sense is 'a loose way of stating the definition' of the phenomenon evidenced by the criterion (*BB* 25).

(2) A criterion in the second sense is, according to Wittgenstein, every *outward* evidence we have for 'inner' processes; Wittgenstein also uses the expression 'evidence' for this notion, and he distinguishes in this context between *sufficient* and *imponderable* evidence. Wittgenstein emphasizes that there is no sharp boundary between these two kinds of evidence (cf., e.g. *RPP* II 614; *Z* 439). There are, however, no outward criteria which could put the presence of a 'sensation beyond doubt; that is to say: there are no such criteria' (*RPP* I 137).

Wittgenstein at first distinguished criteria from symptoms and, in *BB* 24f., he explained that 'to the question "How do you know that so-and-so is the case?" we sometimes answer by giving *"criteria"* and sometimes by giving *"symptoms"* '. If we identify, for example, angina by the presence of a specific bacillus, we get a *defining* criterion for this illness, whereas an inflammation of the throat is a symptom, a 'phenomenon of which experience has taught us that it coincided, in some way or other, with the phenomenon which is our defining criterion'. It is impossible to distinguish sharply between these two kinds of evidence, because 'we don't use language according to strict rules'. In *PI* I 79 and *Z* 438 Wittgenstein notes fluctuations in the usages of the terms 'criterion' and 'symptom', and complains that in science a great deal of confusion arises out of the fact that some measurable phenomena are made defining criteria for an expression. The same oscillation is observed in *PI* I 354, but with opposite indications: 'The fluctuation in grammar between criteria and symptoms makes it look as if there were nothing at all but symptoms'. For the rest, Wittgenstein uses the word 'criterion' only which is sometimes to be understood in the sense of 'evidence', sometimes of 'imponderable evidence' and sometimes in its 'usual' sense.

The sequence of these remarks shows that Wittgenstein gradually changed his mind between 1934 and 1949. He at first distinguished two kinds of evidence, one which we learn to see as being characteristic of an occurrence and which is established by linguistic convention, and one which is discovered to be empirically correlated with evidence of the first kind and parasitic in relation to it; these two kinds of evidence are referred to by Wittgenstein as criteria and symptoms respectively. In the course of his investigations, however, Wittgenstein realized that in our (scientific and non-scientific) *practice* we do not distinguish in this way, but fix whatever pieces of evidence as criteria. For this reason he at some point dropped the distinction drawn in *BB* and absorbed his notion of symptoms into that of criteria (or evidence).[20]

Beyond these pragmatic reasons, Wittgenstein's absorption of the notion 'symptom' into 'criterion' can be explained in different ways. First, a *sharp* distinction between these two notions is indeed impossible (as is best illustrated by medical practice). Secondly, symptoms *are*, in a weak, heuristic sense, criteria (i.e. criteria in the second sense). Finally, Wittgenstein frequently emphasizes his loss of interest in causal explanations (cf., e.g. *PI* I 466). This resignation is well motivated: consider, for example, the criterion for a word like 'bachelor' (in one of its senses). Clearly, a person is correctly called a bachelor if this person is human, male, adult and has never been married; we could also use other criteria, but these would change the meaning of 'bachelor'. If we would like to find out, however, whether somebody attaches a specific meaning to 'bachelor', then it would be unsatisfactory to simply say that he/she has mastered the rules of the English language. How are we to know that a number of people 'follow' the same rules? We can only point to their behaviour within a specific form of life (cf., e.g. *PI* I 190, 344, 504). This gives us the only *evidence* for the meaning of an expression, for 'inner' processes etc. There are no 'genuine' criteria which make sure that someone uses 'bachelor' with a specific meaning or experiences certain 'inner' processes, and this, as Wittgenstein says, 'is a peculiarity of our language-game' (*RPP* I 137). These considerations plainly show the epistemological reasons that motivated Wittgenstein in his use of the notion of 'criterion' in a specific way.

### The Aspectual Character of Psychological Assumption

It is not merely by accident that Wittgenstein introduces the distinction between criteria and symptoms by questioning 'How do you *know* that so-and-so is the case?' (*BB* 24). Since we have no other evidence for knowing that so-and-so is the case, we *fix* some phenomena (which appear important within a language game) and regard them as defining criteria (which may vary for different language games); this seems to hold not only for psychology but also for 'exact sciences' like, for example, physics. However, Wittgenstein makes clear that physical and mathematical evidence is much more certain than psychological evidence; the latter offers only restricted possibilities to explain some outer phenomena by assuming 'inner' processes.[21] In one remark of MS 174 (to be published in the second volume of *LWP*) Wittgenstein even emphasizes that in some sense the 'inner' is an illusion, i.e. that the whole complex of ideas alluded to by this word is like a painted curtain drawn before the scene of the real use of the word.

The uncertainty of any psychological evidence is one problem that has to be taken into consideration by scientists working in the field of AI. Another important question was introduced by Wittgenstein with the following consideration: 'That the evidence makes someone else's feeling (what is within) *merely* probable is not what matters to us; what we are looking at is the fact that *this* is taken as *evidence* for something important' (*Z* 554). The importance of this point is shown by the fact that Wittgenstein several times reflects about it in different formulations (cf. MS 171 and 174 which were written in 1949 and 1950 and form part of the second volume of *LWP*).

Into this very context Wittgenstein introduces a new, important term, i.e. the notion of *aspect* (cf. in particular *RPP* and *LWP*, but also *RFM* III 46-50). Criteria are conventionally fixed pieces of evidence (which in some cases may also be mere symptoms) observable in language use by which we grasp some aspect(s) of the meanings of our expressions. But it is a matter of our language games that we take these pieces of evidence as defining criteria; they are the only evidence we have. Taking this into account we can agree with Wittgenstein that 'the meaning of a word is what is explained by the explanation of the meaning' (*PI* I 560). We should, however, also notice (with Wittgenstein) that we never *have* causal evidence, but *give* a defining character to specific (outward) criteria which only grasp some aspect(s) of meaning. Since there is only outward (public) evidence for language rules we need not distinguish further between 'symptoms' and 'criteria', but may, like Wittgenstein, use the second expression only.

*If* our use of an expression (like 'bachelor') is determined by a specific rule, then we have of course a *criterion* (in the first sense) for the meaning of this expression. On the other hand, we face the epistemological problem of whether a speaker of a language does 'follow' this (or another) rule. By formulating *theoretical* rules within a (linguistic or philosophical) grammar, we try to *explain* the language use. Let us assume that we would be able to explain the uses of the English language completely by grammatical rules. This success would not allow us to assume that a speaker of English 'follows' *these* rules; we not only cannot expect that he/she has the very abstract formulations of a (linguistic or philosophical) grammar at his/her disposal, but, moreover, we have no criterion which could put it beyond doubt that he/she does 'follow' a specific rule.

Therefore, it would be a *mentalistic fallacy* to assume that a grammar could describe the linguistic faculties of a person (or to assume that he/she 'knows' the rules of a grammar). Even if a grammar can explain all the uses within a language and even if the behaviour of a person gives us good (outward) evidence for the assumption that he/she is competent for that language, we have to be aware of the explanatory character of linguistic rules as well as of the fact that these rules grasp only some aspects of the language use which are essential for us. We are never able to grasp *the* meaning of expressions or *the* competence of a speaker-hearer.

## Are There Mentalistic Language Games?

The previous considerations are relevant not only for (theories about) our uses of language, but also for the way in which we use psychological terms (or, in other words, for our assumptions about corresponding 'inner' processes, concerning other people as well as ourselves). Already as children we learn to interpret some observable phenomena as evidence for, for example, pain. What we do then is actually the following: we *explain* the observable phenomena by assuming 'inner' processes. If we succeed with these explanations on the whole (which is presumably the case in everyday life, yet on a very low explanatory level) we are then justified to assume (the *existence* of) 'inner' processes; yet we cannot expect to have a criterion which puts beyond doubt that somebody does feel pain (in the same sense as finding out how much money a person has at his/her disposal by looking into a statement of account of that person).

This fact is relevant not only for the 'folk psychology' of our everyday life but also for scientific psychological theories (which have those experiences as a starting point). It shows that our evidence for 'inner' processes differs from that for outer, observable phenomena. As a result, we get a specific 'logic' (or 'grammar') for psychological terms, for the conditions for the use of such terms are not the same as in other language games. This has been made clear by Wittgenstein in one remark (contained in MS 173) in which he emphatically states that the inner differs from the outer by its *logic* and that the expression 'the inner' is of course explained and made intelligible by logic.

The grammar (or logic) of psychological terms can best be characterized by applying the famous scheme of an explanation for the meaning of linguistic expressions presented by Wittgenstein in *PI* I 43: 'For a *large* class of cases — though not for all — in which we employ the word 'meaning' it can be defined thus: the meaning of a word is its use in the language'. We may continue: For a large class of cases — though not for all — in which we employ psychological terms their meaning can be defined thus: the meaning of psychological terms is the role they play in the explanation of specific observable phenomena, e.g. human behavior. In other words: our psychological language *explains* observable phenomena in assuming that they are based upon 'inner' processes; the very language, however, gives us no possibility to *describe* 'inner' processes, because we have no criteria for *what* processes are 'within'.

The significance of outward criteria for 'inner' processes and the specific use of mentalist terms is illustrated by Wittgenstein most clearly in his famous beetle example (cf. *PI* I 293):

Suppose everyone had a box with something in it: we call it a 'beetle'. No one can look into anyone else's box, and everyone says he knows what a beetle is only by looking at *his* beetle. — Here it would be quite possible for everyone to have something different in his box. One might even imagine such a thing constantly changing. — But suppose the word 'beetle' had a use in these people's language? — If so it would not be used as the name of a thing. The thing in the box has no place in the language-game at all; not even as a *something*; for the box might even be empty. — No, one can 'divide through' by the thing in the box; it cancels out, whatever it is.

This parable contains at least three points which are essential not only for Wittgenstein's psychological approach but also for cognitive science (and AI) in general:

(1) We can only *infer* 'inner' processes from *outward* criteria.[22] If everybody could look *into* his box only, then he would never know what occurs therein. Only if we learn within some form of life to *interpret* some observable phenomena as evidence (or sign) for 'inner' processes, are we able to develop a solid, working picture of (some aspects of) such 'inner' processes.
(2) We can never describe 'inner' processes. When we use psychological terms like 'pain', 'understanding' or 'consciousness' we do not use them in the same way as expressions with which we usually describe something in the world (e.g. 'house', 'tree' or 'mountain'). If we understand psychological terms in the same way as these expressions, then we get the nonsense illustrated by the beetle example as a result. Immediately after this parable Wittgenstein confirms: 'If we construe the grammar of the expression of sensation on the model of 'object and designation' the object drops out of consideration as irrelevant' (cf. also *PI* I 304). Thus, psychological language games are never descriptive, but (at least, some of them) have only their explanatory character in common. There *are*, therefore, psychological language games which make no sense, namely, descriptive language games; on the other hand, it makes *sense* to 'play' some language games in psychology, namely, explanatory ones, and to understand psychological terms as elements of explanations of observable behavior.
(3) Our psychological interpretations always depend upon the *form of life* we grow into. To come back to one of my examples, already as children we learn to interpret some events and kinds of behavior as signs for, for example, pain. Yet in doing so, we grasp specific aspects only which are essential within our form of life; similarly,

even psychologists learn to grasp as evidence for specific psychological phenomena some aspects which are important within the psychologists' (scientific) form of life. We can imagine that other aspects are essential within other forms of life and that other kinds of psychology will be developed. This has been demonstrated, for example, by Harré (1986) and Heelan (1984).


**The 'Intelligence' of Men and Machines**

We have now reached the point at which we can apply Wittgenstein's considerations to AI and its problems. At first glance we receive the impression that according to Wittgenstein there is only one possible answer to the question of whether machines can 'think' or 'understand' something: 'But a machine surely cannot think' (*PI* I 360). Looking at the mass of Wittgenstein's remarks concerning the 'intelligence' of machines, we see that it would be a mistake to take this statement literally, i.e. to conclude that Wittgenstein definitely excludes the possibility of a machine being 'intelligent' for logico-grammatical reasons. We should rather take a more differentiated approach.

*The Human Background of Psychological Assumptions*

Throughout his writings Wittgenstein emphasizes that human beings not only differ from machines, stones and animals (e.g. dogs, lions and parrots) but also from some human-like creatures we would use as slaves or 'reading machines', for it is only man to whom *prima facie* such psychological phenomena like 'thinking', 'uttering and understanding language' or 'feeling pain' are ascribed.[23] In accordance to this, Wittgenstein regards human beings and their language as being 'full of soul', and 'the opposite of being full of soul is being mechanical' (*RPP* I 324; cf. also *RPP* II 292). Therefore, the notions of 'machine', 'mechanism' and 'automaton' seem to form the very opposite to what we regard as 'human'.

What does this opposition consist of? Wittgenstein answers this question by pointing out two features which are specifically human, namely the *complexity* of our behavior and its *openness* (or 'creativity') with regard to rule-systems. The former is illustrated in *PI* I 18 by the picture of an ancient city ('a maze of little streets and squares, of old and new houses, and of houses with additions from various periods'), the latter by the tennis example in *PI* I 68 which is designed to show that 'the "game" . . . is not everywhere circumscribed by rules; . . . yet tennis is a game for all that and has rules too'. Human behaviour differs from mechanical movements 'by the fact that your ordinary movements cannot even approximately be described by means of geometrical concepts'.[24]

It is, however, not only a matter of 'complexity' and 'openness', i.e. a matter of empirical fact, that we do not ascribe psychological phenomena to machines (as well as to animals and inanimate nature), but rather a matter of logic and the conditions imposed by it upon the use of psychological terms. The problem contained in the question whether machines can 'think' is rather 'that the sentence, "A machine thinks (perceives, wishes)": seems somehow nonsensical. It is as though we had asked "Has the number 3 a colour?" ' (*BB* 47). Therefore, it 'would go against the grain' to use the word 'believe' in the same sense when saying 'I believe that he is suffering' and 'I believe that he isn't an automaton' (cf. *LWP* I 321); it makes no sense to apply the notion of 'thinking' as well as other psychological terms to computers.

This is the very assumption computer scientists are opposed to. For example, *pace* McCarthy (1979: 161) ascribing 'certain "beliefs", "knowledge", "free will", "intentions", "consciousness", "abilities" or "wants" to a machine or computer program is legitimate when such an ascription expresses the same information about the machine that it expresses about a person'. McCarthy (1979: 181f.) further affirms that a machine 'introspects when it comes to have beliefs about his own mental state'. According to Wittgenstein, we cannot necessarily express the same *information* by ascribing specific mental states to a machine as when we are making similar ascriptions with respect to a person; hence, it is not at all legitimate to ascribe such mental states to machines.

For Wittgenstein, the main reason why primarily human beings have the 'privilege' of 'having' mental states is that 'thinking', 'understanding', 'feeling pain' and other psychological phenomena are inseparably tied to human life and can only be grasped against this background, namely in two respects:

(1) Psychological language games 'are as much a part of our *natural* history as walking, eating, drinking, playing'.[25] That is, the very features of our minds are in some essential way tied to the specific organization of our physical organization, our *body*: 'The human

body is the best picture of the human soul'.[26] This cannot be the only reason, however, for Wittgenstein distinguishes two meanings of 'being in pain', 'thinking' etc.:

> I can look on another person — another person's *body* — as a machine which is in pain. And so, of course, I can in the case of my own body. On the other hand, the phenomenon of pain which I describe when I say something like 'I have a toothache' doesn't presuppose a physical body. (I can have toothache without teeth.) And in this case there is no room for the machine. — It is clear that the machine can only replace a physical body. (*PG* I 64)

Thus, if the organization of our body alone were crucial for ascribing mental phenomena, the possibility of machines being able to 'think' would still be left. Thus, the salient point of Wittgenstein's argument must be reflected on the other side of the coin.

(2) If we want to know whether a certain being can 'think', we do not only investigate its ability to perform specific tasks but, rather, the total of its (or, better, her/his) *behavior*:

> Our criterion for someone's saying something to himself is what he tells us and the rest of his behaviour; and we only say that someone speaks to himself if, in the ordinary sense of the words, he *can speak*. And we do not say it of a parrot; nor of a gramophone.[27]

If we take the philosophical background presented above under 'Wittgenstein's Philosophy of Psychology' into account, we may interpret this statement as follows: the ascription of psychological states is necessarily connected with the human *form of life*; already as children we learn to *see* some events as *signs* for human behavior as well as some specific behavior as sign for 'inner' states like 'thinking' or 'being in pain'. In other words: we learn to use psychological terms in such a way that their meaning depends upon the total complex of human behavior, to 'the bustle of life. And our concept points to something within *this* bustle' (*RPP* II 625). Let me explain some further points involved in this statement:

(a)   Our use of psychological terms (and, hence, our ascription of 'inner' states) is inseparably tied to the complex interplay of the totality of human behavior. This 'peculiar combined play of movements, words, facial expressions etc., as of expressions of reluctance, or of readiness' (cf. *RPP* I 814) is our *criterion* for ascribing 'inner' states. To be sure, it is not a criterion in the first sense (cf. my discussions above under 'Wittgenstein's Uses of the Notion of Criterion'), but a criterion in the second sense: it is the outward evidence we have for 'inner' processes. And it is *imponderable* evidence (cf. *LWP* I 936): we cannot 'prove' (let alone in a scientific way) that this or that 'inner' process occurs 'within' a person, but can only point to our human experience, to the 'bustle of life', which makes us into some kind of *connoisseur* (cf. *LWP* I 925ff.).

(b) It is this very same experience which tempts us to assume that someone 'has' pains, 'has' certain thoughts, 'has' a soul etc.[28] This is one result of the fact that in ordinary life our psychological hypotheses seem to be confirmed in a way similar to those about, for example, someone owning this or that visible object (e.g. a house, a car, money). Our evidence, however, is not the same in these two cases; hence, this applies also to the respective language games. Although (as I have argued above under 'Are There Mentalistic Language Games?') we can explain important features of human behavior by ascribing 'inner' processes to human agents (i.e. by using psychological terms in an explanatory way), it would be a mentalistic fallacy to conclude that someone 'has' pains etc. (i.e. to use psychological terms in a descriptive way). It seems that our psychological evidence has maliciously set a pitfall where philosophically inclined people are easily caught.

(c) It is the very complexity of the 'bustle' of human life which determines the use of psychological terms, 'and it is the very concept "bustle" that brings about this indefiniteness . . . Variability itself is a characteristic of behaviour without which behavior would be to us something completely different' (*RPP* II 626f.; cf. also *RC* 302f.). Thus, it appears that our ascription of 'inner' processes depends upon the impossibility to describe the behavior, which is to be explained by this psychological assumption, 'by means of geometrical concepts' (*RPP* I 324).

This leads to an apparent paradox with respect to AI: we (or at least the computer scientists) know a lot about the programs underlying the performance of specific tasks by a computer. This knowledge is *necessary* for the success of AI, for the very knowledge of the program should enable us to explain the principles of *human* 'intelligence'. However, it is exactly this knowledge which, at least according to a Wittgensteinian line of reflection, necessarily prevents AI from being successful (or even from being meaningful); for our very *ignorance* about 'inner' processes, which can by no means overcome but 'logically' results from the 'bustle' of human life, underlies our psychological language games in a characteristic way. Thus, we do ascribe 'inner' processes to human beings if this enables us to explain their behavior, whereas we do not ascribe 'inner' processes to a computer, although we do explain its performance of specific tasks by the 'assumption' of an underlying program.

Our result therefore seems to be that within a Wittgensteinian framework no place is left for AI, and we can now turn to the next point of our agenda. However, the subject we are dealing with is as complex as human behavior, and we have to add some more details of Wittgenstein's considerations. For instance, we can apply one of his famous examples to our situation: 'If I say "I have locked the man up fast in the room — there is only one door left open" — then I simply haven't locked him in at all' (*PI* I 99). That is: although the result of the preceding paragraphs was that Wittgenstein denies the possibility that machines are able to 'think', his considerations leave one door (or, more exactly, two doors) open for the good computer scientist to escape from this verdict.

### Do Computers Share a 'Form of Life'?

At first glance it seems that there is one further argument against AI, one which I have already referred to at the end of the section headed 'Some Philosophical Arguments', and which is involved in the considerations of the preceding section, namely that computers cannot 'think' because they 'do not share our human context, what Wittgenstein termed our *forms of life*. For example, computers are not interested in food, humour, or companionship; nor are they hurt when hit, or sympathetically prompted to go to the aid of someone who is'.[29] As should be obvious from our previous discussions, this argument *can* be used against AI; it may not be as obvious, however, that it can also be used *in favour* of AI, namely in the following way.

The question of whether computers share a form of life can be understood in two ways: one interpretation could be whether computers share a form of life *of their own*. Presumably it is very difficult to answer this question; and we may doubt whether we should answer it at all. For it is another question Wittgenstein is concerned with: Do computers share *our* form of life? The salient point expressed in this question is that we can *understand* computers only if they participate in our form of life. This is true for computers as well as for men, i.e. if we share a form of life with some people, 'they are transparent to us'; yet it can also be the case 'that one human being . . . [is] a complete enigma to another'.[30]

Now, although computers are not 'interested' in, for example, food, humour or companionship, we should be aware of the end they are designed for: the 'simulation' of (certain important aspects of) human 'intelligence'. Regarded in this way, computers are not a 'complete enigma' to us, but can exhibit some traits of human behavior. Moreover, there is indeed some evidence that computers are on the way to become an essential part of our (form of) life, so that we shall have to learn to *understand* them (and to understand them better than ourselves or, at least, to understand ourselves increasingly by understanding computers). This evidences a second phenomenon, which also supports the enterprise of AI, viz. a shift in the meaning of our psychological terms.

*Our Uses of Psychological Terms*

Wittgenstein's considerations about (as well as his criticisms of) the uses of psychological terms have to be seen against the background of the ordinary and philosophical practice in the first half of this century. No doubt, our practice has continuously been changing since then. What cognitive scientists mean by the notion of 'intelligence' does obviously not correspond to the everyday usage of this notion at Wittgenstein's time which was essentially the same as ours still is. We may presume that Wittgenstein might have had a lot to criticize about the uses of language within what developed into AI. This is not, however, the point which matters to us. I should rather like to point out the holes through which AI can escape from the prison of Wittgenstein's criticisms:

(1) Wittgenstein himself emphasizes that linguistic expressions in general and psychological terms in particular are not used uniformly: 'If you want to find out how many different things "thought" means, you have only to compare a thought in pure mathematics with a non-mathematical one'.[31] And Wittgenstein

admits the possibility 'that there is a language-game in which I produce information *automatically,* information which can be treated by other people quite as they treat non-automatic information'; he even emphasizes in *RPP* I 817 that this is 'the *important* insight'. It seems therefore that at least some ways of using ordinary language can be 'grasped' or 'simulated' by computer programs, and this to some extent legitimates AI also from a Wittgensteinian point of view.

(2) Even if our sentences were to be interpreted in one uniform way, this would not suffice to make the sentences meaningful; to get meaningful sentences we have to add further determinations (cf., e.g. *RC* 296). For example, the sentence 'I believe that he isn't an automaton', 'just like that, so far makes no sense' (*LWP* I 323). To give meaning to a sentence like this it is necessary to refer to the whole background of the 'form of life' it is embedded in. However, as has been illustrated above under the heading 'Do Computers Share a "Form of Life"?', the computer scientist may choose an appropriately selected 'form of life' which provides him with the right criteria to give the desired interpretations to his sentences.

(3) Although Wittgenstein sometimes seems to deny the possibility of understanding across different forms of life,[32] he does *not* generally defend such a strong view. This would contradict one insight he repeatedly emphasizes, namely that the application of psychological terms is not clearly determined for all cases: 'It is only in normal cases', i.e. in cases of our everyday experience we are sufficiently familiar with, 'that the use of a word is clearly prescribed; we know, are in no doubt, what to say in this or that case. The more abnormal the case, the more doubtful it becomes what we are to say'.[33] Remembering the variability of our evidence discussed earlier under 'Wittgenstein's Uses of the Notion of Criterion', we are well prepared for the uncertainty of whether we can ascribe 'inner' states to this or that being as well as for the possibility that members of different forms of life could understand one another:

> Let us imagine human beings who are unacquainted with dreams and who hear our narrations of dreams. Imagine one of us coming to this non-dreaming tribe and gradually learning to communicate with the people. — Perhaps you think they would never understand the word 'dream'. But they would soon find a use for it. (*RPP* I 101)

Of course, the more similar a 'form of life' is to the one we are familiar with, the better we are able to understand it. However, 'it isn't clear *how much* has to be similar for us to have a right to apply . . . the concept "thinking", which has its home in *our* life', to other creatures or to machines (cf. *RPP* II 186). Thus, the application of psychological terms is not a question of 'yes' or 'no', but there are innumerable degrees of understanding etc.; it is in no way difficult to imagine that we, under this presupposition, are able to understand a computer (and vice versa).

(4) 'Would it be correct to say our concepts reflect our life? They stand in the middle of it' (*RC* 302). This remark, which is characteristic of Wittgenstein, supplies the adherents of AI with a strong argument for the plausibility of their work (and, hence, for the appeal to Wittgenstein as a forerunner of AI). From it, they may conclude that Wittgenstein's views on the (im-) possibility of 'thinking' machines depend upon the background of *his* life, whereas the application of psychological terms to computers depends upon the altered conditions of *our* modern life; it is, then, only a matter of empirical, technical progress that we are successively enabled to apply our common psychological terms to computers. There is indeed some truth in this consideration. According to Wittgenstein, the concepts people use reflect their life; they 'show what matters to them and what doesn't' (*RC* 293). The criteria underlying the uses of language reflect the aspects important within the corresponding form of life; language is a tool to 'organize' the experiences, which can be made within such a framework, in a suitable way. Wittgenstein himself is mainly concerned with the variety of our everyday life (which, in his eyes, is neglected by most philosophers); within this form of life some language games are considered as normal and distinguished from other, abnormal cases. This does not amount, however, to saying that this 'form of life' is the only one possible, 'that we have the right concepts and other people the wrong ones' (*RC* 293); rather, we have at most the right concepts in relation to what matters to us, whereas other people have the right concepts in relation to their interests. Of course, the computer scientist can also point to this state of affairs and, hence, claim that his use of psychological terms is the right one with regard to his purposes.

(5) Finally, let me amalgamate two elements of Wittgenstein's philosophy. On the one side, Wittgenstein makes clear that the 'deterministic' approach to machines is only one possibility: 'We

talk as if these parts could only move in this way, as if they could not do anything else. How is this — do we forget the possibility of their bending, breaking off, melting, and so on?'[34] On the other side, Wittgenstein reflects about the normality of language games in relation to a form of life, and he points out that what is normal for us may become abnormal in different circumstances, and vice versa (cf., e.g. *PI* I 142). Now, in relation to Wittgenstein's 'form of life', it would be abnormal to ascribe the ability of 'thinking' to computers, but this cannot prevent someone to imagine another 'form of life', the world of AI, where this case becomes *normal*, i.e. where the criteria for the use of psychological terms have changed in such a way that computers do think and that the folk-psychological assumptions of the past, which cannot be represented by means of effective procedures (i.e. which cannot be 'simulated' by a computer), lose their point. And, in regard to a possible coexistence of both 'forms of life', we may even conclude from *RPP* I 101 that the possibility of an understanding between these two 'forms of life' still exists.

From the preceding paragraphs we can conclude the following: Wittgenstein in no case *opens* the door for the development of AI; therefore he cannot be considered as a forerunner of AI. Wittgenstein, however, *leaves open* the door for AI to become a meaningful enterprise; the conditions for this have to be clear as well: the aims of AI can only be arrived at after a *radical change* in our form of life. According to a Wittgensteinian line of thinking (and, I should like to add, corresponding to the 'form of life' of our common sense), it makes no sense to call computers 'intelligent' in the *traditional* sense, namely for the following reasons:

(1) Neither do computers exhibit something comparable to human 'intelligence', nor would we regard a man as 'intelligent' who is able to perform exactly the same tasks as a computer.

(2) Computers lack that 'rest of behavior' (cf. *PI* I 344) which is one of our criteria for the ascription of 'inner' phenomena like 'intelligence'; in this sense, they do not take part in the bustle of human life. Therefore, we cannot decide upon the possibility of artificial 'intelligence' by tests like Turing's (1950) that abstract from this context.

(3) The notion of 'intelligence' is an element of the system of our ordinary language, and its meaning is determined within this system in opposition to a number of other expressions like 'knowledge', 'ability', 'education', 'stupidity' etc. What conditions does a com-

puter fulfill to be stupid? No doubt, the semantics of the language used by cognitive scientists differs largely from our ordinary language.

However, this is only a sign for what matters to us in our 'everyday' form of life, but not an obstacle for the development of AI. Indeed, we are at present facing a change in the meaning of psychological expressions which reflects a *change of aspect*,[35] i.e. a change of those aspects we make defining criteria of our language use because they are regarded as *important*. What is going on is a redefinition of psychological terms by the exact means of 'effective procedures'; in this context, it does make sense to call a computer 'intelligent' if it (or he/she?) performs specific tasks or passes a test like Turing's. This exemplifies the accuracy of Wittgenstein's remark that 'if we want to put a concept with sharp boundaries beside our use of this word, we are free to define it, just as we are free to narrow down the meaning of the primitive measure of length "a pace" to 75 cm'.[36]

Although it is plausible to assume that what computers can 'do' does not correspond to 'intelligence' in its usual sense, this does not amount to denying that computers ever could become 'intelligent'. I should like to make explicit, however, that this 'intelligence' will never approximate in any sense to what we usually call 'intelligence', but that the meaning of this notion will change in such a way that it applies to the very tasks computers can fulfill. The problem of 'artificial intelligence' will therefore be solved by an 'appropriate' change in the notion of 'intelligence'. This is the truth underlying Turing's (1950) prediction 'that by the end of the century general educated opinion will be that machines can think', for Turing 'also remarked that by that time the words might have subtly changed in meaning'.[37]

**The 'Simulation' of Human 'Intelligence' by Machines**

Let us neglect for the rest of this chapter the fact that computer scientists use psychological terms in a different way than we do in our ordinary life. Let us simply assume that there is no problem with the application of psychological terms (like 'intelligence', 'thinking' etc.) to machines, i.e. that our life has changed so that computers are important elements of it. We then still face two problems arising from claims which can frequently be found within

AI, namely, that AI programs 'simulate' human 'intelligence' and that those which successfully 'simulate' human 'intelligence' provide computers with mental states similar to those of human beings. For example, McCarthy (1979) is eager to ascribe 'knowledge', 'consciousness', certain 'beliefs' and other mental states to machines if 'such an ascription expresses the same information about a machine that it expresses about a person'; even 'machines as simple as thermostats can be said to have beliefs, and having beliefs seems to be a characteristic of most machines capable of problem solving performance'.[38] Let us consider these two claims separately.

### What Could 'Simulation' of Intelligence by Computers Be?

The notion of 'simulation' is as difficult to grasp as most other terms in psychological theory, in particular because there is no clear definition of what it is to 'simulate' something and of the criteria for a successful 'simulation' of something. As has been pointed out by Taube (1961), we may 'simulate' a piece of cheese by putting it and a piece of metal of the corresponding weight on the two pans of the scales at the same time. What is 'simulated' in this example is the weight of the cheese, but not its odor, taste and nutrifying qualities. Of course, someone might (for some purpose) regard weight as the essential feature of cheese and neglect all other features as inessential once the 'simulation' of the essential feature is possible. I need not emphasize the consequences this argument is confronted with from a Wittgensteinian line of thinking.

Let us for the moment neglect the imprecise way of speaking of 'simulation' within AI. The following question still remains: If a certain model 'simulates' a psychological process, is it plausible to assume that this model, in itself, is (or represents) a psychological process? Sayre (1979: 139) indicates an answer to this question by arguing that

the fact that minds and machines both can recognize patterns, for example, no more implies that minds are material, than the fact that birds and aeroplanes both fly implies that aeroplanes are oviparous. By reverse token, even if it were shown that certain forms of mentality cannot be simulated, it would nonetheless remain a possibility that the mind is material.

Similarly, the fact that machines can possibly 'simulate' the human mind does not imply that the program used for this 'simulation' is mental. The crucial question is whether mentalist assumptions are *necessary* to explain something within AI.

When research in AI started in the 1950s, two kinds of 'simulation', namely *structural* and *functional*, were soon distinguished. Both of them lead to a similarity (or analogy) between the simulated object and the simulating model, i.e. between, in our context, the 'cognitive abilities' of human beings and computers. It is assumed that a computer functionally 'simulates' a certain 'cognitive ability' of human beings if, given the same input (e.g. a specific situation in a game of chess), both exhibit the same (or a similar) output (e.g. a certain move in that game). In addition to this, structural 'simulation' demands that the 'information-processing mechanism' which leads from the given input to the resulting output is proved to be similar for both man and machine.

Very soon it turned out that AI fails to account for structural similarity between human and artificial 'intelligence'; neither 'hardware' nor 'software' can be regarded as structurally similar in man and machine.[39] We are therefore left with the 'functional simulation' of human 'intelligence' by computers as the only possibility. This kind of simulation makes the 'behavior' of man and computer the criterion for successfully simulated 'intelligence', i.e. the fact that computers can perform certain tasks is at the basis of the assumption that they are 'intelligent'. This approach faces, *inter alia*, the following problems:

(1) Is there any evidence that a computer 'behaves' in the same way as a human being? As I have repeatedly pointed out in this chapter, regarding something as 'behavior' of a specific kind is not merely a matter of looking at what happens, i.e. at the physical movements of, for example, a person and a computer. Rather, a great deal of *interpretation* is necessary which rests upon some *criteria* that grasp specific, important *aspects* of what is observed. Now, at least on a surface level, we obviously regard neither the performance of specific tasks by computers as similar to human 'behavior' nor the 'abilities' underlying this performance as similar to human 'intelligence'. It therefore seems that computer scientists select criteria for 'intelligence' and 'behavior' which differ completely from our everyday criteria for the very same phenomena in human beings. That is we face the situation described earlier

under the heading 'Our Use of Psychological Terms'.

(2) For argument's sake, let us assume that it is not only possible to 'simulate' human behavior by computers, but that we have already succeeded in doing so. If we are able to explain a specific trait of human behavior by 'simulating' it with a computer (program), would it be plausible to ascribe 'inner' processes to this computer, i.e. to identify the program as a 'mental state' of the computer? In my opinion, such mentalistic assumptions are in no way necessary for scientific explanations in AI, i.e. computer scientists can explain anything they want to without having recourse to the assumption of 'inner' states in the computer (cf. also under 'Can We Ascribe Mental Processes to Computers?' below). For reasons of scientific economy, we can therefore renounce without any loss mentalistic claims in AI. Yet the situation is not as simple as it may seem at first glance. Let us therefore examine the mentalism of computer scientists in greater detail.

### Can We Ascribe Mental Processes to Computers?

If we remember the restrictions mentioned at the beginning of this section headed 'The "Simulation" of Human "Intelligence" by Machines', it is clear that it at least makes sense to *ask* for (the existence of) 'inner' processes in computers; it makes as much sense as with regard to human beings. To make the question meaningful, two conditions must be met: mentalistic assumptions must help to *explain* something (cf. above 'What Could "Simulation" of Intelligence by Computers Be?' and below); and we must have outward *criteria* which make the mentalistic assumption plausible. Since these conditions hold for 'artificial' psychology as well as for 'natural' psychology, with regard to the ascription of mental states, the same problems 'natural' psychologists are concerned with are also relevant for AI. Consequently, we have to point to some dangers involved in the mentalistic statements mentioned above on pp. 159f.

McCarthy (1979), like many other computer scientists, often speaks of machines 'having' beliefs, knowledge, free will and other 'inner' states. This reflects the very mentalistic fallacy criticized by Wittgenstein with regard to human beings, for McCarthy suggests that machines *have* 'inner' states in the same sense as they have a certain weight, colour or form. However, the computer scientists' evidence (if there is any) for the ascription of 'inner' states to computers differs from other language games in the same way as it is the case in regard to human beings. Therefore, Wittgenstein's verdict against a *descriptivistic* view of 'inner' states is valid for AI too. In this context, too, psychological terms can be used in an *explanatory* way, i.e. to explain something observable. Yet even the best psychological theory never supplies us with a means to describe what is going on 'in' a computer (cf. 'Wittgenstein's Philosophy of Psychology' above).

On the other hand (and once again): do we need mentalistic assumptions to explain something in AI? Computer scientists obviously answer this question in the affirmative, as is demonstrated by their practice. I doubt, however, that there is any explanation in AI for which it is necessary to assume that a computer 'believes', 'thinks' or 'knows' something. For it is the *output* which is to be explained by psychological assumptions. Well, we do explain the fact that a computer performs a specific task by the fact that it was programmed in a specific way, but this does not necessarily involve the assumption of 'inner' states. Only if we adhere to the strongest view of AI, namely to the assumption that a program *is* a mind, do we have to put up mentalism too. However, this position is shared only by few computer scientists; most of them seem to refuse the identification of programs and minds (cf., e.g. Pylyshyn, 1979; Searle, 1980).

If we would like to ascribe 'inner' states to computers we have to meet Wittgenstein's condition that 'an "inner process" stands in need of outward criteria' (*PI* I 580) as it is the case in regard to human beings. What could these criteria possibly be? Our criterion for ascribing certain 'inner' states to a person, according to Wittgenstein, 'is what he tells us and the rest of his behaviour' (*PI* I 344). Does the same hold for computers? It seems that we, for different reasons, have to answer this question in the negative:

(1) As I have pointed out several times, speaking of the 'behavior' of a computer is either naïve, a misleading metaphor or the sign for a use of this term which completely differs from the usual one. The aspects made into criteria by computer scientists are almost incomparable to the aspects which matter to us in our 'everyday' form of life. Unfortunately, computer scientists are seemingly not even aware of their peculiar use of psychological terms.

(2) The outward evidence provided by computers is at least up to now too *poor* to justify taking it as a criterion for mentalistic assumptions. One may object that computers sometimes in the

future will be 'able' to 'do' things they are 'unable' to 'do' now. If this becomes true, my argument could apparently be removed for two reasons: the performance of computers would then supply better outward evidence for mentalistic claims, and their 'abilities' could possibly improve in such a way that, for reasons of complexity, our knowledge of the underlying processes would simultaneously decrease. Let us suppose that both will be the case; indeed, there is some evidence for the increasing 'opaqueness' of computers (cf. Weizenbaum, 1976). It seems that for the very reasons mentioned earlier under 'The "Intelligence" of Men and Machines', we should then have to ascribe 'mental' processes to computers. I admit that considerations like these may be plausible up to some degree. They cannot, however, remove another point involved in my discussions: the criteria for the application of the term 'intelligent' to computers would still differ from those in ordinary-language use. Even in this case, computer scientists would therefore give 'intelligence' another meaning.

(3) Even if we had good evidence that a computer does 'simulate' (specific aspects of) human 'intelligence' this would not necessarily have to be explained by the assumption of 'intelligence' *in* the computer, for what a computer 'tells us' as well as the 'rest of his behavior' are of *no prognostic value* concerning its supposed 'inner' states, i.e. we do not get any information which we would not already have by knowing its program.

Thus, the program itself seems to be our criterion for the 'inner' processes of a computer. But can programs be regarded as outward evidence for 'inner' processes? We can refute this assumption with the following reason: programs are 'outward' in the sense that they are transparent for us; they cannot be regarded as 'outward' if they are identified with minds. In any case, in order to use programs as outward evidence for a supposed 'inner' state of a computer, we should have to have good reasons for assuming that *this* particular program evidences *that* particular 'inner' process. Yet, as has been shown by, for example, Block and Fodor (1972) and Searle (1980), different programs can underlie the same performances. This strongly indicates that programs, too, represent no appropriate outward evidence for mentalistic assumptions within AI.

**Towards the End**

Does it follow from my discussions that we should deny any value to AI? This is the last thing I should like to suggest. Research in the field of AI did provide us with much progress in psychological theory; for example it clarified the role of a lot of conditions for cognitive processes which we were not aware of before because they seemed to be obvious within the context of folk psychology. And it is plausible to expect further insights into *human* psychology by the 'simulation' of *some* cognitive processes by computers. Yet computer scientists, who are trained to evaluate theoretical progress by its technical results, easily neglect the *limits* of their theories. Some of these limits have been discussed in this paper.[40] They can be summarized in the following way:

(1) Even if computer programs can 'simulate' some traits of human 'intelligence', it is not human 'intelligence' in its usual sense which is 'simulated' by them, but (at most) some specific aspects of human 'intelligence' which, in the context of certain purposes, are regarded as important by cognitive scientists.

(2) The language used in AI is extensively perfused with metaphors; this is shown, for example, by the fact that computer scientists call computers 'artificially intelligent'. It is not 'intelligence' which is artificial, but the mechanism designed to exhibit 'intelligence'. When Wittgenstein remarks that 'we do speak of artificial feet, but not of artificial pains in the foot' (*PG* I 64), he not only points to the human background of our use of psychological terms, but also seems ironically to annotate that metaphoric use of language.

(3) Computer scientists seem to use the notion of 'intelligence' in such a way that its application is restricted to the very features exhibited by computers. Consequently, there is a tendency to emphasize the same aspects (important for computers) in regard to men. This leads to an interesting problem which is dealt with in some detail by Born in Chapter 8 of this book: we should not be afraid that sometimes computers may be able to 'think' like men, but, on the contrary, that men begin to 'think' like computers.

(4) Even if AI programs succeed in providing for the performance of specific tasks by a computer (or to take it metaphorically, in 'simulating' human abilities which would underlie the performance of similar tasks), this does not prove that mentalistic assumptions

are necessary for AI; we should therefore be (ontologically) more cautious and renounce the assumption of entities we do not need for explaining.

(5) Even if it made sense to use psychological terms with respect to computers, it would be a mentalistic fallacy to use them in a descriptive way, i.e. to assume that computer programs describe processes (or states) 'in' the computer (or 'in' the human mind 'simulated' by computer programs). To be sure, this problem is faced by psychology in general, but therefore it holds *a fortiori* for 'artificial' psychology.

This critical discussion of the limits of AI owes a great deal to Wittgenstein. Wittgenstein himself, however, pointed out the roads adherents of AI could take without necessarily being worried about his criticism. According to Wittgenstein, we may plausibly assume that our language use (and, hence, our total form of life) changes in such a way that computers, in our opinion, *can* 'think'. This situation fits well into the example given in *PI* I 18:

> Our language can be seen as an ancient city: a maze of little streets and squares, of old and new houses, and of houses with additions from various periods; and this surrounded by a multitude of new boroughs with straight regular streets and uniform houses.

It seems that Wittgenstein parallels our ordinary use of psychological terms with the old part of the city, whereas the new developments are similar to the new boroughs with their straight regular streets and uniform houses.

Wittgenstein admits to both forms of life their own right. We are therefore still allowed to regulate our environment, to draw limits and straighten streets. Yet with such measures, which reflect a change in our interests, we gradually (and in the end radically) change our form of life. And the success of these changes does not prove the old form of life meaningless because of its variety, complexity and uncertainty. On the contrary, it seems that Wittgenstein preferred the traditional form of life, for he not only defends the 'old' language games several times, but also regards 'thinking', for example, as inseparably tied to the 'bustle of human life'.

Moreover, Wittgenstein sometimes criticizes psychological theorizing as well as science in general for taking measurable phenomena as defining criteria of language use. It therefore seems that AI, which had already been born during Wittgenstein's lifetime but developed to a science of high public repute only after his death, would for him have been one element of what he called the 'sickness of a time' (cf. *RFM* II 23). From the context of this quote we can conclude that he meant the sickness of *our* time, to whose therapy he devoted a great deal of his reflections. Seen in this way, it was surely not Wittgenstein's intention to become a forerunner of AI, because he wanted to caution us against a one-sided development, of which AI, together with its scientific, economic and ethical aspects, is certainly an element. Hence, one interesting question mentioned in the introduction to this chapter, i.e. what Wittgenstein thought of Turing's efforts to prove human thinking computable by machines, is to be answered in a more negative way than appeared at first glance.

## Notes

1. I wish to thank Ilse Born-Lechleitner for her efforts to improve my English prose. I owe also much debt to Rainer Born, Georg Dorn, Alfred Kobsa, Kuno Lorenz, Edgar Morscher, Dagmar Schmauks, Gerhard Schurz and Stuart Shanker for their invaluable comments and criticisms; they are, of course, not responsible for the final product.

2. *PG* I 64. Throughout this paper Wittgenstein's works are referred to by the usual abbreviations (listed in the References following these Notes) followed by the number of the corresponding (part and) section; the only exception is *BB*, where page numbers are given.

3. For some central concepts of AI (e.g. 'simulate', 'tacit', 'represent', 'conscious', 'intelligent', 'understand'), I shall use quotation marks throughout this chapter, because they seem to be used in a metaphoric, imprecise way.

4. For the rest of his paper, however, Obermeier (1983) argues (like Wilks, 1976a) that along Wittgensteinian lines programs can be said to have something like 'understanding-as-performance' and therefore can be called 'intelligent'.

5. According to Boden (1977: 424) the term 'Artificial Intelligence' was introduced by John McCarthy in 1956.

6. Some arguments for this interpretation have been presented, e.g. by Canfield (1981), Luckhardt (1983) and Neumaier (1984).

7. In particular, MS 173 and 174 (written in 1950) contain a lot of remarks in which Wittgenstein speaks of the 'world of consciousness', of 'dispositions of our minds', etc. (cf. also *RC* 313ff.), and where he also emphasizes that there is indeed some evidence for 'inner' processes, although this evidence can never be certain. In one remark of MS 174, e.g. Wittgenstein distinguishes mathematical evidence (which is clear and without doubt) from psychological evidence (which is unclear and uncertain).

8. Simon (1984: 25), e.g. believes that 'we all believe machines can simulate human thought'. According to Searle (1980) the proponents of the strong view of AI even believe that a program *is* a mind.

9. This is a rather simplified formulation of Gödel's (1931, 187) theorem VI. For reasons of space I cannot discuss Gödel's argument here at length, but only mention some relevant points. On the application of his argument to AI, cf. e.g. Boden (1977), Born (in this volume), Dennett (1978a), Hofstadter (1980), Lucas (1961), Taube (1961), Turing (1950) and Wiener (1984).

10. This problem is dealt with by e.g. Kobsa (1982), Simon (1979) and Thagard (1984).

11. The assumption of 'tacit knowledge', which is characteristic for some people working in the field of AI, involves in its turn some problems I do not deal with here.

12. This has been shown by aphasic impairment as well as by neuropsychological (e.g. dichotic) experiments; cf. Neumaier (1979). By the way, I am in this context not going to discuss the question whether we may, at some point in the future, be able to build a computer that feels pain (cf. Dennett 1978b).

13. Flanagan (1984: 245). This point has already been discussed, e.g. by Dreyfus (1967) and Sayre (1968).

14. Depending on Sayre (1968) it has been pointed out by Boden (1977: 437) that 'Dreyfus is here confusing the information code with the information coded', cf. also Sutherland (1974) and Wilks (1976b).

15. On descriptivistic mentalism cf. e.g. Bresnan (1978), Bresnan and Kaplan (1982), Chomsky (1965, 1968, 1975, 1980), Halle (1978) and Katz (1964, 1966). It should be noted that these mentalists do not deny the explanatory character of psychological theories; in addition, however, they claim that such theories also describe 'inner' phenomena, although these phenomena cannot be directly perceived.

16. Some of the ideas presented in the following two sections have already been published in Neumaier (1984).

17. Such formulations can be found, e.g. in Baker (1974), Hacker (1972), Kripke (1982), Richardson (1976) and Wellman (1962). Unfortunately, these authors (like many others) neglect some other crucial notions in Wittgenstein's 'later' philosophy which are closely related to 'criterion', e.g. 'aspect', 'evidence', 'justification' and 'sign'. By the way, sporadic use of some of these terms can already be found in *PR*; e.g. in *PR* 7 Wittgenstein emphasizes that language cannot transcend the possibility of evidence, and in *PR* 181 he wonders whether there are criteria for the completeness of a series of numbers.

18. Hacker (1972: 288). For reasons of justice it should be noted that the Oxford philosophers mentioned in the text in the meantime have renounced their earlier interpretations.

19. Resistance to the Oxford interpretation does by no means amount to making criteria inductive grounds, because it makes no sense to apply the usual distinction between logical and inductive grounds to Wittgenstein's argumentation. For reasons of space, however, I cannot discuss this point here in more detail.

20. This development has been denied by some authors, e.g. by Richardson (1976: 110ff.) who holds that 'there are no important changes from the *Blue Book* onwards, in what constitutes a criterion'. I hope to show in this chapter that this assumption is mistaken.

21. Compare, e.g., the remark from MS 174 mentioned in my introduction together with *RPP* I 137 and II 682. In another remark (from MS 173) Wittgenstein emphasizes that it is not the case that the relation between the 'inner' and outer would explain the uncertainty of psychological evidence but that, on the contrary, this relation is only a pictorial illustration of that uncertainty. In the following, the problem of evidence is only dealt with in *psychological* context, i.e. with respect to phenomena like 'understanding', 'feeling pain' etc.

22. To be sure, the notion of inference is used in this context in a technical sense, i.e. as a theoretical, explanatory term which does not necessarily describe what is going on in our brains. This should be clear from the very set-up of this article.

23. Cf., e.g., *BB* 47; *LWP* I 321ff.; *PI* I 25, 157, 283, 357ff.; *RPP* I 96, II 623f. In some remarks of MS 173 (i.e. of *LWP* II) Wittgenstein even considers the case of a man who 'has' no soul. Of course, Wittgenstein thereby does not exclude the possibility of ascribing certain 'inner' processes (e.g. pain) to other beings (e.g. animals); he points out, however, that we learn to do so before the background of *human* life.

24. *RPP* I 324. The same fact is stated by Wittgenstein in *PI* 193 in the following way: 'If we know the machine, everything else, that is its movement, seems to be already completely determined'. So it seems that it is indeterminacy of behaviour (or 'free will') which distinguishes men from machines.

25. *PI* I 25; my emphasis. To be sure, Wittgenstein there speaks not of psychological language games, but of language in general; this does not matter for our purposes, however, all the more so since Wittgenstein uses this argument to show that animals do not talk and, hence, do not think.

26. *PI* II iv (p. 178g). The formulation in *RPP*, the preparatory studies for *PI*, is slightly different: 'The human being is the best picture of the human soul' (*RPP* I 281); this variation, in my opinion, does not change the argument.

27. *PI* I 344; cf. also *RPP* I 841, II 623-7. There is also one remark in MS 173 (i.e. *LWP* II), where Wittgenstein emphasizes that our ascription of 'inner' states depends on the context of human behavior and that it is language which, together with countenance, represents human behavior in its most refined way. In doing so, Wittgenstein refuses the core of Turing's (1950) test (see below).

28. Cf., e.g., *PI* I 283, where Wittgenstein thoroughly emphasizes the word 'has' in the context of mental predicates. This emphasis, which to my knowledge has not sufficiently been taken into account in the exegesis of Wittgenstein, strongly indicates that something is wrong with the assumption that someone 'has' pain etc.

29. Boden (1977: 439). This argument has been introduced by Dreyfus (1979) and is discussed by Boden; it seems to get lost in the course of her discussions, however, for she concludes that 'the philosophical arguments most commonly directed against artificial intelligence are unconvincing', without refuting this particular objection against AI.

30. Cf. *PI* II xi (p. 223f). This statement is less explicit in the preparatory studies: 'So sometimes someone is transparent, sometimes not' (*RPP* II 560; cf. also *LWP* I 193-8).

31. *RPP* II 240; cf. further, e.g. *PG* I 65; *PI* I *passim*; *RPP* I 920, II 194, 216, 220; but also *TLP* 3.323 and 4.002.

32. Cf. *LWP* I 190 (= *PU* II xi, p. 223h): 'If a lion could talk we could not understand him'; cf. also *LWP* I 674f. In the context of AI this example has been discussed by, e.g., Boden (1977), Dreyfus (1979), Hofstadter (1980) and Obermeier (1983).

33. *PI* I 142; cf., e.g., also *PI* I 157 and *RPP* II 186ff.

34. *PI* I 193. In the next paragraph Wittgenstein answers the question about when we think in this way with the following words: 'Well, when one is doing philosophy. And what leads us into thinking that? The kind of way in which we talk about machines'. We can conclude from this remark that with respect to machines other language games than those considered by Wittgenstein are possible and meaningful too.

35. During the last years of Wittgenstein's life 'change of aspect' became one of the central notions in his philosophy which is repeatedly dealt with in *LWP* and *RPP*.

36. *PG* I 69; cf. also *PI* I 69. In two remarks of MS 176, which were written during the last days of Wittgenstein's life, he reconsiders the change from our primitive concepts, which are based on 'imponderable evidence', to clearly defined terms the criteria of which are based on measurable phenomena; e.g. we could define 'lying' by what is measured by a lie-detector. Yet, Wittgenstein asks, if provided

with such means, would we indeed change our form of life? He seems to deny this, for he emphasizes that where measuring does not matter to us, we do not use it even if we *could*.
37. Boden (1977: 423). By the way, this very change in the meaning of the psychological expressions used in AI has as another result the exclusion of the Gödel argument (cf. under 'The Gödel Argument'), for what cannot be expressed by means of effective procedures simply falls out of consideration. This problem is discussed in some detail by Born in Chapter 8 of this book.
38. McCarthy (1979: 161f.). Cf. also Boden (1977), Quillian (1968), Raphael (1968) and Schank (1975, 1979).
39. Cf., e.g., Taube (1961: Ch. vi). Dreyfus's (1979) critique of AI mainly rests on this problem; however, in this respect he is beating the air, because computer scientists seem to have already been aware of this point. Nevertheless, one problem remains, i.e. until today it is not at all clear what is meant exactly by the 'simulation' of human cognitive processes by computer programs, for this concept is mostly used metaphorically.
40. In this chapter I do not deal with e.g. *ethical* problems of AI; these are discussed, e.g., by Boden (1977) and Weizenbaum (1976). I should only like to point to one ethical reason which could prevent us from ascribing 'inner' states to machines: if we did the latter, this would have some ethical consequences; in some circumstances we should e.g. have pangs of conscience with regard to computers. It seems to me that we are not willing to put up with this consequence, but that we would like to use machines for all appropriate purposes without being troubled by any pangs of conscience. Consider in this context Wittgenstein's example of a tribe about whose people we are informed by 'the government and the scientists' that they 'have no souls; *so* they can be used without scruple for any purposes whatever' (*RPP* I 96; my emphasis).

# References

## Works by Wittgenstein

BB     *The Blue and Brown Books* Oxford, 1958
LWP   *Last Writings on the Philosophy of Psychology* vol. 1, G.H. von Wright and H. Nyman (eds); tr. by C.G. Luckhardt and M.A.E. Aue, Oxford, 1982
PG     *Philosophical Grammar,* ed. by R. Rhees; tr. by A. Kenny, Oxford, 1974
PI      *Philosophical Investigations* G.E.M. Anscombe and R. Rhees (eds); tr. by G.E.M. Anscombe, second edition, Oxford, 1958
PR     *Philosophical Remarks,* ed. by R. Rhees; tr. by R. Hargreaves and R. White, Oxford, 1975
RC     *Remarks on Colour,* ed. by G.E.M. Anscombe, tr. by L.L. McAlister and M. Schättle, Oxford, 1977
RFM   *Remarks on the Foundations of Mathematics* G.H. von Wright, R. Rhees and G.E.M. Anscombe (eds); tr. by G.E.M. Anscombe, third edition, revised and reset, Oxford, 1978
RPP   *Remarks on the Philosophy of Psychology,* 2 vols., G.E.M. Anscombe, G.H. von Wright and H. Nyman (eds); tr. by G.E.M. Anscombe (vol. 1), C.G. Luckhardt and M.A.E. Aue (vol. 2), Oxford, 1980
TLP    *Tractatus Logico-Philosophicus,* tr. by D.F. Pears and B.F. McGuinness, London, 1961
Z       *Zettel,* G.E.M. Anscombe and G.H. von Wright (eds); tr. by G.E.M. Anscombe, Oxford, 1967

## Works by Other Authors

Anderson, A.R. (ed.), (1964) *Minds and Machines*, Englewood Cliffs, NJ
Baker, G.P. (1974) 'Criteria: a New Foundation for Semantics', *Ratio*, 16, 156-89
Block, N.J. and Fodor, J.A. (1972) 'What Psychological States Are Not', *Philosophical Review*, 81, 159-81
Boden, M.A. (1977) *Artificial Intelligence and Natural Man*, Hassocks
Bresnan, J. (1978) 'A Realistic Transformational Grammar' in M. Halle, J. Bresnan and G.A. Miller (eds), *Linguistic Theory and Psychological Reality*, Cambridge, MA, pp. 1-59
— and Kaplan, R.M. (1982) 'Grammars as Mental Representations of Language' in J. Bresnan (ed.), *The Mental Representation of Grammatical Relations*, Cambridge, MA, pp. xvii-lii
Canfield, J.V. (1981) *Wittgenstein. Language and World*, Amherst, MA
Cherry, C. (1978) *On Human Communication. A Review, a Survey, and a Criticism*, third edition, Cambridge, MA
Chomsky, N. (1965) *Aspects of the Theory of Syntax*, Cambridge, MA
—— (1968) *Language and Mind*, New York
—— (1975) *Reflections on Language*, New York
—— (1980) *Rules and Representations*, Oxford
Dennett, D.C. (1978a) 'The Abilities of Men and Machines' in Dennett (1978c), pp. 256-66
—— (1978b) 'Why You Can't Make a Computer that Feels Pain' in Dennett (1978c), pp. 190-229
—— (1978c) *Brainstorms. Philosophical Essays on Mind and Psychology*, Montgomery, VT
Dreyfus, H.L. (1967) 'Why Computers Must Have Bodies in Order to Be Intelligent', *Review of Metaphysics*, 21, 13-32
—— (1979) *What Computers Can't Do. The Limits of Artificial Intelligence*, 2nd rev. edition, New York
Flanagan, O.J. (1984) *The Science of the Mind*, London
Gödel, K. (1931) 'Über formal unentscheidbare Sätze der Principia Mathematica und verwandter Systeme, I, *Monatshefte für Mathematik und Physik*, 38, 173-98.
Hacker, P.M.S. (1972) *Insight and Illusion. Wittgenstein on Philosophy and the Metaphysics of Experience*, London
Halle, M. (1978) 'Knowledge Unlearned and Untaught: What Speakers Know about the Sounds of Their Language' in Halle, Bresnan and Miller (eds), (1978), pp. 294-303
—— Bresnan, J. and Miller, G.A. (eds), (1978) *Linguistic Theory and Psychological Reality*, Cambridge, MA
Harré, R. (1986) 'The Social Construction of Mind' in R. Barcan-Marcus, G. Dorn and P. Weingartner (eds), (1986) *Logic, Methodology and Philosophy of Science*, Amsterdam
Haugeland, J. (1981) 'Semantic Engines: an Introduction to Mind Design' in Haugeland (ed.), (1981), pp. 1-34
—— (ed.), (1981) *Mind Design. Philosophy, Psychology, Artificial Intelligence*, Boston, MA
Heelan, P.A. (1984) 'Is Visual Space Euclidean?' in Neumaier (ed.), (1984), pp. 1-12
Hofstadter, D.R. (1980) *Gödel, Escher, Bach: an Eternal Golden Braid*, New York
Katz, J.J. (1964) 'Mentalism in Linguistics', *Language*, 40, 124-37
—— (1966) *The Philosophy of Language*, New York
Kenny, A. (1967) 'Criterion' in P. Edwards (ed.), (1967) *The Encyclopedia of Philosophy*, vol. 2, New York, pp. 43-73
Kobsa, A. (1982) 'On Regarding AI Programs as Theories' in R. Trappl (ed.), (1982) *Cybernetics and Systems Research*, Amsterdam, pp. 933-5

172    *A Wittgensteinian View of Artificial Intelligence*

Kripke, S.A. (1982) *Wittgenstein on Rules and Private Language*, Oxford
Lucas, J.R. (1961) 'Minds, Machines and Gödel' in Anderson (ed.), (1964), pp. 3-59
Luckhardt, C.G. (1983) 'Wittgenstein and Behaviorism', *Synthese*, 56, 319-38.
McCarthy, J. (1979) 'Ascribing Mental Qualities to Machines' in Ringle (ed.), (1979), pp. 161-95
Minsky, M. (ed.), (1968) *Semantic Information Processing*, Cambridge, MA
Nedo, M. and Ranchetti, M. (eds), (1983) *Ludwig Wittgenstein. Sein Leben in Bildern und Texten*, Frankfurt am Main
Neumaier, O. (1979) *Biologische und soziale Voraussetzungen der Sprachkompetenz*, Innsbruck
—— (1984) 'The Problem of Criteria for Language Competence' in Neumaier (ed.), (1984), pp. 85-102
—— (ed.), (1984) *Mind, Language and Society*, Vienna
Obermeier, K.K. (1983) 'Wittgenstein on Language and Artificial Intelligence: the Chinese-Room Experiment Revisited', *Synthese*, 56, 339-49
Pylyshyn, Z.W. (1979) 'Complexity and the Study of Artificial and Human Intelligence' in Ringle (ed.), (1979), pp. 23-56
Quillian, M.R. (1968) 'Semantic Memory' in Minsky (ed.), (1968), pp. 227-70
Raphael, B. (1968) 'SIR: Semantic Information Retrieval' in Minsky (ed.), (1968), pp. 33-145
Richardson, J.T.E. (1967) *The Grammar of Justification: an Interpretation of Wittgenstein's Philosophy of Language*, London
Ringle, M. (ed.), (1979) *Philosophical Perspectives of Artificial Intelligence*, Brighton
Sayre, K.M. (1968) 'Intelligence, Bodies, and Digital Computers', *Review of Metaphysics*, 21, 714-23
—— (1979) 'The Simulation of Epistemic Acts' in Ringle (ed.), (1979), pp. 139-60
Schank, R.C. (1975) *Conceptual Information Processing*, Amsterdam
—— (1979) 'Natural Language, Philosophy and Artificial Intelligence' in Ringle (ed.), (1979), pp. 196-224
Searle, J.R. (1980) 'Minds, Brains and Programs' reprinted in this volume.
Simon, H.A. (1984) 'Why Should Machines Learn?' in R.S. Michalski, J.G. Carbonell and T.M. Mitchell (eds), (1984) *Machine Learning. An Artificial Intelligence Approach*, Berlin, pp. 25-37
Simon, T.W. (1979) 'Philosophical Objections to Programs as Theories' in Ringle (ed.), (1979), pp. 225-42
Sutherland, N.S. (1974) 'Computer Simulation of Brain Function' in S.C. Brown (ed.), (1974) *Philosophy of Psychology*, London, pp. 259-68
Taube, M. (1961) *Computers and Common Sense. The Myth of Thinking Machines*, New York
Thagard, P. (1984) 'Computer Programs as Psychological Theories' in Neumaier (ed.), (1984), pp. 77-84
Turing, A.M. (1937) 'On Computable Numbers, with an Application to the Entscheidungsproblem', *Proceedings of the London Mathematical Society*, 42, 230-65
—— (1950) 'Computing Machinery and Intelligence' in Anderson (ed.), (1964), pp. 4-30
Weizenbaum, J. (1976) *Computer Power and Human Reason. From Judgement to Calculation*, San Francisco
Wellman, C. (1962) 'Wittgenstein's Conception of a Criterion', *Philosophical Review*, 71, 433-47
Wiener, N. (1948) *Cybernetics, or Control and Communication in the Animal and the Machine*, New York
Wiener, O. (1984) 'TuringsTest. Vom dialektischen zum binären Denken', *Kursbuch*, 75, 12-37

Wilks, Y. (1976a) 'Philosophy of Language' in E. Charniak and Y. Wilks (eds.), (1976) *Computational Semantics: an Introduction to Artificial Intelligence and Natural Language Comprehension*, Amsterdam, pp. 205-33

—— (1976b) 'Dreyfus' Disproofs', *British Journal for the Philosophy of Science*, 27, 177-85

Winograd, T. (1972) *Understanding Natural Language*, Edinburgh

Winston, P.H. (1977) *Artificial Intelligence*, Reading, MA

# 7 WHAT IS EXPLAINED BY AI MODELS?[1]

Alfred Kobsa

## Introduction

It is sometimes argued, both inside and outside of Artificial Intelligence research (AI), that if one has succeeded in building an AI program which is pretty good at carrying out some specific task, then one has also accounted for a theory (usually it is not specified, of what). See for example Winston (1977, p. 259): 'Occasionally after seeing what a program can do someone will ask for the theory behind it. Often the correct response is that the program *is* the theory' (Winston's emphasis).

Similarly, it is often claimed that a program for simulating some cognitive behavior which is both 'input-output-equivalent' to the human behavior and 'structurally equivalent' to the processes generating that behavior (whatever that means) would also be an explanation.

Such claims are sometimes called into question by counter-intuitive examples like Weizenbaum's (1976) benighted medieval clockwork-builders who will never be able to discover the Newtonian laws underlying the operation of their apparatus by merely building more and more sophisticated clockwork mechanisms.

Or take the plastic bird example presented in Kobsa (1982b): some years ago an 'artificial bird' was very popular as a children's toy in Austria. Inside its body there was an elastic string connected to the plastic wings of the bird. This could be released. Having been let loose, the bird slowly flew to the ground in a way which looked quite natural, by fluttering its wings. Can we regard this bird as an explanation of 'flying' (natural birds' flying, artificial birds' flying, flying in general)? Nevertheless, we are certainly able to state structural relationships between our bird and natural birds!

In the last few years the goal of AI has shifted somewhat from 'making computers smarter' (Raphael, 1976) to 'understanding intelligent processes independent of their particular physical realization' (Goldstein and Papert 1977, p. 85). So Artificial Intelligence also attempts to account for our 'real world', i.e. has not

174

only technological, but also scientific goals. But then the results of AI and their interpretation cannot be judged only by technological criteria, viz. their contribution to technological progress; instead we also have to expose these results to generally accepted meta-theoretic criteria which have proven useful in other disciplines.

In the following sections I will attempt to do this with respect to the notion of "explanation" (and in some extent also to the notion of "theory") and investigate whether and in what way the thesis that a program can be regarded as an explanation holds true. I will try to place the intuitive objections mentioned above on a firm base and to show their correctness in many interpretations of this thesis. Using functional analysis as a meta-theoretical framework, I will moreover attempt to exemplify what explanations based essentially on AI modelling might look like. I thereby do not want to advocate functionalism, though a 'functional stance' is at present nearly unanimously accepted in Computer Science and Cognitive Psychology. My primary concern is to demonstrate the need for high-level generalizations, functional generalizations might serve as promising candidates.

**What is an Explanation?**

In ordinary language the term 'explanation' is used in a very broad and vague sense. Usually it is related to the notion of 'making something more intelligible', which is sometimes also required for scientific explanations (e.g. Boden, 1962). We have to be somewhat careful with such a claim. Also the view that 'explanation is reduction to the familiar' raises some problems. The terms 'intelligibility' and 'familiarity' involve a strong cognitive or even subjective-emotional component which make them dubious criteria for the acceptability of presumptive explanations. 'One person's familiars are another's marvels' (Rescher, 1970). And the appeal to God may sometimes cause 'deeper' subjective understanding than elaborated theories.[2]

Of course, the claim that new theories should be compatible with, or preferably rely upon or support established theoretical constructions is correct. Also, the problem that sometimes in the process of scientific explanation one ultimately has to appeal to 'intuitively intelligible' assertions is not at all called in question.

For Nagel (1961) 'explanations are answers to the question "Why?" '. But science can only answer a specific interpretation of this question, namely 'How, in accordance with what rules did some event occur?'; it cannot account for the 'deeper reasons' why they occurred (*ratio essendi*). Eysenck (1970, p. 389) even argues that "why" questions in the latter sense 'are meaningless and cannot, by definition, have any answer, "how" questions do have answers, discoverable by science.'

So for the present purpose a first minimum requirement for an explanation will be not only to describe individual cases of our 'real world', but also to enable us to see them as instances of some regular pattern. Thus, an explanation usually makes use of a set of generalizations (the *theory*) under which one can subsume these individuals. The generalizations will not be required to have any specific formal character, e.g. to be proposition-like. They only have to render possible the derivation of representations of all individuals which are claimed to be explainable using the theory.

Nor are these generalizations required to be 'laws which nature obeys'; we can primarily regard them as abstract constructions, the appropriateness of which has to be established in practice.

The derivability of representations of individuals is certainly only a minimum requirement for an adequate explanation. Explanation is not only deduction, i.e. not only a two-termed relation between theory and fact. An acceptable explanation, moreover, must meet certain pragmatic conditions, i.e. the acceptability of an explanation is context-dependent. An interesting analysis of this characteristic is provided by Van Fraassen (1980).

One of these pragmatic criteria is the appropriateness of the language in which the theoretic generalizations are formulated, viz. the appropriateness of the level of language. This stems from the demand that explanations should uncover the essential and leave out the inessential, a requirement worth keeping in mind when investigating the value of AI models for explanation.

To substantiate this claim let us consider an example proposed by Putnam (1973, p. 131) as an argument against reductionism:

My example will be a system of two macroscopic objects, a board in which there are two holes, a square hole 1″ across and a round hole 1″ in diameter, and a square peg, a fraction less than 1″ across. The fact to be explained is: The peg goes through the square hole, and it does not go through the round hole.

One explanation is the peg is approximately rigid under transportation and the board is approximately rigid. The peg goes through the hole that is large enough and not through the hole that is too small. Notice that the micro-structure of the board and the peg is irrelevant to this explanation. All that is necessary is that, whatever the micro-structure may be, it be compatible with the board and the peg being approximately rigid objects.

Suppose, however, we describe the board as a cloud of elementary particles (for simplicity, we will assume these are Newtonian elementary particles) and imagine ourselves given the position and velocity at some arbitrary time $t_0$ of each one. We then describe the peg in a similar way. (Say the board is 'cloud B' and the peg is 'cloud A'.) Suppose we describe the round hole as 'region 1' and the square hole as 'region 2'. Let us say that by a heroic feat of calculation we succeed in proving that 'cloud A' will pass through 'region 2', but not through 'region 1'. Have we explained anything?

Putnam argues that we have only *deduced* the fact but not explained it. For 'whatever the pragmatic constraints on explanation may or may not be, one constraint is surely this: That the relevant features of a situation should be brought out by an explanation and not be buried in a mass of irrelevant information' (Putnam, 1973, p. 132). The relevant features in this example are described by theorems of geometry and not by theorems of physics. So we shift perspective and use some different language. But note, in order to be allowed to do so we had to presuppose the rigidity of the peg and the board, which is 'so to speak, an organizational result of microstructure' (Putnam, 1973, p. 133) and which is perhaps explained by this microstructure. But, as Putnam put it: 'Explanation is not transitive.'

## What is an AI Model?

To begin with, let us start with a black box together with something called input ("*i*") and output ("*o*"). Both input and output consist of a set of discrete atomic signs, some of them usually concatenated according to the rules of some grammar. As outside spectators, we are able to give some interpretation for these signs by attributing meaning or reference to entities of our 'real world' to them. (By "real world" I simply mean a set of potentially acquireable data, i.e. I presuppose no structure in it.) Thus, we can interpret a binary array as 'representing an image' (e.g. of an apple) and the character string "GOD IS DEAD" as representing some proposition in English. By "*I*" and "*O*" I henceforth will refer to the interpretation of "*i*" and "*o*", respectively.

The signs are in principle arbitrarily interpretable. But as Fodor (1980) pointed out, they must at least meet the condition that every semantic distinction which is found appropriate to draw must be expressible by a syntactic distinction.

Let us now render the box a little bit more transclucent. We find a mechanism performing processes of a special kind, namely effectively computable procedures, which is the only well worked-out notion of process we have up to now. Accepting Newell's (1980) coextensive definition, we can also regard the mechanism as a '(physical) symbol system'[3] which performs syntactic operations on uninterpreted signs, accepting "*i*" as input and "*o*" as output.

What is the task of this mechanism? We have designed it in order to reconstruct an aspect of a situation in our real world: whenever we see a specific relation between "*I*" and "*O*" in our world (we always talk about this relation using 'meaningful' terms, so we do not use the syntactic language of our model) we want our mechanism to produce M("i"): = "o" given input "*i*". So, for example, whenever we accept a binary array "*i*" as a representation of an image we require our mechanism to produce output signs "*o*" interpretable as "apple" or "yes" if and only if that image is for us an image of an apple.

Thus, we require this mechanism to be *complete*, i.e. to infer syntactically "*o*" from "*i*" whenever we see that particular relation between the corresponding "*I*" and "*O*". Of course we will also require it to be *sound* in the sense that every "*o*" it infers from an "*i*" we accept as a valid representation of some "*I*" be interpretable and have a specific interpretation "*O*" only if "*I*" and "*O*" are in the specific relation we wanted to reconstruct.[4]

Principally, there is no fixed interpretation for our mechanism's input and output signs. Therefore the interpretation of the operation of the system as a whole, which depends on the interpretation of the input and output signs, is also arbitrary. Think of Searle's (1980) manipulator for Chinese-character-like symbols and not of the binary array which for us is a 'natural' representation of an image of an apple; of course in AI (unfortunately, because seductive — see ELIZA?) we mostly choose 'natural' symbol structures as input and output signs, which have an 'intuitive' and (usually) unique meaning for us. To explore why they are 'natural representations' (i.e. which of their features bring about that we automatically attribute meaning to them) is one of the tasks of AI, amongst other disciplines.

## What is Explained by AI Models?

Our box gulping "$i$" and yielding " $o$", if and only if there is a specific relation between "$I$" and "$O$" in our 'real world', already has two important characteristics, regardless of what mechanism there is in the box:

First, it is certainly predictive: whenever we want to know what "$O$" a specific "$I$" is related to in our world we only need to feed the corresponding "$i$" into our mechanism. The interpretation of the resulting "$o$" gives us the answer.

Secondly, we can regard it as a generalization of the behavior it is able to produce. Every input-output pair we can deduce from it is subsumable under it. So we may claim the model to be a theory about these input-output pairs and the deduction to be an explanation of these input-output pairs.

Apart from the fact that one may doubt whether the language of computer programs or low-level flowcharts is appropriate for stating generalizations, i.e. whether it is capable of revealing the essential and leaving out the inessential, I believe there is little sense in regarding a computer program as an 'explanation' of the input-output pairs we can deduce from it. The interesting question is: What makes it possible for an AI program to exhibit a certain behavior, i.e. what characteristics enable it to carry out some specific task? But no matter how difficult it is to design them, AI programs are not theories about structures, mechanisms and processes capable of generating certain behavior: they *are* these structures, mechanisms and processes.

Of course, one may try to identify the input and output signs of an AI model with their 'meaningful' interpretations and regard the AI model as a generalization about "$I$"-"$O$" pairs, i.e. — as we consider AI models — human input-output pairs. So we see our model as a reconstruction of how people produce "$O$" from

"*I*". Very roughly one can regard this as a first-hand goal of psychology. In doing so we have subsumed these behavior patterns under some regularity; according to our criterion we are therefore able to explain this behavior through our AI model. (Here, I ignore the problem of the appropriateness of language and other pragmatic criteria which one may set up for an adequate explanation.)

This explanatory content of an AI model is independent of the kind of mechanism used in the interior of the model. What is achieved if we can state morphisms between the working of some AI model and the way the corresponding behavior is produced by people ('simulation models')? If we accept that explanation is not only structural analysis and a description of our world, but also has to relate the discovered (postulated!) individuals to some regularity, then we do not thereby extend the explanatory scope of our model. In this case as well, I suggest, neither the AI mechanism nor the morphism is a theory about the structures, mechanisms and processes (or whatever else one supposes might enable people to exhibit certain behavior), and can therefore not explain them.

A somewhat opposed view claims that this kind of analysis would provide a special style of explanation, recently called 'systematic explanation' (Haugeland, 1978). The characteristics of this kind of explanation are suggested to be that an ability is explained through appeal to a specified structure of a mechanism, and to specified abilities of any mechanism having the same structure and interaction among its sub-parts. I will accept this definition, but I want to shift the emphasis to its second part. The first half requires only the description of an individual; a structurally or functionally equivalent AI model may be of considerable help in that task. Assertions as those specified in the second part of the definition require generalizations *about* mechanisms, structures and interactions, which certainly cannot be identical to one of these individuals.[5]

In the following sections I hope to be able to clarify these important distinctions.

## Functions, Decomposition, and Functional Explanation

In order to answer the question as to what makes it possible for an AI model to exhibit certain behavior, i.e. in order to make AI models the object of our investigation, we have to invent a new language and find a new perspective from which we can resume our efforts of explanation.

To explain the abilities of computer models in general, people in computer science usually refer to the function of sub-parts of the model. The function (or purpose) of a mechanism thereby is seen as the effects of the mechanism which are necessary for a proper operation of the whole system or some component of it. In order to name these features one has to create some abstract vocabulary, so one leaves the language of the computer model.

To give an example: upon asking for the purpose of some part of a program one will usually hear answers like: 'This part checks whether a client has already settled his open accounts before accepting his new orders.' The answer is apparently formulated in a task-related language. It specifies a function by referring to some background knowledge of the characteristics of a task and of properties of systems capable of carrying out that task. (It is therefore somewhat difficult to present examples from AI.)

Functional analysis is not restricted to abstracting from mechanisms only: the result of the interaction of several functions can itself be subsumed under some higher-level functional term. The result is some functional decomposition, the lower-level functional terms being closely related to the specific mechanism, the higher-level functional terms indicating the contribution of the specific function to the accomplishment of the task.

Thus, when defining functional concepts in computer science we have to consider their decomposability into a system of lower-level functions or their realizability by effective procedures, their role in some organizational context and, if possible, their contribution to the overall operation of the system. Having defined them via abstraction from mechanisms, we are sure not to have evoked demons with miraculous powers; we are always able to refer to physical realizations of these concepts. The choice of functional concepts is essentially pragmatic, they are abstract constructions which have to prove their appropriateness in practice.

I want to emphasize that I by no means want to vote for any sort of reductionism via functional decomposition, viz. type functionalism. I think there are two main arguments against the fruitfulness of such efforts:

First, as pointed out by Haugeland (1978), a successful functional reduction does not render the higher-level functional terms superfluous. A multi-level perspective contributes to revealing the essential and leaving out the inessential, as illustrated by Putnam's (1973) example cited above. Every new level adds new information about functional interaction at this level. The decomposability of these functions is presupposed, but details of the specific decomposition are irrelevant.

Secondly, I doubt whether for many complicated mechanisms a 'precise' hierarchical functional decomposition (in the sense of complete deducability of higher-level functional types from lower-level functional types) is possible at all levels. The subsumption of some functional interaction under some higher-level functional term will often be 'approximative' (but precise enough to allow for a scientifically interesting description).

Or vice versa, in order to account for higher-level types by means of lower-level types one usually has to use appropriate idealizations and add 'boundary conditions' accidental from the perspective of lower-level terms (see Putnam, 1973, 1974; Lugg, 1974).

So going from the bottom up through several levels we may finally arrive at what can be called a 'nearly-decomposable system' (not exactly in the sense of Simon, 1969!), i.e. a system in which the functional types can only be imprecisely decomposed, while the functional tokens can be accounted for without any problems by referring to lower-level functional tokens.

To illustrate this, let us take an example from biology where we also find thoroughly explored functional decompositions: one can account for the notion of (mammalian) digestion — an opaque natural kind of somatology — by referring to the interaction of the digestive organs, presuming that an energy supply is necessary for their proper functioning. For certain purposes this is doubtlessly an adequate level of description. But there is no sense trying to account for the term 'digestion' at the cellular or even subcellular level. The question whether the transport of oxygen by erythrocytes has to be included in the reduction of the type 'digestion' can hardly be answered.

Functional terms are independent of the mechanisms underlying them. So given an accepted functional decomposition we can set out looking for 'functional alternatives', i.e. mechanisms with the same function (and no side-effects hampering parallel functions) which we can use as substitutes for the original mechanism. The set of possible functional substitutes for a mechanism forms a functional equivalence class.

We can now set out stating generalizations based on these

equivalence classes, thus conferring explanatory power upon our notion of function. Up to now they were merely abstractions or categorizations.

Adapting the deductive scheme presented by Hempel (1959) we get:

(a) at time *t*, a model *M* adequately infers "*o*" from "*i*";
(b) given an accepted functional decomposition of *M*, *M* adequately infers "*o*" from "*i*", only if a specific requirement *n* is satisfied;
(c) *F* is the equivalence class of mechanisms, the function of which satisfies *n*, and *F* is not empty;
(d) one of the mechanisms of *F* is present in *M* at *t*.

Using this scheme, we can account for the presence of a particular mechanism in our model *M* by pointing out that this mechanism serves a certain function (purpose) which — given a particular functional decomposition of *M* — we regard as absolutely indispensable. Thus, we have subsumed the occurrence of that mechanism under some regularity.

Since the interaction of several functions can also be subsumed under a functional term, we can form equivalence classes from systems of functions serving the same higher-level function and hence account for the presence of such a system in the model by the above explanatory scheme, if we regard the result of this functional interaction as indispensable.

And how can we justify that a particular function is indispensable in a functional decomposition? We supply appropriate reasons by referring to the role it plays in some major context, viz. its contribution to the presence of some higher-level function which itself is regarded as indispensable. The terminal function in this sequence is the working of the model as a whole.

To put the above statements more precisely: in a strict sense we can only deduce (and according to our criteria therefore explain) functions and functional decompositions or sets of mechanisms capable of exhibiting some behavior. We cannot explain why a specific mechanism of a functional equivalence class is present in a model *M*, nor — more general — why *M* is the realization of a specific functional decomposition. (As we have only considered computer models up to now, we can preliminarily leave this problem aside, considering it to be a 'design decision'.) I will henceforth use the terms "explanation of mechanisms" and "explanation of a realization of a theory" having these provisos in mind.

The reasons we give to justify the generalizations will be empirical, referring to the nature (constraints) of a task and the contribution of the functions of a functional decomposition to the accomplishment of that task. In many cases this will probably include assumptions about the structure of our world and specifications for which parts of a functional decomposition implicitly embody or explicitly represent these assumed structures.

Thus, by combining what Cummins (1975) has called *analytical strategy* (our search for an appropriate functional decomposition) with *subsumption strategy* we have finally arrived at a multi-level hierarchy of explanation through subsumption under generalizations, which is also *systematic* in the sense of Haugeland (1978).

A single functional decomposition need not be appropriate for all models capable of carrying out some task. As Marr (1977) pointed out there may be several entirely different algorithms for a task. In that case one may try to carefully change the functional framework in order to account for these models as well, and arrive at what Marr (1977) seems to have meant by 'computational theory', or one may try to give reasons why this is not possible. If we are able to do either, then we have probably understood the characteristics of the models and the nature and constraints of the task, by virtue of which the models are capable of carrying out that task (see Pylyshyn, 1978, 1980).

### Trying to Account for Real World Relations

Up to now we have defined a deductive scheme based on the notion of function, which we used to explain mechanisms which syntactically inferred a sequence of signs "$o$" from a sequence of signs "$i$". With "$I$" and "$O$" we referred to the interpretation of "$i$" and "$o$", respectively. The task of this mechanism was to reconstruct some relation between "$I$" and "$O$" in our real world by syntactic means.

Having developed our multi-level explanatory scheme, we are not content with only being able to explain syntactic reconstructions, i.e. how mechanisms are able to infer "$o$" from "$i$". We are somewhat more ambitious and would also like our explanatory framework to account for the way "$I$" and "$O$" are related in our world, e.g. — as we consider AI models — the way in which people produce "*O*" from "*I*". We do so by postulating that the functional language and the generalizations developed for explaining syntactic mechanisms are also explanatory in respect to the way people produce "*O*" from "*I*".

In order to be justified in doing so, we have to presuppose that there is something in man which can be adequately referred to by our functional vocabulary. As good luck would have it, contemporary cognitive psychologists widely agree upon regarding human cognitive behavior as being the result of processes which may be studied at some abstract ('mental') level, i.e. independently of their particular physical realization (see Kobsa, 1982a). Moreover, current Cognitivism assumes that the effect of these processes can be adequately referred to by what is called *intentional interpretation* (see Haugeland, 1978), corresponds to our notion of function. We therefore postulate the 'human realization'[6] to be one of the many functional substitutes of our functional decomposition, thus we can explain it with the scheme described above. Also in this case we usually cannot deduce specific mechanisms, but only functions or sets of mechanisms. It will be left to other disciplines, e.g. biology, to state generalizations by which we can explain the presence of specific mechanisms.

It is important to note that the notion of function is so vague that it does not from the start require effective, 'mechanistic' or 'deterministic' realizations. Thus, in applying functional terms to human abilities one does not presuppose that 'man is a machine'. But now it becomes apparent that our approach has some considerable advantage: we have acquired our theoretical functional terms via multiple abstraction from symbol-manipulating mechanisms and systems of functions realizable through symbol-manipulating mechanisms. Therefore, as pointed out above, we are certain not to have conjured up homunculi with miraculous powers in our explanatory language. There is at least one possible (viz. effective) realization for every function we have postulated.

Of course, the functional decomposition(s) we chose for explaining our set of possible mechanical models, may be totally inappropriate in accounting for human cognition. In this case there may be some functional decomposition in which both artificial mechanisms and the human mind can be seen as functional alternatives; otherwise we must try to account for why this is not the case.

How can we find out whether a functional framework or

individual functions are appropriate descriptions for human cognition as well? We must design empirical test strategies which, as Pylyshyn (1980) pointed out, can be based only upon abstract processes and not on their spatio-temporal realizations (i.e. mechanisms) or characteristics thereof (e.g. reaction-time). So our tests will mainly rely on the effects of processes, i.e. functions, and maybe, also on results of developmental psychology. Seen from the opposite side, methodological constraints obviously support our functional scheme.

As the notion of function is an appropriate abstraction over any sort of process, I see no reason at present why we should suppose that man performs computations, as suggested for example by Pylyshyn (1980) and Fodor (1980). The argument that this is the only well worked-out notion of 'process' which we have to date is not very convincing. For psychological purposes the opaque notion of 'process' will certainly do at present. In order to constrain the set of possible basic functions, as suggested by Pylyshyn (1980) for the purpose of explanation, we also need not consider the set of these functions as a 'virtual machine'.

**What Could be Explained Via AI Modelling?**

With the meta-theoretical framework developed above (which is based mainly on functional analysis) we have accounted for a theory about 'intelligent processes independent of their particular physical realization' (Goldstein and Papert 1977, p. 85). It is a theory about the nature of some ('intelligent') task and the characteristics of models capable of carrying out that task or showing some 'intelligent' behavior.

In our framework, an AI model is merely one instantiation of some functional decomposition, i.e. one member of a (perhaps infinite) set of mechanisms subsumable under this decomposition. Its behavior can be explained by the regularities linking the functions of this decomposition to higher-level functions and to the accomplishment of the task. So an AI model, in model-theoretic terms, is exactly what we have always called it, namely a *model of a theory*. As we can see, this is completely different from a theory.

According to current cognitivistic assumptions, a natural organism capable of exhibiting the same behavior would also fall under some functional decomposition and its generalizations. The reason why we could state functional relations between an AI model and the processes which, according to our postulate, are used by the organism to exhibit that behavior, is simply because their functional decomposition is the same up to an equivalence of one or more functions. So we are now able to specify because of what features these realizations are related models of a theory.

Thus, we can see that in current AI research — apart from the restricted sense described on p. 179 — we do not state theories or explanations but create artificial individuals, comparable with the sophisticated clockworks or the plastic bird. The capabilities of these individuals have to be subsumed under (perhaps functional) explanatory generalizations.

AI modelling is undoubtedly an extremely useful tool in our task of understanding 'intelligent' processes. A successful AI program is a proof that it is possible to realize (better: to reconstruct) some 'intelligent' behavior through effective procedures or '(physical) symbol systems', and that it is possible to realize this behavior in the very way specified by these procedures. Moreover, AI research has certainly revealed many problems which psychological and philosophical research had not previously exposed. But we should be careful not to be seduced into saying more than we justifiably can. In some ways our current situation truly is similar to medieval alchemy, as was suggested by Dreyfus (1965): guided mainly by our intuitions, we mix together computational mechanisms and strive for 'intelligent systems'.

AI modelling certainly does provide us with deeper experience in recognizing what makes it possible for a system to produce certain 'intelligent' behavior. It can be assumed that efforts to make this background experience explicit and to state it in form of generalizations will eventually lead to theories. One may moreover suppose that without such theories, the technological goals of AI cannot be reached. However, there is no guarantee that these conjectures are correct.

## Notes

1. This paper was written while the author was affiliated with the Department of Computer Science, University of Linz, Austria. Much of its content has been inspired by fruitful discussions with R. Born (Univ. of Linz).
2. Eysenck (1970) suggests that the subjective feeling of intuitive understandability of a description depends essentially on the visualizability of that description. See similar results of Johnson-Laird (1975) and Johnson-Laird and

Steedman (1978) in regard to the influence of visualizability on the acceptance of logical syllogisms.

3. I do not see these symbols as 'standing for something', having 'meaning', 'reference', etc. I regard them only as meaningless signs being identifiable entirely by their shapes.

4. This requirement, which I believe to be fundamental whenever we try to reconstruct 'meaningful phenomena' by syntactic means, is lacking in Newell's (1980) exposition of a physical symbol system, though I perceive it as being implicitly presupposed in his somewhat opaque definition of 'designation': according to Newell (p. 156) 'an entity X designates an entity Y relative to a process P, if, when P takes X as input, its behavior depends on Y.' So in order to determine whether X designates Y we have to judge whether the behavior of P 'depends on' Y, ignoring X. The only way to determine that the behavior of P 'depends on' Y and not on Ȳ is to look at what was 'intended' with P and whether P meets these intentions. So at some appropriate step of P (without loss of generality: after P has finished) I will take the results, interpret them and compare them with my intentions. If there is no correspondence I will reject the assertion that the behavior of P depends on Y. But here I presuppose that P is both *sound* and *complete*, so this presupposition is implicit in Newell's definition. The same defect also applies to his definition of 'representation'.

5. Thus AI models do not 'explain the possibility of various kinds of mental processes, including learning, perceiving, solving problems, and understanding language', as was suggested by Sloman (1978, p. 27). For Sloman an explanation of (the possibility of) X is (roughly) some theory or system of representation which generates (the possibility of) X (p. 45). But even if we find equivalences between human behavior and the interpretation of a model's input-output pairs we do not generate (i.e. explain) 'mental processes', but only human input-output pairs.

As for Sloman (1978, p. 45) a 'request for an explanation of a possibility or range of possibilities is characteristically expressed in the form "How is X possible?"' AI models, for the same reasons, also do not give answers in *his* sense to questions like 'How is it possible to *interpret* an untidy collection of visual data as representing such and such a scene?' or 'How is it possible for locally ambiguous image fragments to *generate* a unique global interpretation' (more precisely: How is it possible for a *mechanism to generate* . . .; Sloman 1978, p. 254; emphasis mine). A similar inexactness in the use of the notion of 'explanation' can be observed in Brachman and Smith's (1980) questionnaire (Thesis 44.c, which was supported by most respondents).

6. For the sake of simplification I will presuppose that 'all minds are equal' and that the same behavior is always realized in the same way. Of course, an acceptable functional analysis should also account for individual differences and give reasons why and under what circumstances different 'strategies' are used.

## References

Boden, M.A. (1962) 'The Paradox of Explanation', Proceedings of the Aristotelian Society S.A., vol. 62, pp. 159-78. Reprinted in M.A. Boden (1981) *Minds and Mechanisms: Philosophical Psychology and Computational Models*, Brighton, Sussex, Harvester, pp. 113-29

Brachman, R.J. and Smith, B.C. (eds) (1980) *SIGART Newsletter No. 70* (Special Issue on Knowledge Representation)

Cummins, R. (1975) 'Functional Analysis', *Journal of Philosophy*, 72 (20), 741-65

Dreyfus, H. (1965) 'Alchemy and Artificial Intelligence', Report P-3244, Santa Monica, Rand Corporation

Eysenck, H.J. (1970) 'Explanation and the Concept of Personality' in R. Borger and F. Cioffi (eds), *Explanation in the Behavioral Sciences*, Cambridge, Cambridge Univ. Press, pp. 387-424

Fodor, J.A. (1980) 'Methodological Solipsism Considered as Research Strategy in Cognitive Psychology', *The Behavioral and Brain Sciences*, 3, 63-109

Goldstein, I. and Papert, S. (1977) 'Artificial Intelligence, Language and the Study of Knowledge', *Cognitive Science*, 1 (1), 84-123

Haugeland, J. (1978) 'The Nature and Plausibility of Cognitivism', *The Behavioral and Brain Sciences*, 2, 215-60

Hempel, C.G. (1959) 'The Logic of Functional Analysis' in L. Gross (ed.), *Symposium on Sociological Theory*, New York, etc.; Harper & Row, pp. 271-307, reprinted in M. Brodbeck (ed.) (1968) *Readings in the Philosophy of the Social Sciences*, New York, Macmillan, pp. 179-210

Johnson-Laird, P.N. (1975) 'Models of Deduction' in R.J. Falmagne (ed.) *Reasoning: Representation and Process in Children and Adults*, Hillsdale, N.J. Erlbaum

—— and Steedman, M. (1978) 'The Psychology of Syllogisms', *Cognitive Psychology*, 10, 64-99

Kobsa, A. (1982a) 'Künstliche Intelligenz und Kognitive Psychologie' (Artificial Intelligence and Cognitive Psychology) in H. Schauer and M.J. Tauber (eds.), *Informatik und Psychologie*, Wien-München, Oldenbourg, pp. 133-68, reprinted in J. Retti *et al.* (1984) *Artificial Intelligence — Eine Einführung*, Stuttgart, B.G. Teubner, pp. 99-124

—— (1982b) 'On Regarding AI Programs as Theories' in R. Trappl (ed.) *Cybernetics and Systems Research*, Amsterdam-New York, North-Holland, pp. 933-5

Lugg, A. (1974) 'Putnam on Reductionism', *Cognition*, 3 (3), 289-93

Marr, D. (1977) 'Artificial Intelligence: A Personal View', *Artificial Intelligence*, 9, 37-48

Nagel, G. (1961) *The Structure of Science*, New York, Harcourt, Brace & World

Newell, A. (1980) 'Physical Symbol Systems', *Cognitive Science*, 4, 135-83

Putnam, H. (1973) 'Reductionism and the Nature of Psychology', *Cognition*, 2 (1), 131-46

—— (1974) 'Reply to Lugg', *Cognition*, 3 (3), 295-8

Pylyshyn, Z.W. (1978) 'Computational Models and Empirical Constraints', *The Behavioral and Brain Sciences*, 1, 93-127

—— (1980) 'Computation and Cognition. Issues in the Foundations of Cognitive Science', *The Behavioral and Brain Sciences*, 3, 111-69

Raphael, B. (1976) *The Thinking Computer: Mind Inside Matter*, San Francisco, W.H. Freeman

Rescher, N. (1970) *Scientific Explanation*, New York, The Free Press

Searle, J.R. (1980) 'Minds, Brains and Programs', *The Behavioral and Brain Sciences*, 3, 417-57

Simon, H.A. (1969) *The Sciences of the Artificial*, Cambridge, MA, MIT Press

Sloman, A. (1978) *The Computer Revolution in Philosophy: Philosophy, Science and Models of Mind*, Hassocks, Sussex, Harvester

Van Fraassen, B.C. (1980) *The Scientific Image*, Oxford, Clarendon Press

Weizenbaum, J. (1976) *Computer Power and Human Reason: From Judgement to Calculation*, San Francisco, Freeman

Winston, P.H. (1977) *Artificial Intelligence*, Reading, MA., Addison-Wesley

# 8 SPLIT SEMANTICS: PROVOCATIONS CONCERNING THEORIES OF MEANING AND PHILOSOPHY IN GENERAL

Rainer P. Born

Nothing is more difficult and nothing needs more character than to be in open conflict with one's time and openly say: 'No!' (Tucholsky)

## Summary

In the context of a general scheme explicating the relation between language, information and reality, two components important for the way in which understanding of meaning is brought about are identified, namely theoretical and vernacular background knowledge. The conflation of explanatory and descriptive (operative) conceptions in the context of applying theories to reality is made responsible for a series of problems concerning the relation of theory and reality.

## The Philosophy of the Silent Majority

The starting point of my considerations and my point of departure from ordinary reflections is a strictly speaking *explanatory analysis* of the functioning and of the methods of (formal) semantics. At the same time, it is an analysis of the methodology of *analytic philosophy* in general. Though the latter can hardly be characterized by a special content, it can well be characterized by a special approach (a searching strategy) for the solution of diverse problems. This is particularly evident in the field of epistemology, where, in the framework of analytic philosophy, the original question as to *what* knowledge/cognition is has been replaced by the question, '*How* knowledge *is acquired?*'

When adopting this approach, we concentrate primarily on the

190

role and the expressive power of language(s), in so far as this 'expressive power' or 'linguistic resolution level' can be considered as decisive for the *acquisition* of knowledge. In general, one could say that what I am concerned with is the dependence of what knowledge is on those (e.g. linguistic) *means,* the application of which brings about, justifies and perhaps explains the *grasping* of the content of meaning or content of information (or simply of the meaning in the sense of significance) of a linguistic expression.

Starting from this background, I shall deal with the claim that (formal) semantics can contribute essentially to the clarification of the role which 'understanding meaning' plays in the context of communicating information (with the help of written or verbal means of expression). In a tentatively summarized way one could say that I am here concerned with how *grasping* the 'meaning of (linguistic) expressions occurs' and how the reference of (linguistic) expressions is fixed on the grounds of grasping their meaning (with regard to content). My concern, therefore, originates in a definitely theoretico-explanatory point of view.

Furthermore, I wish to suggest that the philosophy or theory of science should be understood as 'meta-theoretical investigations' into the model-theoretical or even mathematical *structure* of special scientific disciplines. Philosophy of science might also be regarded as a theory to 're-construct' the arrival at decisions about the acceptance and enforcement or spread of certain scientific results in so far as these are understood to be caused by rational arguments. If we accept these presuppositions, the relevance of investigations into an analysis of the *cognitive content* of scientific results is evident. This fact explains the interest in theoretical considerations concerned with how the 'grasping of meaning' occurs and with how the 'reference of linguistic expressions becomes fixed' in scientific inquiries.

In order to implement these themes, I shall concentrate on a general scheme for the discussion and integration of considerations about the relations between 'language', 'information' and 'reality' (LIR for short). In this framework a series of *conceptual split-ups,* i.e. distinctions which are crucial for our objectives, can be introduced. Since the scheme has already been introduced in Born (1982, 1983), at least in a semi-technical way, I want to concentrate here on examples, consequences and possibilities of application and turn to technical formulations at the end of this chapter.

As a first example of a series of 'distinctions' (more or less explicitly contained in the scheme LIR) I want to mention the fact that the *means* we apply in order to *study* the 'meaning' (or significance) of linguistic expressions are not normally those with which we build up or convey 'meaning'. For explanatory purposes only this much need be considered for the time being: If we study, for example in the framework of the so-called statement view of theories, a special scientific discipline as a 'system of true sentences between which there exist relations of deduction', then it does not by any means follow that we can convey an understanding of the cognitive content of a certain theory by starting from definitions and axioms for such a 'system of sentences' and by generating all meaningful statements from it with the help of (formal) deductions. The failure to recognize this fact has in many cases led to mistakes in the transformation or misapplication of results from philosophy of science.

The rules which are used to justify knowledge are (normally) not the ones we may use in order to generate knowledge. According to this analysis, theories are *not* directly or literally *descriptive* 'systems of rules'. They need an *interpretative transformation*. This means that we have to learn how to handle theories (cf. M. Polanyi's remarks on 'Tacit Knowledge'). The correct understanding *of the content* or the significance of the results of a special scientific discipline — in a time when their technical transformations invade the remotest spheres of our private lives — requires other means, at least in analysis, and other mechanisms than those provided by the practical application of information in the context of everyday life. (In the zone where these two fields merge fatal misunderstandings do occur — at least occasionally.)

Under normal conditions, the philosophy of science cannot be transformed directly into epistemology.[1] With the help of the scheme LIR (which will be introduced in an intuitive manner with the help of the computer poetry example, see below) the different influences of theoretico-explanatory (scientific) and everyday background knowledge, as well as of metaphors and heuristics, on the way in which the reference of (linguistic) expressions becomes fixed shall be identified as the cause for the phenomena in question. The way in which one fixes reference indicates an understanding of the meaning of expressions, and can be considered as the manifestation of an understanding of the information about the world encoded in those expressions. Furthermore, possibilities for a systematic avoidance of mistakes will be demonstrated.[2]

**Heresies on the Topic: Science and Semantics**

The heresies that will be described by the following example predominantly concern false expectations as regards the efficiency of science. The *ultimate objective* of the example is to turn the tables (cf. the quoted journalist-example) and to show that the same — *wrong* — expectations also apply to the receptions of our so-called 'everyday knowledge'. These false expectations express themselves in the transformation of folk-knowledge into long-term 'cooking recipes for the solution of standard(ized) problems in stereotype(d) situations'.

Therefore, a strategy of *reductio ad absurdum* underlies the construction of the example. I intend to make us aware of tacitly accepted (absurd or simply false) ideas, presuppositions and assumptions. I am thinking of presuppositions which — as I want to impute — seem to underlie many ideas about the 'functioning of science' and which are *manifested* in the assessment and the *understanding* of the asserted content of the results of a special scientific discipline (more precisely: the use based on it).

In my opinion the same applies to the results of considerations in the philosophy of science in general, and especially to the field of formal semantics (as I will show later).[3]

*Computer Poetry — or: Causes and Symptoms*

Let us imagine a 'centre of interdisciplinary computer-communication' (CIC for short), maybe in Tarocania.[4] Tarocania is a fictitious country where the mother tongue is certainly not English. Suppose that the cabinet of Tarocania has decided to have the CIC purchase a computer program P from the MIT (Massachusetts Institute of Technology). This program P is able to simulate and generate English poetry (or literary texts). P should now be studied at the CIC and developed further. Our task, however, is to study the CIC, i.e. the procedures and methods of investigation employed there.

To begin with, the computer specialists (whose knowledge of English may correspond to the interests of a modern general education in Tarocania) will test the P-program (primary program). For this purpose they polish the computer outputs and send them off to various English literary magazines for publication. The replies of the editors, who, not knowing the origin of the poems, interpret and judge them by their content, may be restricted to 'accepted' or 'rejected' (as it is the custom when judging the validity of rational arguments). In any case, there is to be *no* feedback in regard to the content, aesthetic theme or whatever of the poems.

Suppose the result of these tests is a success-rate of 80 per cent positive reactions from the editors. What could our computer engineers do now (given the boundary conditions mentioned above and the technical means at their disposal) in order to improve the given P-program in such a way that the probability of success is raised to 90 per cent?

They will (probably) try to *identify symptoms* (characteristic traits or parameters) which they assume are characteristic for those poems assessed positively (through acceptance).[5] After this, one could systematically try to change the rules contained in the P-program (i.e. the algorithm and perhaps the reservoir of the basic signs admissible for the formation of syntactically well-formed sign-sequences as well) in such a way that a new program ($P_1$-program for short) is the result. This program would then be able to generate those sign-sequences or text figures which could be brought into agreement with the chosen characteristic symptoms.

These symptoms are now used as *criteria* for the *selection* of admissible text figures. If this procedure proves to be successful when tested by sending in the poems and having them judged by the literary experts of the magazines; (i.e. *if* the probability of success is actually raised by 10 per cent), then our computer experts will be able to say — and rightly so, from the point of view of the means at their disposal and the frame of their objectives — that their 'analysis of poems according to characterizing symptoms' has obviously hit the target (or grasped) of what seems to be essential for the generation of good poetry.[6]

Let us now suppose that a secondary program $Q_0$, based on the Tarocanian background-knowledge C, has been developed for the technical assessment of the 'poeticity' of computer outputs. This program takes over the C-assessment just mentioned and is able to enhance the construction and sophistication of the $P_i$-programs ($i = 1, 2 \ldots$).

A real example demonstrating the 'grasping and simulating of unconscious processes of assessment' (in our case the development of $Q_j$-programs ($j = 0, 1, 2 \ldots$) by reason of C-conceptions and everyday background knowledge) is given in Frude (1983: 43), who describes an early machine for the 'differentiation of visual impressions' developed by the physicist John Taylor:

He invented a machine which sexed people's photographs. Pictures were placed beneath a lens which focused the pattern of light and shade on to an array of light-sensitive devices. In an initial training period, as well as having all the data from the array, the machine was informed whether the photograph was that of a man or a woman, but after a hundred or so training trials the machine had learned to identify the sex of the portrait correctly. Clearly it was recognising the sex from some pattern in the data from the array of photo-sensors, but quite what this pattern looked like was unknown even to the man who invented the machine. Perhaps we shouldn't be too surprised at this for many human skills, like sexing of faces, are performed reliably without the individual being able to formulate the implicit rules which must be followed for such a feat to be possible.

Of course we now have to ask a few questions: Has the system (machine) *grasped* what a woman or a man *is*? Does it have to do this for the accomplishment of its task? Have we ourselves grasped, by restricting the formulation of the problem, what is essential for the recognition of patterns?

If we now make an interim evaluation of the situation of computer poetry, we could say that the computer experts departed from a purely syntactical sign-language L and from rules for the transformation of signs (in the $P_i$-programs) and in the end had the results judged. It was, however, the message of the poems which was assessed, namely what they seemed to express for the interpreters (readers) in their own world B. The positive feedback of the readers (not, however, in regard to content!) was used to identify 'formal' characteristics which could be used for the selective generation of suitable text-figures. The main ingredients of the procedure at the CIC may be summed up in Figure 8.1, where L designates the realm of signs (or a syntactical, formal language), e.g. restricted English over which the primary programmes $P_i$ operate. C contains the tacit presuppositions and the everyday background knowledge which has been used for the construction of the secondary programs $Q_j$. $Q_j$ was developed by inserting the $P_i$-results ($i = j + 1$) into a field of communication B, in which the L-figures generated by $P_i$ could be read (*interpreted*) as poems of a natural language $L$ (e.g. English), i.e. they could be evaluated (judged) in regard to their *content*, and understood and used in $L$. We could oversimplify by saying that the readers of the poems, when looking at the L-figures,

Figure 8.1

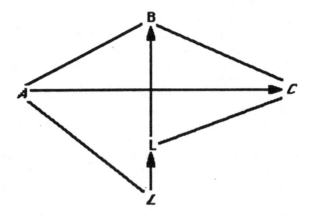

read into them something like a *reference of the content* of information to their own (possible) world B and used a *background knowledge referring to the content A* about their world B for this. *A*
therefore contains 'meaning constitutive' heuristics of assessment,
so to speak, which have led to the selection of meaningful and
therefore acceptable poems (i.e. those fit for publication). *A* therefore *explains* the fixing of reference of *L*-expressions by *L*-language
users.

For further illustration, let us imagine *L* to be the language of
a group of nuclear physicists who discuss the latest experiments in
quantum physics in a rather casual way at a party. We ourselves
are, for the sake of the example, fictitious journalists who were
sent to the party to report on the importance of these experiments
and on their reception by the specialists.

Let it be the case that a certain percentage of the *L*-expressions
is unknown to us so that we can only understand them as *syntactic*
*L*-figures, and so do not know precisely what they refer to or what
they actually mean. We assume, however, that the physicists relate
them to reference objects (or reference-situations) of their world
B with the help of their *A*-background knowledge, i.e. content.
As experienced party-lions we will quickly be able to learn how
to *identify* these ominous expressions by their form and the incom-
pletely comprehended *L*-utterances in which they occur, and
together with the help of our *C*-background knowledge, we will
develop rules for their use at the party. Encouraging nods from

the experts will serve as feedback and guide-lines, and we will learn when to utter the expressions and insert them skilfully at suitable moments during the party-talk so that our linguistic behavior in regard to the use of these expressions will, at least in the small party-world, hardly be distinguishable from that of the experts. We assume, of course, that the experts use the expressions in question correctly on the strength of an $A$-background knowledge in regard to content. Basically, the rules which are developed with the help of $C$ and our native skill for the discreet use of incomprehensible terms are something unconscious, just as is the recognition of sex 'from some pattern in the data from the array of photo-sensors' of the Taylor machine. In a somewhat extreme way we could say that university students similarly grow into the correct use of a technical language long before they really know exactly what all those terms mean.

I hope that this simulates in a straightforward way the situation of the computer example in terms of the everyday experience of students.

As an intermediate result I wanted to show the *different* ways in which the comprehension (or creation) of meaning comes about with the help of an $A$-channel, which is concerned with contents and a simulative $C$-channel using characteristic symptoms or characterizing features. The point of both examples is to identify those ideas and assumptions about the structure of the assumed realms of reference for B which are *built up* with the help of $C$ (respectively the $Q_j$-programs or rules for the use of terms imitated by it). The sign sequences from L (L-figures) are interpreted in B by a detour via $A$ by the users of $L$. If we place a journalist and a Tarocanian computer expert into real B-worlds — i.e. a journalist in a lab and a computer expert in a publishing house — it would quickly become evident that the ideas and assumptions about the meaning of the L-figures built up via $C$ do not lead to the same *behavior* as a B-world picture built up via $A$.

The different ideas and assumptions about B become evident in a different behavior of orientation. Since an $A$-understanding in regard to content does not underlie either the generation or the assessment of poetry (except in a rudimentary sense based on Tarocanian school-experiences), a computer expert transplanted to a publishing house will, because of his insecurity, have to observe the rules developed by himself *like a slave*. Only on reaching an understanding in regard to content will he be able to handle his rules more freely. In any case, we could characterize his behavior as ritualization due to a deficient or incomplete understanding of the content(s) or meaning of the poems.

In order to realize the full potential of the example and the presented conceptions about the 'occurrence' and 'communication' of results of a special scientific discipline caricatured in it, let us suppose that rumours about the success of the $Q_j$-programs have reached an American publishing house. They now want to rationalize the firm by replacing their literary experts (referees) by the $Q_j$-programs. It is sufficient to point out that the probability of success can thereby be raised to 100 per cent, and that in the long run nobody (except in a very trivial sense) needs to understand the message of poems or needs to know what they really express (i.e. needs to understand the intended meaning of poems at all). Through the feedback of acceptance and rejections and their own success (e.g. public recognition, social prestige, money etc.) in producing poetry the writers will be trained to send in such poems as are compatible with the 'tastes' of the computer. *The problem is therefore not that computers will learn to 'think' like human beings but that human beings would start to think like computers.*

We realize now how far we could get away with rules for the controlled generation of artefacts without having to *understand* the content or information of these artefacts.

We could say that, strictly speaking, formal philosophy of science *studies* that kind of rational 'argumentation-behavior' which leads to success and general acceptance of scientific results (within special scientific disciplines). The latter is generally referred to as *context of justification*. The rules for the simulation and reconstruction of this 'argumentation-behavior' (within a 'community of scientists') are, in general, therefore — except for trivial examples — *not directly* (or literally) *descriptive* of the ideas *actually* used by the scientists. The *rules* for an adequate use of scientific expressions in the journalist-example were also not directly descriptive.

*Suppositions/assumptions* about the causal *structures* of the realm B which the members of the respective language community *refer to*, enter — explanatorily speaking — the actual argumentation behavior of scientists and are encoded in $A$, considering the latter as a means of investigation. We seem to believe, however, (or at least one sometimes has that impression) that we could *grasp* those contentual conceptions (the *cognitive content*) *completely* with *purely descriptive* formal-syntactical means (cf. the $Q_j$-programs) by inventing formal rules. These should lead to the same argumentation *behavior* and be able to evoke a benevolent affirmative behavior of experts in restricted test-situations. Considered from this point of view, one could say that we learn rules to pretend or fake knowledge and not rules to produce knowledge. This situation expresses itself in the fact that the existing procedures for *justifying knowledge* which have been developed for checking the correctness of arguments and which originally went hand in hand with a knowledge of the significance and of the coming about of the results of a special scientific discipline, which were interpreted in a natural, unconscious manner via the repertoire of the experiences of a specific science, are now used in a ritualized, detached manner; i.e. they are used as generative procedures for the fake production of knowledge and are transferred to the so-called *context of discovery* of scientific research.

In the following sections I want to show, among other things, that the problems resulting from this situation can be overcome if we concentrate instead on the confrontation between the *explanatory* and the *descriptive* elements in scientific theories and on the role they play in the arrival at an understanding of the meaning of the results of a special scientific enterprise.

*Theory and Reality — or: If There is Something Like a Sense of Reality, There Has To Be Something Like a Sense of Possibility*

A completely different approach to the central ideas of this article, already implicitly contained in the computer poetry example and hinted at in the preliminary account can be found in the major opus of the no-doubt most important philosophical writer of this century, namely in *The Man without Qualities* by Robert Musil.[7] Musil's philosophical inclinations are manifest from his doctoral thesis, a critical analysis of Mach's doctrines (Musil, 1908). Ernst Mach, the founder of Neopositivism, is, so to speak, the missing link to that school of analytical philosophy originating in the Vienna Circle with which we are concerned here.

Musil's life and his main work could be regarded as dedicated to the 'failure of intellectualism'. In our context, we could address this failure in the following way: Misunderstandings lead to an inadequate practice in certain fields at least, which results in a failure to 'turn theories into reality'.

In a passage which is especially revealing as far as our present problems are Ulrich (the main character of the book — a man without qualities, in whom the spectrum of all possible intellectual qualities merge into the whiteness of none) toys, in a sort of intellectual *étude*, with the following idea[8]:

> Let us assume that in matters of morality it is exactly the same as in the kinetic theory of gases: everything swirls about chaotically, each thing doing what it likes, but if one calculates what in the manner of speaking has no cause to arise out of it, one finds that is the very thing that does really arise! Let us therefore assume too that a certain quantity of ideas is swirling about in the present time. It produces some most probable average value. This shifts very slowly and automatically, and that is what we call progress of the historical situation. But what is most important is that our personal, individual motion doesn't matter in the least in all this. We may think and act to the right or to the left, high or low, in a new way or an old way, wildly or with circumspection: it is of no consequence at all to the average value. And to God and the universe *that's* all that matters — *we* don't count! (Musil's emphasis).

A first fatal consequence of these *theoretico-explanatory* considerations would be to regard the 'gas example' as a literal description of our situation in general, and to infer from it direct *rules* or *instructions for acting*. For this would mean that we could at any rate stop to think, act or deal with the world we live in (with regard to content). As is often the case with the understanding of examples, the 'deeper meaning' becomes evident through an intensive study of the implied picture. If we — regarding ourselves as molecules of a gas — cease to move at all, the average value Ulrich is concerned with does not come about, and we can easily picture the consequences. Commitment and dedication is therefore necessary for everyone. The mistake of a superficial analysis consists in relating the term 'average value'[9] *directly* to the individuals and therefore in misunderstanding this term in a *directly* (instead of indirectly) *descriptive* way in the sense of applying it to the organization of one's own life.

The discrete handling of our theoretical results of the 'intellectual game' is therefore obviously in need of additional knowledge or of understanding which cannot be *verbalized* completely. It has to be learned in the practical application of the 'handling of theoretical knowledge'. For doing so we have also to concern ourselves with the way in which such an understanding can be developed. M. Polanyi has dealt with these problems under the heading 'tacit knowledge' and given a number of examples.[10] Polanyi is here concerned with 'skills' in the practical transformation of knowledge/cognition, something that can be explained by an at least tacit 'grasp' (or interpretation) of that information-content (or that *meaning*) which one ascribes to cognitive statements about a certain section of the world. In the computer poetry example this fact exhibits itself in the 'behavior' of using information as demonstrated by the natural interpreters of *L*-expressions (cf. intuitive versus non-intuitive understanding).

If one grows organically into a 'practice' or a community of speakers, then the 'problem of applying' information (or knowledge) does not seem to matter. By a constant feedback from one's social environment one learns adequate rules for the generation of, say, poems — as well as correct interpretations and rules for their use. Thus, the behavior of 'having understood' corresponds to an actual grasp of what might be called the original intentions (or the message) of a poem. In this case, symptoms and causes correspond to each other, i.e. judgement or evaluation of poems or formal features according to symptoms, *grasps* or *meets* certain intentions. Within such a linguistic 'practice', reflections about certain situations and their explanatory understanding can seemingly be used as literal descriptions and therefore as prescriptions (rules) for acting in a considerate manner in 'typical' situations. Failing this, one could easily draw the wrong conclusion that one could construct a realistic picture of the world (with the help of the 'intellectual game' of providing an explanatory analysis).

Musil himself distinguishes in this context between a *sense of possibility* and a *sense of reality*. The sense of possibility — transferred to our problems and translated into our language — refers to the understanding of structures of situations (or of their rational characteristic features); the sense of reality concerns the manifestations of such structures in real situations or rules for the handling of them, that is, rules which operate in such situations. The difference between thinking in 'possible worlds' constructed with the help of a theoretico-explanatory understanding and the transformation of these thoughts into reality (by using descriptive rules) becomes especially clear by the following passage, in which Arnheim (= Rathenau) talks (Arnheim is the prototype of the clear and active realist):[11]

I myself never play billiards . . . but I know that one can play the ball high or low, from the right or from the left. One can strike the second ball head on or merely graze it. One can hit hard or lightly. One may choose to make the cannon stronger or weaker. And I am sure there are many more such possibilities. Now, I can imagine each of these elements being graduated in all directions, so that there are therefore an almost infinite number of possible combinations. If I wished to state them theoretically, I should have to make use not only of the laws of mathematics and of the mechanics of rigid bodies, but also of the law of elasticity. I should have to know the coefficients of the material and what influence the temperature had. I should need the most delicate methods of measuring the co-ordination and graduation of my motor impulses. My estimation of distances would have to be as exact as a nonius. My faculty of combination would have to be more rapid and more dependable than a slide-rule. To say nothing of allowing for a margin of error, a field of dispersal, and the circumstance that the aim, which is the correct coincidence of the two balls, is itself not clearly definable, but merely a collection of only just adequately surveyable facts grouped round an average value . . . And so you will see, . . . I should need to have all the qualities and to do all the things that I cannot possibly have or do. You are, I am sure, enough of a mathematician yourself to appreciate that it would take one a lifetime even to work out the course of an ordinary cannon-stroke in such a way. This is where our brain simply leaves us in the lurch! And yet I can go up to the billiard-table with a cigarette between my lips and a tune in my head, so to speak with my hat on, and, hardly bothering to survey the situation at all, take my cue to the ball and have the problem solved in a twinkling!

Let us consider this situation from the point of view of the difference between *explanations* and *descriptions* as mentioned several times, i.e. from the point of view of the explanatory roles of theories in regard to the billiard game and the rules for acting, i.e. playing billiards. The trivial point seems to be that the theoretical explanations in no case *express rules for the generation* of those results which should be explained by the theory. If we take the example we have just discussed as our background, the 'meaning' of the *difference* that has been introduced and therefore the dictum 'explanation versus rules for the generation' becomes literally illustrative. In the sense of a non-technical explication of split-semantics we could, developing this difference, say the following: if we want to express the model-theoretical semantics, especially when studying the significance of scientifically meaningful terms, we have to split up the relation of these terms, namely in regard to *structure-models* and *concrete* (or material) *models*. Structure-models correspond to theoretical explanations, material models correspond to realizations or operationalizations.

The main problem in this context is how meaning (or significance), which is given via theoretical insights (given in structural models) can be transferred into material models, i.e. in a correct and promising way. In this respect, mistakes often carry far-reaching consequences.

When considering theories of meaning which claim to explain how we are able to understand new expressions within our system of communication, it is important to bear in mind that they are not, strictly speaking, *direct* descriptions of how the understanding of an information-content of utterances can be built up or brought about. (Not rules or recipes, but instructions for the identification of suitable rules.)

I am thinking here especially of the 'reception' of the doctrines of logical empiricism which has led to the widespread positivistic cushion (cf. Einstein's *Ruhekissen*) that a theory is nothing but a set of true sentences (understood as statements) among which there exist deductive relations (please note that I am talking about the reception of logical positivism only). In order to *mediate* or convey the meaning (significance) of a theory, one therefore only has, according to this approach, to formulate definitions and axioms and *deduce* statements from them. Following these methods should automatically lead to the building up of 'understanding' and 'insight' since there is nothing to be understood apart from the syntactical deductive relations. The only thing one would have to worry about was empirical checks of the deduced results.

In this case, a theory for the explanation and characterization of meaning (e.g. of what a theory is),[12] was turned into a method for the generation of meaningful statements with the help of characterizing symptoms. This meant, however, that explanatory conceptions were misconstrued as directly descriptive.

The whole procedure has eliminated the (human) *interpreter*, i.e. someone who has to be able to *understand* and *use* those

expressions which have been generated and characterized as meaningful (cf. the journalist-example). An interpreter *reacts* to the
presentation of certain expressions. *He* has to *use* them! If a physicist prepares an experiment and waits for and watches the reactions
of mother nature, he to some extent prepares 'meaningful expressions' which he expects mother nature to understand. One should
not overdo this anthropomorphization, however. What is important
is the difference, which is that human interpreters are not very
reliable in their reactions to the presentation of an expression and
that a great deal of feedback (communication) is necessary in order
to stabilize these reactions in the social context. Yet even in this
case we cannot be sure that we are dealing with genuine understanding or merely with a certain behavior which we interpret as a
symptom for 'having understood' the 'information-content' of those
expressions (compare once more the journalist-example).

In conclusion, I want to come back to Musil and the difference
between explanation and action in connection with Musil's sense
of possibility and reality. Just like Musil, we could call somebody
who dreams in a world of possible explanations yet does not act,
a 'nihilist' — from a literary point of view — and somebody who
interprets these dreams in a direct way and impatiently, without
considering their meaning, and who regards them as *prescriptions
for actions* ('rules') and transforms them directly, an 'activist'. A
'realist' (in Musil's sense) would then be somebody who is able to
relate both realms in a realistic way to each other and (at least
locally) reconcile them. We could regard the end of the chapter
'Atemzüge eines Sommertages', on which Musil was working on
the morning of his death, as a visionary answer to the problem in
question (or at least as an identification of its causes):[13]

Of course it was clear to him that the two kinds of human
being . . . could mean nothing else than a man 'without qualities'
and, in contrast, the man with all the qualities that anyone could
manage to display. And the one might be called a *nihilist*, dream-
ing of *God's dreams* — in contrast with the *activist*, who is,
however, with his impatient way of acting, a kind of God's
dreamer too, and anything but a *realist*, who goes about being
worldly-clear and worldly-active. 'And why aren't we realists?'
Ulrich wondered. Neither of them was, neither he nor she: their
*thoughts* and *actions* had for long left no doubt of that. What

they were was *nihilists* and *activists*, and now one, now the other, according as it came.


## Split Semantics

I have already abstracted in outline from the computer-poetry example a scheme which illustrates the basic idea of split semantics. This idea consists of assuming the existence of (at least) a 'vernacular' *component* of meaning (built in as manipulatory *rules*) and a 'technical' (theoretico-explanatory) one. The *vernacular component* manifests itself in *rules* for handling and using information and therefore in a certain *folk*-knowledge.[14] It is the expression of folk-knowledge in contrast to certain scientific or theoretico-explanatory knowledge which is a systematic restriction and local enrichment and therefore a supplementation to folk-knowledge. Both components are assumed to be necessary for a successful explanation of certain aspects of the 'behavior' of language users, and are also regarded as a useful literal heuristics in order to understand what is essential for comprehending the meaning or content of information of some presented linguistic expressions. In the scheme LIR these components are represented as $C$ resp. $A$.

In each case we can ascribe a concrete $A$- and $C$-background knowledge to those theoretico-explanatory concepts. This background knowlege acts as a filter for selecting and for fixing the reference of expressions, especially when dealing with (resp. identifying) *concrete models* in the realm B. $A$ resp. $C$ can therefore (in an explanatory way) be regarded as responsible for the 'behavior of users' with respect to B. $A$ as well as $C$ can be understood as more or less explicit ways of uttering assumptions about the 'structure' of the given world B with which we concern ourselves or to which we refer.

In this respect we could — in anticipation of formal semantics and the semantic (or structural) approach to philosophy of science (Sneed-Stegmüller, van Fraassen and others) — say that $A$ formulates *structure models* (in contrast to real models) and therefore *studies the reference of our respective languages of science onto real models via the detour of structure models.*

Using the methods of formal semantics (in its special elaboration for the purposes of a theory of sciences) assumptions about the structure of B which are implicit in $A$ can be explicated in a technical way. These *A*-assumptions (e.g. about the causal structure of B) underly the reference of certain theories to reality. The corresponding *C*-assumptions determine the actual reference-behavior (the way in which we talk about our results and their *significance*) in the context and practice of our labs. They do so in the form of heuristics, metaphors and everyday background knowledge and can then on the one hand be identified with the help of the resolution level of the scheme LIR, and on the other hand they can be modified according to the circumstances. Thus the creative initiatives, impulses and even influences of philosophical reflections can be understood much better; i.e. we can understand and watch what goes on.

Since *A* and *C*, as means of expression, have a different expressive power or resolution level, we are here confronted with a problem of translation from a field rich with distinctions and means of expressions into a field that does not contain the same expressive power. This problem can be solved by a local enrichment of *C* with pictures, metaphors, heuristics and above all, experiences. The scheme shown in Figure 8.2 is therefore a sort of meta-frame for discussing the way of proceeding, and therefore also the significance of the results of formal semantics and philosophy/theory of science.[15]

To begin with, I want to embed the way in which formal semantics works into the scheme. For this purpose we imagine a pre-systematically chosen section L of some natural language (abbreviated as **L**) as the *object* of our investigation. We suppose that the users of L refer to a realm B and that we want to *study* the *manner* of information-processing in L made evident by the 'behavior of (rationally) *drawing conclusions*'. What is *de facto* done (but seldom said explicitly) is that concrete expressions $\Phi$, $\Psi$ from L or sets of expressions $G = \{\Phi_1, \Phi_2, \ldots \Phi_n\}$ are *mapped* (in a suitable way) onto well-defined sign-sequences $\varphi = t(\Phi)$, $\psi = t(\Psi)$ respectively $\Gamma = t(G)$ of a *formal language* L. ($\varphi$, $\psi$ are elements of L). In the diagram this mapping is given as a (structural) translation t from L to L. It is called structural because it maps an expression $\Phi$ from L onto its logical structure $\varphi = t(\Phi)$ in L, which is the result of a logical analysis of $\Phi$ and only expresses the result of an analysis of $\Phi$ under a certain *aspect*. It should be made clear that $\Phi$ and the relation between $\Phi$, $\Psi$, *G* etc. is *investigated* under this aspect[16] (Tarski, for example, talks of a mapping of relevant terms of an object language onto structural and *descriptive names* taken from

# Figure 8.2

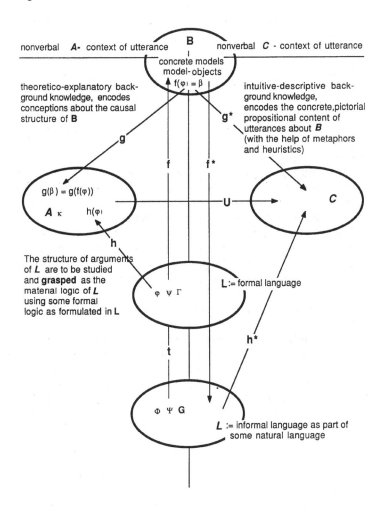

nonverbal **A-** context of utterance **B** nonverbal **C** - context of utterance

concrete models
model- objects

$f(\varphi) = \beta$

theoretico-explanatory background knowledge, encodes
conceptions about the causal
structure of **B**

intuitive-descriptive background knowledge,
encodes the concrete, pictorial
propositional content of
utterances about **B**
(with the help of metaphors
and heuristics)

$g^*$

$g$

$f$ $f^*$

$g(\beta) = g(f(\varphi))$

**A** κ $h(\varphi)$

—U—➔ **C**

$h$

The structure of arguments
of **L** are to be studied
and **grasped** as the
material logic of **L**
using some formal
logic as formulated in **L**

$\varphi$ ψ Γ

**L** := formal language

$h^*$

$t$

Φ Ψ G

**L** := informal language as part of
some natural language

the syntactical part of the meta-language).

The mechanical manipulation of sign-sequences in L can therefore be used to *determine* the *existence* of a relation (e.g. a logical
conclusion) between concrete expressions of *L*. The mechanical
*rules* (*syntactical operations*) for the transformation of signs in L
are therefore to a certain extent able to 'capture' the concrete

relations between expressions of $L$, without, however, literally describing the internal linguistic mechanisms of $L$.

From this point of view it should be possible to say that $\Psi$ follows from $G$, (or is a consequence of $G$-- in signs $G \vDash \Psi$) if and only if the sign-sequence $t(\Psi) = \psi$ (as element of the formal language L) can be *generated* (deduced) in a controlled and reproducible way from the sign-sequence $t(G) = \Gamma$. In any case, it should be clear that *no arbitrary* L (with a formal calculus for the transformation of sign-sequences contained in it) and *no arbitrary* structural-translation t (form $L$ to L) is suitable for such a task. Strictly speaking, we are dealing here with a theory about the *linguistic (argumentation) behavior* in $L$, a theory which is formulated in the formal language L. Formal logic (compare the proof of the completeness of predicate-calculus of the first order) concerns those parts only of the argumentation behavior in $L$ which can be reconstructed theoretically, prognosticated and explained without suppositions about the structures of the realm of reference B which the $L$-speakers refer to in their utterances $\Phi$, $\Psi$. Yet as soon as we want to grasp 'argumentation in regard to content' in $L$ (which refers to B with the help of L), we need a possibility to *represent* suppositions about B in L, e.g. in the form of non-logical axioms, so we can continue to use L for studying the argumentation behavior of $L$ (as part of some natural language L).[17]

One could create a 'program' out of this which eliminates all those linguistic terms which contain signs without a (direct) meaning. Any philosophical problem based on reflective and explanatory attempts to understand the world could thereby either be shifted onto empirical problems (provided that the chosen descriptive concepts correspond to explanatory concepts) or could be eliminated as meaningless given the proof of the impossibility of such a translation. The excess of such a 'philosophy of rules' leads to a reduction in *creativity* and *flexibility* as regards new situations of problem solving, knowledge-acquisition and knowledge transfer.

This 'program' is above all based on the assumption of a direct translation (or correspondence) between *explanatory and descriptive (operative) concepts* (compare the original problems of the theoretical and the empirical terms of a theory within philosophy of science).

In the scheme, these problems are taken care of by the mapping U from $A$ to $C$, which is to be understood as an *indirect* translation or transformation of explanatory concepts 'into' descriptive (operative) ones, in the sense of Musil's 'realist'.[18]

So as not to leave the choice of such syntactical representations of $L$ quite in the air, we could imagine that they were reached via a representation of *assumptions* about the structure of B. In a technical manner this is done in the framework of (mathematical) model-theory (i.e. by the presupposition of set-theoretical structures in $A$ (cf. the scheme LIR), consequently of *structure models A* is the *domain of interpretation* of the formal language L. We could therefore say that the relation of the informal language $L$ to B is *simulated* by the relation of the formal language L to $A$ (i.e. we study the relation of $L$ to B with the help of L to $A$ and render it explicit). What we miss, however, is the connection between the *real models* in B and the *structure models* in $A$. For this, we can assume a — in general — many-to-one mapping g from B to $A$, which strictly speaking assigns structure models in $A$ to model objects in B. In practical applications g can be realized by *measurements* which constitute the graph of a mapping g from B to $A$. Furthermore, the connection between the formal language L and B is realized by a function f which simulates the reference-behavior f* of $L$ towards B.

Technically speaking, it seems rewarding to restrict the interpretation mapping h from L to $A$ to predicate letters of L. f should then take over the task of designation $f(\varphi) = \beta$ as a mapping of individual constants in L to individuals in B. If furthermore we assume a correspondence $\kappa$ between the elements $g(\beta)$ and $h(\varphi)$ defined upon $A$, whereby $\kappa$ is determined partly empirically (via the mapping g from B to $A$) and partly theoretically (via the mapping h from L to $A$), then we may reach the truth-definition given below. We assume that $g(\beta) = g(f(\varphi)$ and that $h(\varphi)$ corresponds to $g(\beta)$ from $A$ (in signs $h(\varphi)\kappa g(\beta)$) if the pair $(h(\varphi), g(\beta))$ is an element of the graph $\kappa_G$ of the 'correspondence' $\kappa$. $\kappa_G$ consists (mathematically speaking) of all those *pairs* (of elements in $A$) for which it is the case that $h(\varphi)$ and $gf(\varphi)$ correspond to each other (empirically). Let W designate the set of (deductively) true sentences of $L, W \subseteq L$. $\varphi$ is element of W iff $h(\varphi)\kappa gf(\varphi)$ is the case. With the help of h one can select assumptions in $A$ about the structure of B so that some $\Phi \in L$ is accepted by the users of $L$ if the correspondence $\kappa$ holds.

This fact should express itself in the behavior of the *users* of the *information* about B which is assumed to be encoded in some $\Phi$.

If, e.g. $\varphi$ = Pa is the structural descriptive name t($\Phi$) of the statement $\Phi$: = 'Tony is blue', then h($\varphi$) equals h(Pa) where h($\phi$) is a proposition or rather the content of a psychological conception — be it a political statement or an assertion about the mood Tony is in. This proposition h($\varphi$) may be considered to be valid if one regards e.g. an object (or, in our example, a subject) $\beta$ from B, such that $\beta$ = f($\varphi$) = f(Pa). The fact that $\Phi$ is valid with respect to $\beta$ is expressed as g($\varphi$)$\kappa$h($\varphi$), where $\kappa$ is a correspondence between g(B) and h(L) — or more precisely h(t($L$) ) — such that $\kappa_G$ (the actual graph of the correspondence $\kappa$) is a subset of the Cartesian product g(B) × h(L) of g(B) and h(L).

As soon as we have understood the basic idea of the left side of the scheme LIR we are free to distinguish any structures and theories in $A$ and to investigate their prognostic and explanatory potential in regard to the behavior of language users of $L$ *vis-à-vis* B. The *technical explication* of those aspects of 'meaning', e.g. of $\varphi$ in $A$, which enables us to forecast the $L$-behavior with respect to B, can now be used to identify those everyday conceptions (compare the mapping U : $A \rightarrow C$ in the scheme LIR) which function as background knowledge to determine our concrete reference behavior and the actual use of $L$-expressions with respect to B. This is, above all, important in *learning-situations*, if, for example, an *understanding* of the *meaning* of some linguistic expressions has to be *built up* (or if a different background knowledge leads to a different behavior of the users of $L$ — compare the computer-poetry example and test-situations).

With the help of these explications of the manner in which formal semantics operates as a frame of reference, we are able to realize the positive contribution of formal semantics in regard to theories that deal with explaining the way in which an understanding of the meaning of linguistic expressions arises (although the contribution by itself is not a direct one).

This fact becomes especially clear with applications in the field of the philosophy of science. There too the empirical content of information of scientific theories is — strictly speaking — not given directly. The formal philosophy of science can therefore be identified within the scheme LIR as the relation between L and $A$. Basically — and this refers to the methodology of analytic philosophy in general — it is the *behavior of (linguistic) argumentation* in a regulated (or regimentated) language which is studied. Statements about the content of meaning of corresponding utterances are inferred from them. In doing so, however, the *A*- and *C*-(meaning-)component of expressions are in general not distinguished. They are sometimes deliberately regarded as the same. Musil's interpretation of the connection of the direct transformation of explanations into advice for actions should be taken into consideration in this context.

## Notes

1. Unless, of course, one creates a philosophy out of the fact that one naturalizes explanatory concepts as directly descriptive ones. In this case, one learns to use *symptoms* — e.g. for the correctness of arguments — in such a way that one conceives of oneself as directly handling or manipulating objects according to certain rules. Yet is it possible to state these symptoms, which should correspond to natural sets, for every field of knowledge in such a way that some theoretical, not directly descriptive *understanding* becomes superfluous and could be replaced by *rules* for acting? Is it possible to find (or invent) these rules *before* one knows the (exact) field of knowledge one has to deal with?

2. The title of the scheme, *split semantics* (the right hand is not to know what the left hand does) or *schizo-semantics* (in certain disciplines one does things which contradict the tacitly assumed 'working philosophy' one refers to as an explicitly expressed 'positivistic pillow') resulted, in a sort of self-baptizing (contrary to the practice of baptizing in S. Kripke's philosophy of language) in a natural way from discussions with Otto Neumaier, to whom an at least maeutic function in finding the title must not be denied.

3. It remains to be shown that the claim to, e.g., *the primacy of everyday language* with respect to the grasping of meaning is 'ideologically' just as stupid as the reverse claim to the primacy of science over everyday knowledge. A universally *complete* translation of both realms (of language) into each other is to my mind impossible for factual and to some extent logical reasons. The enforcement of such a translation would necessarily lead to an 'impoverishment' of language and therefore to a wanton restriction and limitation of the reservoir of possibilities for problem-solving (by way of reducing the expressive power of both realms). It would also lead to a reduction of creativity and flexibility in the face of new situations. What we need in contrast to this Orwellian situation is a mutual, positive stimulation of both fields, which would lead to a local increase of the expressive power of languages and a sophistication of our methods of gaining knowledge.

4. Detailed information about Tarocania which can be used for touristic purposes may be found in Fritz von Herzmanovsky-Orlando's *Maskenspiel der Genien*.

5. At this stage, I suppose, expectations of a *common-sensical knowledge,* (of the *C*-area in the scheme, see below under 'Split Semantics') in regard to content as well as aesthetic considerations about poems in the Tarocanian mother-tongue and the Tarocanian cultural background in general will enter in a *tacit form.* (Compare below the example of a machine that recognizes patterns.) Furthermore compare Michael Riffaterre's *Text Production* as an example of the Formalist tradition of descriptive poetics where the *literariness* of a literary text is primarily defined by formal means.

6. In doing so, *one* aspect of the everyday-language use of 'grasping' has been selected and been transferred into a specific context. This is a natural and unconscious way of generalizing everyday semantics. It would, however, be nonsensical

to maintain that the computer is an instantiation of reflection and understanding, just because of the fact that the ordinary language use of grasping information suggests that grasping of knowledge has to be accompanied by consciousness. This piece of polemic is especially directed against such philosophers as do not want to recognize the completely different mechanisms for the stipulation of the meaning of the terms of a special scientific discipline in the practical grinding of the scientific mill.

7. I quote from the English edition of Robert Musil's *The Man without Qualities*.

8. Musil (1979: 231), second book, Part Two, Ch. 103: 'The Temptation'.

9. 'Average value' is a theoretico-explanatory term which expresses an understanding of a situation and deals with or refers to the *analysis* of that *situation*.

10. Polanyi (1958, 1966). These papers have been brought to my knowledge by Rom Harré.

11. Musil (1979: 331f), second book, Part Two, Ch. 114: 'The state of affairs gradually becomes critical. Arnheim is very gracious to General Stumm. Diotima prepares to sally forth into the illimitable. Ulrich indulges in fanciful talk about the possibility of living in the same way as one reads'.

12. In regard to special expressions one could say that a sentence is meaningful if it can be deduced.

13. Musil (1979: xxii-xxiii), end of Part Three and beginning of Part Four, the English edition quotes this in the foreword. My italics.

14. 'Folk-knowledge' is not intended as depreciatory. It is intended as an aspect with different emphasis.

15. The arrows in the diagram are set-theoretical mappings.

16. One could also consider the consequences of 'ontologizing' the logical structure.

17. Such 'representations' are, however, by their status, theoretico-explanatory, technical means of reconstruction and are therefore not to be considered as directly descriptive (except in trivial contexts). It is admittedly understandable that one looks for such representations, and therefore theories accommodate an understanding of being *direct descriptions* of reality and therefore instructions for acting (respectively *rules* for the manipulation of reality).

18. And in a perhaps playful and wilful generalization of some of Wittgenstein's conceptions (compare Wittgenstein, 1921: 6.53) and the spirit of the Vienna Circle.

# References

Born, R. (1982) 'Sprache — Information — Wirklichkeit' in R. Born (ed.), (1982) *Sprache — Information — Wirklichkeit*. Wien, pp. 109-24

——(1983) 'Physikalische Semantik: Kausalität kontra Quantenlogik' in J. Czermak and P. Weingartner (eds) (1983) *Akten des 7. Internationalen Wittgenstein Symposiums*. Wien, pp. 416-20

Frey, G. (1982) 'Identität: Ontologische Voraussetzungen, theoretischen Denkens' in W. Leinfellner, E. Kraemer and J. Schank (eds) (1982) *Akten des 6. Internationalen Wittgenstein Symposiums*. Wien, pp. 240-4

Frude, N. (1983) *The Intimate Machine*, Close Encounters with the New Computers, London

Herzmanovsky-Orlando, F. von (1958) *Maskenspiel der Genien*, Bearbeitet und hg. von F. Torberg (Gesammelte Werke, 2), München

Musil, R. (1908) *Beitrag zur Beurteilung der Lehren Machs*, Berlin (Neuausgabe: Reinbek 1980)

——(1979) *The Man without Qualities*, vols. 1, 2, London (*Der Mann ohne*

*Split Semantics* 213

*Eigenschaften,* ed. by A. Frisé, Hamburg (Neubearbeitete Ausgabe: 2., verbesserte Auflage. Reinbeck 1981))
Polanyi, M. (1958) *Personal Knowledge. Toward a Post-critical Philosophy,* London
—— (1966) *The Tacit Dimension,* London
Riffaterre, M. (1983) *Text Production,* New York (Französische Originalausgabe, La production du texte, Paris 1979.
Wittgenstein, L. (1921) 'Tractatus logico-philosophicus' in L. Wittgenstein (1960) *Schriften 1.* Frankfurt and Main, pp. 7-83

# FURTHER READING

Abelson, H., Sussman, G.J. with Sussman, J. (1985) *Structure and Interpretation of Computer Programs,* Cambridge MA.
Austin, J.L. (1975) *How to Do Things with Words,* 2nd edn by J.O. Urmson and M. Sbisa, Cambridge MA.
Babbage, H.P. (ed.) (1889) *Babbage's Calculating Engines,* London.
Baker, G.P. and Hacker, P.M.S. (1980) *Wittgenstein: Understanding and Meaning,* Oxford.
Bamme, A., Feuerstein, G., Genth, R., Holling, E., Kahle, R. and Kempin, P. (1983) *Maschinen-Menschen, Mensch-Maschinen: Grundrisse einer sozialen Beziehung,* Reinbek bei Hamburg.
Barwise, J. and Perry, J. (1983) *Situations and Attitudes,* Cambridge MA.
Benner, P. (1984) *From Novice to Expert: Excellence and Power in Clinical Nursing Practice,* London.
Block, N. (ed.) (1980) *Readings in Philosophy of Psychology,* Vol. 1, Cambridge MA.
Block, N. (ed.) (1981) *Imagery,* Cambridge, MA.
Block, N. (1983) 'Mental Pictures and Cognitive Science' *The Philosophical Review,* 499–541.
Boolos, G. and Jeffrey, R. (1980) *Computability and Logic,* 2nd edn, Cambridge.
Brownston, L., Farrell, R., Kant, E. and Martin, N. (eds) (1985) *Programming Expert Systems in OPS5: An Introduction to Rule-Based Programming,* Reading MA.
Bruner, J.S., Goodnow, J.J. and Austin, G.A. (1956) *A Study of Thinking,* New York.
Campbell, J. (1984) *Grammatical Man: Information, Entropy, Language and Life,* Harmondsworth.
Canfield, J.V. (1981) *Wittgenstein: Language and World,* Amherst.
Charniak, E., Riesbeck, C.K. and McDermott, D.V. (1980) *Artificial Intelligence Programming,* Hillsdale NJ.
Cresswell, M.J. (1985) *Structured Meanings: The Semantics of Propositional Attitudes,* Cambridge MA.
Cummins, R. (1983) *The Nature of Psychological Explanation,* Cambridge MA.
Daiser, W. (1984) *Kuenstliche Intelligenz Forschung und ihre epistemologischen Grundlagen,* Frankfurt/M.
Davidson, D. (1970) 'Mental Events', in L. Foster and J. Swanson (eds) *Experience and Theory,* 79–101, London.
Davies, R. and Lenat, D.B. (1982) *Knowledge-Based Systems in Artificial Intelligence,* New York.
Davis, M. (1965) *The Undecidable. Basic Papers on Undecidable Propositions, Unsolvable Problems, and Computable Functions,* Hewlitt NY.
Dennett, D.C. (1978) *Brainstorms,* Cambridge MA.
Dretske, F.I. (1981) *Knowledge and the Flow of Information,* Oxford.
Dreyfus, H. (1979) *What Computers Can't Do,* New York.
Dreyfus, H.L. with Hall, H. (ed.) (1982) *Husserl, Intentionality, and Cognitive Science,* Cambridge MA.
Dreyfus, H. and Dreyfus, S. (1986) *Mind over Machine,* London.
Ericsson, K.A. and Simon, H.A. (1984) *Protocol Analysis, Verbal Reports as Data,* Cambridge MA.
Fauconnier, G. (1985) *Mental Spaces: Aspects of Meaning Construction in Natural Language,* Cambridge MA.
Fetzer, J.H. (1981) *Scientific Knowledge: Causation, Explanation and Corroboration,* Dordrecht.
Fetzer, J.H. (1984) *Principles of Philosophical Reasoning,* Totowa NJ.
Field, H. (1972) 'Theory Change and the Indeterminacy of Reference', *Journal of Philosophy* 70, 462–81.

Fodor, J. (1979) 'Methodological Solipsism Considered as a Research Strategy' in *Cognitive Psychology, The Behavioral and Brain Sciences*, 63–109.

Fodor, J.A. (1981) *Representations: Philosophical Essays on the Foundations of Cognitive Science*, Brighton.

Gibson, J.J. (1950) *The Perception of the Visual World*, Boston.

Goodman, N. (1978) *Ways of Worldmaking*, Indianapolis.

Graham, N. (1985) *Introduction to Computer Science*, 3rd edn, St Paul, Minn.

Grice, P. (1975) 'Logic and Conversation', in P. Cole and J. Morgan (eds), *Syntax and Semantics 3: Speech Acts*, 41–58, New York.

Gunderson, K. (1985) *Mentality and Machines*, 2nd edn, London.

Harris, M.D. (1985) *Introduction to Natural Language Processing*, Reston, Virg.

Heims, S.J., Von Neumann, J. and Wiener, N. (1980) *From Mathematics to the Technologies of Life and Death*, Cambridge MA.

Hintikka, J. (1979) *Logic Language-Games and Information: Kantian Themes in the Philosophy of Logic*, Oxford.

Hornstein, N. (1984) *Logic as Grammar*, Cambridge MA.

Johnson-Laird, P.N. (1983) *Mental Models: Towards a Cognitive Science of Language, Inference and Consciousness*, Cambridge.

Kosslyn, S.M. (1975) 'Information Representation in Visual Images', *Cognitive Psychology* 7, 341–70.

Kowalski, R.A. (1979) *Logic for Problem Solving*, Amsterdam.

Kripke, S.A. (1980) *Naming and Necessity*, 2nd edn, Oxford.

Kursbuch 75 (1984) *Computerkultur*, Berlin.

Kursbuch 84 (1986) *Sprachlose Intelligenz? Worte und Medien*, Berlin.

Lappin, S. (1981) *Sorts, Ontology, and Metaphor: The Semantics of Sortal Structure*, Berlin.

Lawler, R.W. (1985) *Computer Experience and Cognitive Development: A Child's Learning in a Computer Culture*, Chichester.

Lyons, J. (1981) *Learning, Meaning and Context*, Fontana Paperbacks.

MacCormac, E.R. (1985) *A Cognitive Theory of Metaphor*, Cambridge MA.

Marr, D. (1982) *Vision*, San Francisco.

McCarthy, J. and Hayes, P.J. (1969) 'Some Philosophical Problems from the Standpoint of Artificial Intelligence', in B. Meltzer and D. Michie (eds) *Machine Intelligence 4*, Edinburgh.

McCarthy, J. (1960) 'Recursive Functions of Symbolic Expressions and Their Computation by Machine', in *Communications of the ACM 7*, 184–95.

Michalski, R., Carbonell, J.G. and Mitchell, T.M. (1983) *Machine Learning: An Artificial Intelligence Approach*, Palo Alto, Calif.

Minsky, M. (1975) 'A Framework for Representing Knowledge', in P.H. Winston (ed.) *The Psychology of Computer Vision*, New York.

Mitchell, S. and Rosen, M. (eds) (1983) *The Need for Interpretation: Contemporary Conceptions of the Philosopher's Task*, London.

Monk, A. (ed.) (1985) *Fundamentals of Human-Computer Interaction*, London.

Montague, R. (1974) *Formal Philosophy*, New Haven.

O'Shea, T. and Eisenstadt, M. (eds) (1984) *Artificial Intelligence: Tools, Techniques and Applications*, New York.

Ortony, A. (ed.) (1979) *Metaphor and Thought*, Cambridge.

Otto, P. and Sonntag, P. (1985) *Wege in die Informationsgesellschaft: Steuerungsprobleme in Wirtschaft und Politik*, Muenchen.

Plantinga, A. (1974) *The Nature of Necessity*, Oxford.

Putnam, H. (1974) 'Language and Reality', repr. in Putnam 1980, pp. 272–90, Princeton.

Putnam, H. (1975) 'The Meaning of "Meaning"', repr. in Putnam 1980, pp. 215–71, Minnesota.

Putnam, H. (1976) 'Realism and Reason', repr. in Putnam 1978, pp. 123–38, Harvard.

Putnam, H. (1978) *Meaning and the Moral Sciences*, London.

Putnam, H. (1980) *Mind, Language and Reality: Philosophical Papers*, vol 2, Cambridge.

Putnam, H. (1983) *Realism and Reason, Philosophical Papers*, vol 3, Cambridge.

Reichman, R. (1985) *Getting Computers to Talk Like You and Me*, Cambridge MA.

Rich, E. (1983) *Artificial Intelligence*, New York.

Rock, I. (1983) *The Logic of Perception*, Cambridge MA.

Rosen, S. (1980) *The Limits of Analysis*, New Haven.

Salmon, N.U. (1982) *Reference and Essence*, Oxford.

Sandström, G. (1985) *Towards Transparent Data Bases: How to Interpret and Act on Expressions Mediated by Computerized Information Systems*, Lund.

Schank, R.C. (1975) *Conceptual Information Processing*, Amsterdam.

Schank, R.C. and Abelson, R.P. (1977) *Scripts, Plans, Goals, and Understanding*, Hillsdale NJ.

Schank, R.C. (1982) *Dynamic Memory: A Theory of Learning in Computers and People*, Cambridge.

Schwartz, S.P. (ed.) (1977) *Naming, Necessity, and Natural Kinds*, Ithaca.

Sowa, J.F. (1984) *Conceptual Structures: Information Processing in Mind and Machine*, Reading MA.

Toulmin, S. (1972) *Human Understanding: The Collective Use and Evolution of Concepts*, Princeton.

Tversky, A. and Kahneman, D. (1975) 'Judgment under Uncertainty: Heuristics and Biases', *Science* 185, 1124–31.

Tversky, A. and Kahneman, D. (1982) *Judgment under Uncertainty*, Cambridge.

Van Fraassen, B.C. (1980) *The Scientific Image*, Oxford.

Weiss, S.M. and Kulikowski, C.A. (1983) *A Practical Guide to Designing Expert Systems*, London.

Winston, P.H. and Horn, B.K.P. (1984) *LISP*, 2nd edn, Reading MA.

# INDEX